How to Landscape Your Home

Donald J. Bushey

Illustrated by the author

McGraw-Hill Book Company
New York Toronto London

A GUIDE TO HOME LANDSCAPING

Library of Congress Catalog Card Number: 55–9536

Published by the McGraw-Hill Book Company, Inc.

Printed in the United States of America

First McGraw-Hill Paperback Edition, 1964

This book is dedicated to homeowners. I have stopped
at many hundreds of their places and met with many
more in public meetings in the course of my work in
extension teaching in landscaping. I have come to
know them, they have described their many different
landscape problems to me, and it has been a joy to
work with them. I have seen the interest these people
have had in their families and in their immediate surroundings. Because of this mutual interest, I have felt
a close relationship to them.

In spite of the diversified situations encountered,
certain similarities were evident, and the solutions,
with slight variations, were found in one or another
of several somewhat standard patterns. It is such ideas
as these that are presented in the ensuing pages, with
the hope that they may be helpful to other homeowners.

Preface

This book is written with the sincere hope that it will be a guide to you, as a homeowner or prospective homeowner, from the initial stages of planning through the final planting of your property for use and attractiveness. Part of the fun of planning a new home and its surroundings comes in the challenges it presents. There are certain ways to meet these challenges and to find the solution for each with relative certainty. The plans and procedures illustrated and described here in a step-by-step sequence are simple, easy to follow, and can be adapted to many situations.

It is suggested that you first read through this book in order to get the general feeling of the entire problem. Then, as you approach each phase of your project, study the appropriate portion of the book in detail.

It will be of most help to those of you whose home is still in dream form, to guide your decisions and help you avoid pitfalls leading to disappointment. Some people begin with a mental picture of the house they want, while others select the location and then plan the house. Many of you will employ an architect in order to obtain a home planned especially to suit the requirements of your family. Others will select a house plan from the various ones available. In any case, the text points out facts which will help you to develop for it the setting which will do it justice and make you as happy with it as you had hoped.

This book emphasizes that the selection of a site, with or without a house, is of primary importance in this project which most families undertake only once in a lifetime. It describes how to obtain a satisfying relationship between the house and grounds through the suitability of the property for the type of house, the placing of it on the lot to take advantage of the best features of each, the approaches to it, the plantings around it, and the views from it.

For you who have your home and wish to do new ornamental plantings, this book will help you plan them to your own liking and avoid mistakes often made. Careful selection of the plants you use and planting them in appropriate places produce an effect that will remain satisfactory for many years to come with a minimum of maintenance in pruning and transplanting.

Next, you who have had your own homes for many years, or have purchased homes with mature plantings, have problems in fertilizing, pruning, transplanting, and general care. Some plants may have become overgrown or have been improperly used through lack of careful original planning. Those who have these problems will find suggestions about the care of such shrubs and directions for transplanting them to more appropriate locations.

You who wish to have your property planned in a more intricate and individual manner should consult with a professional landscape designer. He will be of special help on unusual or perplexing problems. Reading this book will help you confer more intelligently with him. He will be of most help if he is employed in the early stages of your planning, and the results usually are far superior if he is engaged before construction is begun.

You will all want to know when and how to start and maintain your lawns, plant or transplant your trees, shrubs, and flowers and how to care for them from year to year as they mature. Much of this information is given in this book.

Landscaping pays. Realtors claim that, when properly done, it adds 10 to 15 per cent to the value of the property. Even more important is the factor which cannot be measured in dollars and cents—the satisfaction it offers for pleasant family living.

It is my earnest hope that your results will provide years of satisfaction and give you a new interest in gardening, a most healthful hobby and outdoor recreation.

The models pictured in this book have been originated by the author. The plywood base is surfaced with sheet metal covered with green felt to represent the lawn. Other colored fabrics have been used for driveways, sidewalks, and cultivated beds, similar to the way in which "flannelgraphs" have been used for many years. Houses of various styles of architecture have been constructed to the scale, ¼ inch equals 1 foot. A complete "nursery," including vines, shrubs, and trees, has been made. Each plant is mounted on a magnet sufficiently strong to hold it in place and in an upright position on the metal base.

The flexibility of this method has many advantages. It enables the designer to duplicate precisely a three-dimensional effect for any plan he creates. The appearance of new plantings can be demonstrated with small plant sizes. The small sizes can be replaced in a few seconds by larger specimens of the same type, to show the effect after several years' growth. Various types of plants can be studied in any location.

A long time is required to construct most landscape models. With this system, after the original work is done, practically any landscape plan for a reasonably level property can be constructed in miniature, quickly and easily. It may then be studied from any desired angle.

Deepest appreciation goes to my wife, Esther, for her patient and capable help. Her ability and knowledge of the subject have been a big factor in the preparation of this manuscript. Thanks also go to my sister, Lucile, for her helpful suggestions.

Various members of the Floriculture and Ornamental Horticulture staff at Cornell University have contributed information, both verbally and as authors of extension publications. Plant lists arranged in size groups, originally prepared in 1919 by Emeritus Professor R. W. Curtis, were used as a guide in selecting plants to be included in this book.

D. J. B.

Contents

Selecting a Site

The ideas presented in this STEP can be used to advantage by those interested in buying a property on which they will build their own home as well as those who are buying a home already built. It is important to select land wisely in either situation.

So you are thinking of building a new home or possibly finding one to your liking already built, one that contains the proper number of rooms and of a size that will meet the requirements of your family. Just thinking about it and discussing it is the beginning of a thrilling project. It will pleasantly occupy your thoughts until the home is finished and from then on to its complete interior and exterior decoration.

For some people, building a new home is a headache from start to finish; others enjoy it. Probably the severity of the headache and the degree of pleasure is proportional to one's ability to visualize accurately the final product of the building plans the contractor is to follow. You can visualize the result more clearly by building a scale model of the house and grounds to study from all angles, inside and out. Sometimes this is easier than to try to picture from a blueprint the size, shape, and arrangement of rooms. Plan the house and grounds together to form a harmonious unit.

Some prefer to buy a house that most nearly meets the needs of the family. If you decide to follow this course, an architect or building contractor can give you a reliable estimate on the value of the building and advise you as to whether it can be adapted to your needs at a reasonable cost.

Most of you will not, and none of you should, allow your enthusiasm to interfere with sound judgment and calm consideration when selecting your new property. There are a number of important factors any one of which could make, break, or slightly mar the complete success of your project. Seldom will any one home property have all of the desirable and none of the undesirable features described here. You will have to select the site that most nearly meets your requirements. Many of the things you should investigate will take only a short time. The right person can give you the answer in a few minutes; and having the right answer may save you money and concern in the years to come.

No doubt you have set up certain ideals for your house. In a similar way, you should set up your ideals for the size, character, and general location of the site. While riding around the city, village, or rural area of your choice, be on the lookout for a location where you believe you would like to live for several years, or possibly for life.

Whether you decide to locate in a more or in a less densely populated area is a matter of personal choice. That decision may be governed somewhat by your interest in gardening, in other outdoor activities, a little extra space, the distance from neighbors, from library, playgrounds, or shopping. Your interest in community affairs and the frequency of city activities may influence your choice.

RURAL PROPERTIES

The present trend among city and village workers to buy property and build homes in rural districts has merit for those who want large sites. Small properties are available in the country, but the smaller the lot, the greater the loss of country benefits.

Rural property values are likely to be lower than those in densely populated places. However, in order to make a fair cost comparison with city and village real estate it is necessary to add to the purchase price the cost of drilling a well, installing a septic tank and tile lines for sewage disposal, and securing other needed conveniences that are included in the price of a city or village lot. Differences in the tax rate, transportation to and from work and school, and other expenses should be considered.

Frequently there are opportunities to buy, at a low price, an abandoned farm or a farm with a poor land classification, with or without buildings. Most of the soil on such farms is not of high quality, but a portion of it might be satisfactory or could be improved to provide food for the family and possibly supplement the income. Also, if a farm is suitable in character and sufficiently near a growing community, several acres could be purchased and held for subdividing and sale to others interested in rural living.

CITY AND VILLAGE PROPERTIES

If your family is not the outdoor type and still wishes to have a home of its own rather than live in an apartment, it is probably best to look for a place in a city or suburb near your employment. If you believe that a certain location is the place for your family, you may know the community well enough to search for a site in a part of it familiar to you. However, time may be saved by first going to see the city or village clerk or other public officials for information about zoning regulations. Most local governments control, by an ordinance, the purpose for which real estate may be used. This practice is known as "zoning." A zoning ordinance contains many technical details and regulations made for the protection of the residents of the community. For your immediate purpose it is not necessary to go into all the details, but you should know something of the portion which affects the property you are considering. Public officials can show you on a map what sections of the community can be used for residential, business, or industrial developments. Usually these main classes of land are subdivided. For instance, some portions of residential zones may be restricted to single-family dwellings and others to multiple-family dwellings, including apartment buildings. In this way the zoning ordinance controls the growth of a community in a practical way and protects health and property values.

When you know what areas in your chosen community are set aside for a residence such as you propose to build, you can confine your search for a site to these districts. You can then be reasonably sure that no large apartment will be built on a property adjacent to your home, overshadowing it and obstructing sunlight and views. No business or industry detrimental to your property value will be built nearby. Any such nonconforming use of real estate is not permitted under a zoning ordinance unless the growth of the community in years to come makes necessary a change in the local regulations. Then the fringes of residential properties nearest the business or industrial zones generally are the first ones affected.

Few rural areas are controlled by a zoning ordinance.

In most cases the cost of land is greatest in a city or village and usually includes public utilities and services. The property tax rate in some areas is higher than in others. Where taxes are higher, the public school systems are likely to be better equipped and staffed; public parks, golf courses, and other recreational facilities are maintained at a high level; public services such as police and fire protection are modern; and the community is a desirable one in which to live.

Properties just outside the limits of a high-tax area usually have lower direct taxes, but if this property is served with water, sewer, and other conveniences operated by the community, a fair premium rate usually is charged for them.

Occasionally there are hidden costs about which the city or village clerk can give you information. If all the improvements such as pavements, sidewalks, street lights, water and sewer connections are made and paid for, the value of the lot is greater. If they are not made and paid for, the cost of the land should be less, but you will have to supply them sooner or later. In addition to charges for public improvements, there may be back taxes held against the property in which you are interested. Any such unpaid bills may be transferred to the purchaser unless other arrangements are made.

There are other minor charges that may be added to the cost of a building site. They include legal fees for tracing the title and registering the deed. A surveyor should be employed to verify the location of the boundary lines with the description in the deed and, if necessary, prepare a topographical map which shows accurately the slope of the ground.

General Considerations

When you have narrowed your choice of a site to a few possibilities, it is well to consider next some of the details that usually make for congenial living and maintenance of property values.

It is best to look for a property within a locality where other homes are about the same size and value as the one you plan to build. If you should build a more elaborate and more costly home than those that occupy nearby lots, the sale value of your property will decrease toward the value of the less expensive homes. If the families living nearby are within the same general income range and have about the same standards of living, there will be more congenial neighborliness.

Homes occupied by the owners usually are well maintained and made otherwise attractive by well-kept lawns and ornamental plantings. These are the things that hold values of real estate in the area at a high level.

Most residential sections of a city or village and some nonfarm rural areas include some homes that are tenant-occupied. If these are attractive and well maintained, they are not detrimental to the value of nearby private property, but those that are run down and occupied by irresponsible tenants depress values considerably.

Whether or not the community is zoned, it is well to survey the surroundings to avoid nearby dumps, railroads, or industrial areas. Sometimes fine residential subdivisions have been built several miles from a heavy industrial section only to find that the prevailing winds carried smoke and odors across these homes. Once a situation of this kind is known, it is somewhat harder to sell such real estate except at a financial sacrifice.

Unless you prefer the noise and confusion of heavy or fast traffic, you will find it more pleasant to locate on a side street or side road. This is especially desirable if the safety of the children and other members of the family is considered. The side road, however, should be paved to avoid dust and dirt.

In years gone by, hardships were encountered by those who chose to live two or three miles away from their work, schools, church, and shopping centers. Today nearly everyone has a car, and paved roads extend in every direction. Several miles of travel to and from these centers of activity is no longer a great hardship. With school buses and other public transportation facilities available, the family car does not always need to be used. Neither is it difficult to travel a few miles to an evening at the movies nor to drive several miles to a social evening.

Nearness to schools is not of particular concern to families without children or to those whose children have nearly completed their schooling. In a like manner, people who have retired or are about to do so need not consider nearness to work.

PUBLIC UTILITIES

Practically all properties within city boundaries are supplied, or can be easily supplied, with a variety of public utilities such as water, electricity, gas, telephone, sanitary sewers, and storm sewers. Most village lots have available water, electricity, and telephone; some have gas and sanitary sewers, but few will have storm-sewer connections. They are dependent upon surface drainage to carry off rain water. Many rural properties have only electricity and telephone connections available, and homeowners must supply other services for themselves. The city or village engineer can give the needed information.

An adequate supply of water is essential. Reservoirs, streams, lakes, springs, and the like, supply all cities and most villages with water for general household use. It is filtered and treated to make it clean and safe. If a public system is not available, it usually is necessary to drill a well unless a good, free-flowing spring is located on the property. A well driller may strike a good supply at a relatively high level, but in some locations it is necessary to drill several hundred feet. The cost increases with the depth it is necessary to drill. The experience of nearby neighbors may be a guide, but not a perfectly reliable one, since water levels and soil conditions vary. Water obtained from any private source should be tested, usually by a state health department.

It is convenient, but not necessary, to have both electricity and gas available. Occasionally, a consumer may have to pay for the extension of a power line. Even in the most inaccessible places, private electric plants may be installed so no one need go without this important commodity. If natural or manufactured gas is not piped to the property, oil or tank gas for cooking and heating is available to places located on an all-weather road.

Telephone connections, another taken-for-granted essential for our way of life, are available even in the most distant and unpopulated parts of this country. Here again the consumer may be charged for extending the line.

All cities and most villages are equipped with sanitary sewers for the disposal of kitchen and bathroom waste. In localities where there is a sanitary sewer, find out from the city engineer how deep it is opposite the property in which you are interested, in order to be sure it is deep enough for drain connections.

If sanitary sewers are not available, private sewage disposal can be provided by a septic tank and tile lines. The successful operation of a septic tank depends upon its construction and the natural drainage of the soil. Sandy and gravelly subsoils provide good drainage and require relatively short tile lines. A larger system is needed in clay soils as they do not drain well. A simple and relatively sure way to determine whether a soil has naturally good drainage is to take samples with a soil auger at each foot of depth to a total of 4 feet or dig a hole about 4 feet deep and examine the subsoil. If it is mottled in color, usually browns, yellows, and reds, natural drainage is not good, and great lengths of tile are needed. Usually a soil of uniform color is an indication of good natural drainage. The experience of neighbors who depend upon septic tanks may be helpful.

Storm sewers such as a city provides, with street gutters and tile connections for the disposal of surface water, may not be installed in outlying portions of cities, most villages, and rural areas. Where they are not available, it is necessary to dispose of excess surface water by means of correct grading, sometimes supplemented by tile lines. Suggestions for difficult drainage problems are given in STEP 3.

SIZE OF THE SITE

Whether your house is to be in a densely populated area or in a rural district, study the details of the site. A rectangular-shaped property, about twice as deep as it is wide, with the side boundary lines at right angles to the highway, is best as it can be planned for more efficient use than an irregularly shaped lot. Irregularity and shallowness are greater problems on small lots than on large ones. Usually, the more irregular the shape, the more difficult is the planning.

When making plans for your house, you consider the size of your family and its requirements to be sure the house will have enough rooms of the right size for convenient living. In a similar way, you should consider the family requirements when selecting the site. Do you want lawn areas for games and general outdoor living? Will it meet the children's interests as they grow older? An area that is first used for swings, teeters, sandbox, and other equipment for children may, in later years, be used for badminton, tetherball, and other active games. Will flower and vegetable gardens provide a needed hobby, be enjoyed, and be useful? What services, such as a clothes-drying yard, a place for refuse cans, incinerator, and compost pile, are needed? When you have answered such questions, you are ready to select a property that will satisfy the interests of your family.

Most homeowners want some lawn areas and a place for ornamental plantings. If you want these, the building site should be at least 60 by 120 feet for homes of conventional design. Properties of this size usually are available in urban places. Many persons who want a larger property may find it only in a rural area or in a residential subdivision consisting of large lots. Keep in mind that a one-story house requires more land area than does a two-story house with the same number of rooms. A lot about 150 feet square, or the equivalent, can be planned to include everything most families want, and can still be maintained without a great amount of work. A fairly level lawn 50 by 100 feet is adequate for a variety of lawn games and other outdoor recreation. A vegetable garden of 5,000 square feet is large enough for most families. A clothes-drying yard requires 225 square feet, more or less. Some may want enough property so that they can keep poultry or other livestock and have a vegetable garden large enough to produce a full year's supply of vegetables and small fruit.

SLOPE OF THE GROUND

The slope of the ground requires careful consideration. If your family wants a vegetable garden and lawn for games, the site should be relatively level, sloping only enough for surface drainage. Part of it might be somewhat steeper. Slightly sloping property, with a 2- or 3-foot rise in 100 feet, adapts itself to interesting landscape effects and involves little grading.

On nearly level property, the grades for drives and walks are easy. A sloping walk or steep driveway such as one that drops sharply into a basement garage is difficult to use, especially during freezing, wintry weather.

For most families, steeply sloping land, 5 or more feet to each 100 feet, is undesirable, particularly if play areas and a vegetable garden are needed. Even for good landscape effects, you may have to do a large amount of grading and wall construction between different levels. Such grading and construction is expensive or requires a lot of work for the owner. Also, unless the house and landscape plans are cleverly prepared, the upkeep on such a property is rather difficult. It is hard to mow a lawn on steep slopes, and high banks may need to be planted densely to prevent soil erosion. The greater the slope of the land, the more difficult will be the development of that property.

Do not be satisfied just to look at a property and decide that the land is level enough. Regardless of where you stand, level land will appear to incline toward you. Sloping land is equally deceiving. A fairly accurate estimate of the grade can be obtained with a carpenter's level. Place it on a standard, in a level position, at a measured height, possibly 4 feet high. Sight along the upper edge and, with a stake, mark the point at which the line of sight intersects the ground. Measure the horizontal distance from the level to the stake. If this distance is 40 feet, the rise is equivalent to 10 feet in 100 feet, or a 10 per cent slope (Figure 1). If all the property slopes at about this same rate, it is too steep for most families whose interest is in gardening and lawn games.

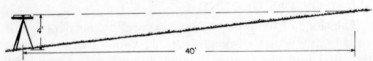

FIGURE 1. Slope of the ground. This slope, having a 4-foot rise in 40 feet, is the equivalent of a 10-foot rise in 100 feet, which is a 10 per cent grade.

Property having a rather undulating surface should be surveyed and a topographic map prepared. This map shows the slope of the land and is essential for accuracy in planning the house and grounds.

Homes built on land considerably above or below the highway must be planned skillfully to avoid a considerable cut or fill. Any financial saving made in purchasing a lot of this kind should be weighed against the cost of moving the soil.

Do not select a property on low land where experience indicates that high water sometimes causes damage either by flood or by heavy rainfall flowing into cellars. Probably some of the old-timers in the community can tell you whether any such situation has occurred in the past.

SOIL

The soil on the property you are considering should be one that will produce thrifty plants. A sandy loam is best for most purposes. Your county agricultural agent can give you technical information about soils and fertilizers. For the amateur, probably the best way to determine productive soil is to observe the growth of native plants on the prospective site and others nearby. Late summer or a period following several weeks of dry weather is the best time to make these observations. Trees, shrubs, and grass in good condition at this time are an indication that your plantings will do well.

In general, sandy and gravelly soils are not productive, largely because water and soluble fertilizers quickly leach downward beyond the depth of roots of plants. Clay soils, which may be identified by their sticky and smooth character when they are wet, hold moisture and fertilizers for long periods, hence require smaller amounts and less frequent applications of fertilizers than do sandy soils. Clay soils are difficult to work whether they are dry or wet, but on a relatively small property this condition can be improved by yearly applications of barnyard manures, peat, and other organic materials. New soil conditioners now available are said to be more effective on clay soils than on sand.

TREES

One or more large shade trees of a good variety are a real asset to a home property. If trees are so located that they will shade the house from the south and west, so much the better. Sometimes a new home can be located advantageously with respect to the position of the tree or trees on the lot. A wooded site is a poor choice for a family wanting a vegetable garden, flowers and shrubs, or a large lawn for games, unless an area sufficiently large for the purpose can be cleared. Small plants are shaded from overhead, and their roots cannot compete favorably with those of large trees.

VIEWS

Occasionally a distant view is available from city properties, but rural homes frequently overlook a lake, river, distant hills, or valleys. Most homeowners value such properties highly and make the most of them.

GETTING OPTION BEFORE BUYING

When you have decided on the site you would like to own, tell the owner or real estate agent with whom you are dealing that you would like to have an option to buy the land pending the results of your investigation into such matters as unpaid taxes, assessments, title, and boundaries. You should have a competent attorney trace the ownership to be sure the title is clear. If this is not done until after you have signed a contract to buy it, you may become entangled in serious difficulties. The deed should include a clear description of the location and extent of the property. An experienced surveyor should check the property lines and outline them with permanent markers. After these details are taken care of, you can buy the site with assurance that everything is in order.

Locating the House on the Property

This STEP is particularly for those who are going to build a new home and for those who plan to remodel an existing house.

PLANNING THE HOUSE TO FIT THE SITE

When you buy a site with the idea of building a home, you should be sure that the size, shape, and room arrangement of the house you plan to build are suited to the property. Sometimes it is discovered too late that the plans that appealed to you on paper do not fit the chosen location. Thinking in terms of narrow lots and wide lots must be done in a relative manner. A 60-foot lot may be wide for some homes and a 100-foot lot may appear narrow, depending upon the size and shape of the structure to be built.

The house to be erected on a narrow lot must be planned carefully to conform to building regulations so as not to be too close to the property lines. If it is to be a one-story house, it must be narrow across the front and extend deep into the property. A one-story house requires more ground area than a one-and-a-half- or two-story house containing the same number of rooms (Figure 2).

The trend is to have the living and dining rooms face the rear or side lawn with a door or doors located to provide easy access from one or both of these rooms to the outdoor living areas. With this arrangement it is frequently neces-

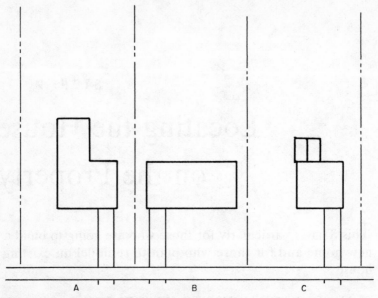

FIGURE 2. Houses fitted to the site.
   A. This one-story house is narrow and deep and fits a narrow lot.
   B. This one-story house is too wide for a narrow lot.
   C. This two-story house, with the same number of rooms as A and
B, takes up less ground space.

sary to have the kitchen face the street. Also, for one-story houses, at least one bedroom may need to be at the front.

If you want picture windows in your new or remodeled home, it is well to consider the nearness of the neighbors and the street. You will have little privacy if the view into the rooms is as clear as that toward the outside. The outlook from within is the one most valued. The view advantage from within the house increases proportionately with the distance from the street and the height above it. In this respect homes in rural areas have the better opportunities because the neighboring dwellings are not close and the house usually is located some distance from the street. This makes it possible to have a large window face in any direction offering the best picture with no loss of privacy.

In situations where the lots are small and the homes are close together, as in cities and villages, picture windows in a front or side wall frequently are a disappointment, while one on a back wall, where it overlooks a rear lawn, is enjoyed.

BOUNDARY LINES

When your property has been surveyed and permanent markers set at the corners, you know the extent of your land. You can accurately outline it with strings connecting the markers. The side and rear boundary lines are probably about where you expected, but the front line may be somewhat different from the one you had visualized.

In cities and villages the street sidewalk is on public property and the front boundary usually is a few inches toward the house from the inside edge of the sidewalk (Figure 3, A and B). Many deeds for rural properties, farm or nonfarm, describe the front line as being the center of the road it faces. Actually the owner's front line probably is 30 feet or more from the center of the road and parallel to it. For example, if the highway is 60 feet wide, this measurement is 30 feet; if it is a 100-foot highway, the measurement is 50 feet, and so on (Figure 3, C and D).

BUILDING-LINE RESTRICTIONS

Regulations in your deed or in a local ordinance specify the minimum distance which must remain between a building and the boundaries whether the property is urban or rural. The distance frequently varies from one community to the next, from one street to another. In rural areas the front setback usually is greater than in cities. This allows for possible future widening of the road (Figure 3, C and D).

If no such regulations are in effect, it is wise not to crowd the side or rear boundaries any more than is necessary and to set the house back from the street about the same distance as other nearby homes. If the value of this precaution is not immediately obvious, it probably will be as soon as someone builds a structure on the adjacent lot.

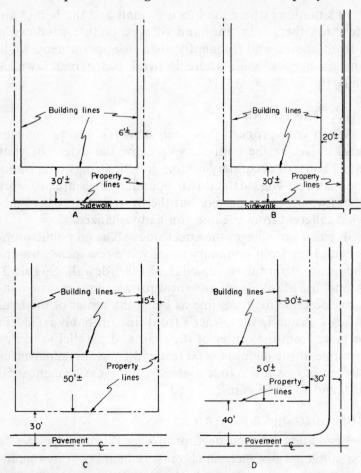

FIGURE 3. Property lines and building lines.

A and B. On a city or village lot the front property line usually is a few inches toward the house from the inside edge of the sidewalk. The building lines are specified in local ordinances and will vary from one community to the next, from one street to another. Plan B is a corner lot. The building setback is specified to be 30 feet on one street and 20 feet on the other.

C and D. On rural properties the front private property line usually parallels the road on a line one-half the width of the highway measured from the center of the road. The property in plan C faces a 60-foot highway, and plan D is on a corner where an 80-foot highway intersects a 60-foot highway. The building setback is 50 feet on the wider highway and 30 feet on the other.

POSITION OF THE HOUSE ON THE LOT

On narrow lots there is little choice in determining the lateral position of the house, as it will absorb practically all of the available width. The garage and driveway should be placed as close to one side of the property as is permitted, leaving all possible space at the other side (Figure 4, A and B).

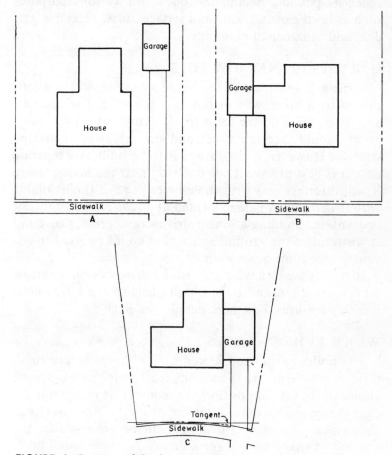

FIGURE 4. Position of the house on the lot—setback from the street. A, B, and C. On small lots the house usually is located as near the street as regulations permit. In A and B the house front parallels a straight street; in C it parallels the tangent to a curved street.

With few exceptions it is best to have the front of the house parallel the street, especially on narrow lots. On curving streets the front of the house should be parallel to a tangent of that curve (Figure 4C). Also, it is usually best to locate the front of the house as near the street as regulations permit. It is seldom better to place the house farther back because the dwellings on the adjacent properties will block the distant view of the street. It is wise to reserve as much space as possible behind the house for various purposes such as lawn games, picnic and service areas, vegetable garden, and ornamental plantings.

GARAGES ON NARROW LOTS

If the garage is part of the house structure, whether connected by a breezeway or not, it is considered as one unit and its position on the lot is fixed accordingly. The garage doors should face the street and the driveway should be straight. However, if the garage is to be built as a separate unit, it is best to have it conveniently near the house, where it will interfere less with the efficient use of the available yard (Figure 4). A garage located at a rear corner of the lot necessitates building a longer driveway at greater cost and is wasteful of the ground space that could be used to advantage for some other purpose.

It is possible to have a "Y" in the driveway on a narrow lot (Figure 27, A and B) but both plans shown have objectionable features. For more details, see STEP 4.

WIDER BUILDING SITES

The building sites considered here, either urban or rural, farm or nonfarm, are those sufficiently wide to have some choice in the lateral position of the house. It is better to locate the house to one side of the property, not directly in the center. The precise distance will be governed by the amount of space needed for a driveway, turnaround or Y, adequate in size and shape to give easy access into the garage. Few things are more annoying than to be forced to maneuver the car back and forth several times in order to line it up parallel with the garage before being able to enter.

Frequently it is desirable to provide space for some service areas on the garage side of the property.

There is a simple method for determining whether or not there is sufficient room to drive into the garage easily. Set a stake into the ground at each of the proposed four corners of the garage. Define the position of the door or doors with one stake at each side, and outline the sides of the proposed driveway. When the ground is sufficiently hard, make the test by driving your car along the "driveway" into the "garage" to see if your car can be guided into it without difficulty. If the land is sloping, this test is an indication of how hard it will be to "make the grade." Actual tests of this kind frequently bring out flaws in a plan, and corrections can be made before it is too late. Both the degree of the slope and the amount of space required for a Y in the driveway are deceiving.

If the street or road extends in a general north-and-south direction, the house should crowd the north side of the lot with the service portions of the house (kitchen, garage, basement entrance, and driveway) on this side. This allows for convenient delivery of groceries, fuel, and the like, and leaves a greater amount of lawn space on the sunny side of the house. An outdoor terrace, ornamental plantings, and outdoor living equipment of a type the family enjoys are appropriate in this space.

If the street or road extends in a general east-and-west direction and there is some choice in the lateral position of the house, it usually is best to crowd the east side of the lot and have the service parts of the house on this side. Then the larger lawn space on the west will have the afternoon sun. However, the advantage here is not so great, and, if preferred, the house may crowd the west side of the lot. The dwelling will then shade the terrace or other living area immediately east of the house, and an ample amount of sunlight is available for ornamental plantings (Figure 5).

Many object to the noise of major thoroughfares and prefer to locate their home farther from the street than the minimum distance required. This is permissible, but the house should be placed far enough forward and to one side

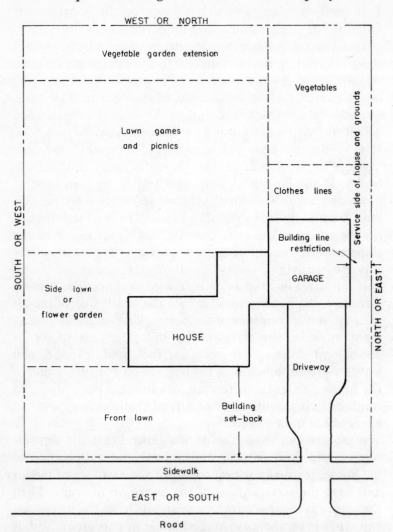

FIGURE 5. Position of the house on the lot—distance from the side property line. If the service side of the house and grounds (garage, kitchen, clotheslines, refuse cans, vegetable garden, and the like) is close and concentrated at one side of the lot, preferably north or east, more space is available in the balance of the lot for outdoor recreation and ornamental plantings.

to allow ample room for the various activities desired. Both situations may be satisfied if the lot is sufficiently deep.

The state or county highway superintendent can inform you about the width of the highway and plans for any future widening of the road. If there is any indication that the highway may be changed, set the house far enough back from the road to allow for it.

The front wall of houses on large lots need not face the road if there is any advantage in facing them otherwise. The slope of the ground, the position of existing trees, views from the house, direction of the prevailing winds, and the compass directions are some of the things that may influence the direction the house is to face.

CORNER LOTS

With corner lots the specified setback must be observed on both streets. It is usually best to have the house face the more important street, with the driveway entrance at the side where there is less traffic. In some situations, however, it may be better if house and garage face the same street.

SLOPING GROUND

Because of the extreme variation in the natural characteristics of sloping properties, it is not possible to do anything more in this book than give a few general ideas in planning for them. Such places are best planned by qualified architects and landscape designers who are trained to prepare clever, imaginative plans for each individual property. No two house plans or landscape plans will be the same; no more than two properties have identical natural features. Appropriate buildings and plantings can be planned either in modern or in the traditional manner, but difficulties in grading and in general appearance are encountered when a home of more or less standard design is built on a steep slope. A more pleasing result is obtained if the house is so designed that it blends with its surroundings, with the natural slope accepted and changed no more than is necessary.

There are at least two general characteristics which identify homes designed for sloping property.

1. They have different floor levels. Sometimes one floor is superimposed over the other. In this case only one story is exposed above the soil at the higher side, and two full stories show at the lower level. This is most likely to be the case if the slope is steep (Figure 6A). Here a basement garage may be suitable.

On less precipitous slopes there usually is less difference between the elevations of the floor levels, and one is placed beside the other with only a few steps between (Figure 6B). In this way the design of the house conforms to the slope of the ground.

2. The exterior finished siding usually does not continue at the same level on all sides of the house. It conforms to the slope of the ground so that the same approximate height

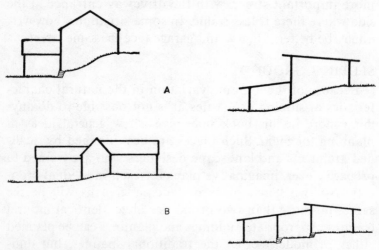

FIGURE 6. Homes on sloping land.

A. On steeply sloping land a house may look like a one-story house on the high side and a two-story house on the low side. This appearance may be minimized by adding a one-story wing to the low side of the house.

B. On moderately sloping land a house sometimes is built with different floor levels, one beside the other.

of basement wall shows above the soil level all the way around the house. An alternate but less satisfactory method is to paint the exposed portion of the basement wall the same color as the finished siding so that the line between the two is less obvious.

LAND ON WHICH TREES ARE GROWING

Building sites with a few good shade trees present special problems, but their value far outweighs any difficulties involved. A house usually can be located to avoid one or two trees. If you have found a site with large trees located where they will shade the house from the south or southwest, you are fortunate indeed. At this stage the location of the house can be adjusted a few feet this way or that to utilize the shade from the tree or trees. Ideas for the position of trees with relation to the house are found in STEP 7.

For comfortable shade the house may be placed within 10 feet of a tree if the variety is such that it has upright, arching branches which will not require too severe trimming. The house would have to be placed farther, possibly 15 or 20 feet, from a tree with a wide-spreading, horizontal branching habit.

Building sites with several trees growing on them, including those in a wooded area, may be a little more perplexing. Usually some of the trees have to be sacrificed. If there are one or two particularly fine specimens, they should be saved, and it may be possible to build near them even though it may be necessary to design a house to fit the particular situation. Other than that, locate the house as described at the first of this STEP and cut down all trees that do not conform to this plan. You can well afford to sacrifice a large tree of an undesirable variety, especially if it is not well shaped or is in poor condition because of cavities and broken branches. Sometimes good trees have to be removed when they interfere with the best position of the house. Small trees, 2½ inches in diameter or less, that conflict with the best use of the property are not worth saving unless they are good specimens and can be utilized elsewhere.

Grading

Although this STEP is chiefly for the new home builder, it is not uncommon for a homeowner to decide to regrade an established lawn. The general ideas presented here can be applied to either situation.

TREE PROTECTION

Before any grading or construction work is done, any trees to be saved should be protected. The site may have appealed to you largely because of the beauty of the trees growing there, and it would be heartbreaking to lose them. It takes many years to produce large trees, and they add considerably to the value of the land.

Trees located far enough from construction operations may not be subject to damage. However, operators of heavy soil-moving equipment and hand laborers sometimes accidentally break low branches or tear large pieces of bark from the tree. Damage to broken branches can be corrected quickly by proper pruning, but a scar left by the removal of a large piece of bark, if it is not properly and quickly cared for, will take several years to heal.

A fence may be built around each tree or clump of trees to be protected (Figure 7). If practical from the contractor's point of view, enclose approximately the full spread of the branches with posts spaced about 6 feet apart and with two or three wires connecting them. The fence may also prevent an invisible damage often disregarded. Soil added above the root system of trees may be fatal to them during even temporary storage. Trees sometimes have been so badly dam-

aged that they later succumbed because of soil left there
during one growing season while the house was being constructed. The reason for this is perfectly clear when we
realize that tree roots naturally grow in the soil at a depth
where they have available the required amount of oxygen,
water, and plant nutrients essential for root and top growth.
Adding soil to the original surface places these roots at a
lower level with regard to the new surface, and they are de-
prived of their required amount of these vital materials.

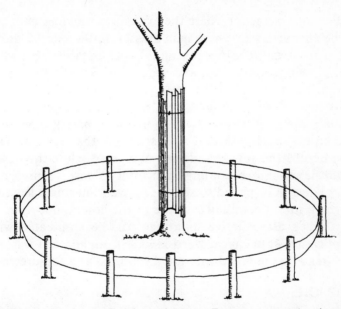

FIGURE 7. Tree protected from damage. Trees near construction operations should be protected from damage by a fence placed around
them or by boards secured around the trunks.

The fence also serves to keep heavy machinery from driving under the trees, a practice which packs the surface and
retards the flow of oxygen and water into the soil.

Where there is no opportunity to protect trees with a
fence, another method is used to protect them from aboveground damage. Boards, about 1 by 3 inches in size, are
placed vertically around the trunk of the tree and wired into

position. These boards should extend from near the ground level to a height of about 7 feet (Figure 7).

SOIL SAMPLES AND TESTING

If you are developing your lawn from the beginning on a new property or rebuilding an old lawn, soil samples should be taken for testing at this time. Information on this is given in STEP 5, p. 60.

THE UNSEEDED LAWN

Portions of the lot where the existing grade does not need to be changed, and where field grasses and weeds are growing, can be made into a reasonably presentable lawn without plowing, cultivating, and seeding it. Start in the spring when the stems are soft and mow the area regularly. This kills the tall-growing field weeds, and the grasses survive. Thus it may not be necessary to live with bare ground over the entire site for several weeks or months. Such a place can be utilized for a children's play yard while the newly made lawns are becoming sufficiently dense to use. You may later be surprised to see the mowed but unseeded area develop into a good lawn. Some of the common low-growing weeds may survive, but they can be eliminated with application of chemical weed killers. Roughness in the surface may be smoothed with good soil used as a top-dressing.

TOPSOIL

Preliminary grading on the home property begins with the first moving of the soil. The important rule here is to save all the available topsoil, hoping there is enough. None should be wasted as it would be expensive to buy enough for the thrifty growth of the lawn and other plants. Of course, if you are fortunate enough to be able to get an ample amount of it for the hauling from a nearby source, you need not save all you have on the lot.

The depth and quality of topsoil varies considerably from place to place. It consists largely of decomposed grass, leaves, twigs, and other organic matter. Usually topsoil is dark gray or black in color and may be from 3 to 12 or more inches deep, below which the color of the soil usually is yellow, brown, or red. There is quite likely to be a distinct line between the two colors.

GRADING THE LAWN

The ideal situation is one where the natural grade does not need to be changed extensively. If this is the case, you have done careful and excellent planning. You will be more likely to have good plant growth and will be saved from extensive grading and soil conditioning.

When heavy soil-moving equipment is on the property to excavate for the building, it is well to do any necessary rough grading that may be done at that time. The topsoil where the house is to be located, and for about 8 feet beyond, should be removed and deposited where it will not interfere with building construction or places where any cut or fill is needed in grading the lawn areas. Remove the topsoil from any places on the lot where the grade will be changed except around existing trees that are to be saved. Do not bury good topsoil under a fill of subsoil.

The lawns sufficiently far from construction operations can be done at this time or after the building is completed. In either case the rough grading is done with subsoil, the surface of which should be from 2 to 4 inches lower than the finished lawn to allow for a proper depth of topsoil (Figure 8). For variations of this procedure see STEP 5, p. 63. Under driveway locations, the rough grade should be from 9½ to 12 inches lower than the finished surface; under side-

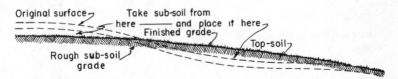

FIGURE 8. Grading uneven ground. Broken lines show the original surface and depth of topsoil. The full line shows the finished grade. The cross-hatched area is the topsoil for the new lawn, below which is the rough grade of subsoil.

walk locations, it need be only 4 inches below the finished surface.

At this stage it is best to do a thorough job of adding certain fertilizers. Broadcast 30 pounds of 0-10-10 fertilizer on the rough-graded subsoil and work it into the top 5 or 6 inches with a rotary tiller, or fork it by hand. These two major fertilizer materials, phosphorus and potash, do not seep into the soil readily, and it is well to mix them in thoroughly and deeply at this time. This places these materials at a depth where a high proportion of the roots will be growing. The available topsoil is then spread evenly over the surface to the finished grade.

Profiles A through F, Figures 9, 10, and 11, suggest solutions to various grading problems. The one which is best suited to your need, or a variation of it, is determined by the natural slope and the amount of soil available from the excavation. The amount of soil from this source varies with the size of the basement. Economies are effected by redistributing the soil on the property to equalize any necessary cut or fill. The ideas given in the various profiles shown here can be used around any house whether on a large or small lot or in a city or rural setting. They may all be adapted to the front, the rear, or either side of the house.

Grading on a relatively level lot usually is not much of a problem. Illustrated in profile A, Figure 9, is a simple and gradual reverse curve suitable for most such places. A grad-

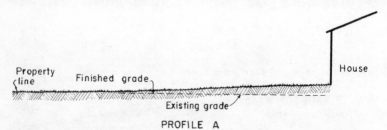

PROFILE A

FIGURE 9. Profile A. Grading about a house on level land. Grading around a house on level land is simply done. Add only enough topsoil to give surface drainage away from the house.

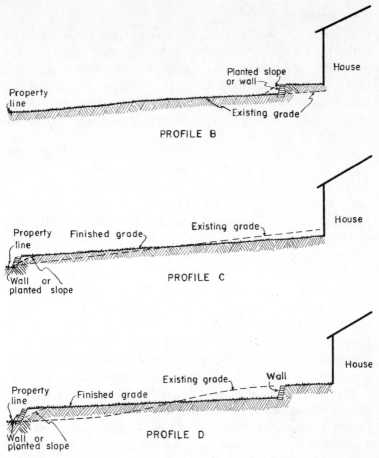

FIGURE 10. Grading about a house located above the adjacent land.

Profile B shows a slightly sloping lawn and a terrace near the house. The terrace simply covers what would otherwise be an exposed high foundation wall.

Profile C shows a slightly sloping lawn made from land that was rather steep. The house was placed lower than the original grade. The soil level was lowered near the house and raised near the property line, equalizing the cut and fill.

Profile D. This house is placed high on rather steeply sloping ground. A terrace near the house is at the level of the original grade. The balance of the lawn is made more level by lowering the grade near the terrace and using this soil to raise the grade near the property line. Retaining walls or planted slopes divide the different levels. The lower wall may be near to or some distance from the property line.

ual incline also would be appropriate. Here the house is located only slightly higher than the adjacent property. The pitch may vary from an average of 1 to about 3 per cent, that is, a 1- to 3-foot rise to each 100 feet of horizontal distance. The 1 per cent grade is suitable for lawn games and other outdoor living; the 3 per cent grade is better for an ornamental lawn only.

Profile B, Figure 10, shows a house above the adjacent land. The terrace next to the house is built up with soil taken from the excavation or obtained elsewhere. The terrace should be a minimum of 8 to 10 feet wide if it is to be used for outdoor living, and usually extends the full width of the house or more. The retaining wall may be a dry stone wall, one laid without mortar, or a masonry wall, with mortar. Instead of a wall, a steep slope planted with ground covers may be used. It is best not to use grass on a slope as it is hard to mow. If the terrace is at the side or behind the house it might be paved and provided with an outdoor fireplace. If the area between the foot of the wall and the property line slopes only enough for surface drainage, about 1 per cent, it would be suitable for lawn games.

Profile C, Figure 10, shows grading which may be done near a house located about the same distance above the adjacent land as the one in profile B but with a greater amount of soil to be used. The wall or planted slope is made near the property line rather than near the house. The slope from the top of the wall to the house may vary from about 1 to 3 per cent.

The grading shown in profile D, Figure 10, provides for a greater difference in elevation between the house and the adjacent land. It may be a combination of profiles A and C or B and C. Depending upon the height of the slopes or walls and the difference in elevation from one side to the other, the lawn may or may not be level enough for all outdoor activities.

Profile E, Figure 11, illustrates the grading that may be done on any of the four sides of the house in situations where it must be located below the adjacent property. The land slopes upward from the house. Redistribution of the soil on the site provides a pleasing setting for the house and proper surface drainage. A wall may be preferred to a gentle slope and would provide an attractive background for a flower garden. If this lawn is quite large, the wall or slope may be 8 or more feet inside the boundary line and the border planting be done on the higher level.

Another possibility for grading a site where the house is located below the adjacent property is shown in profile F, Figure 11. As with all the other plans, the slope between the wall and the property line can be adjusted to be more nearly level or more steeply sloping, depending upon which will be best for your use. If the low area is against a side or rear

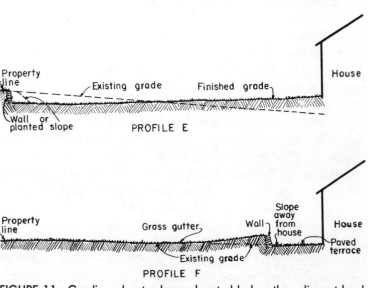

FIGURE 11. Grading about a house located below the adjacent land.

Profile E. The house is placed higher than the existing grade. The cut and fill is equalized by lowering the grade near the property line and raising it near the house, covering the high foundation wall and making a more level lawn.

Profile F. In this plan the existing grade has been changed very little. The space near the house was graded to slope outward, and a fill made beyond the wall was shaped to carry surface water toward the property line and off to one side.

wall of the house, it might be developed into a paved terrace with flagstone, brick, or other material used as the surface. Also, if desired, an outdoor fireplace could be built into the wall.

The grass gutter above the wall is smoothly curving so that it can be cut easily with a lawn mower. It is just deep enough and correctly graded to catch surface water and carry it away to one side or the other to a suitable outlet, rather than permitting it to drain over the wall toward the house. The low portion of the slope away from the house also is graded to carry excess water to one side. If feasible, it usually is better to locate the wall or steep slope near the property line or just far enough away from the house to allow ample space for the desired use.

DETERMINING THE GRADE NEAR THE HOUSE

The difference between the desired soil grade and the finished first-floor level of the house will be determined largely by the type of construction, the existing grade, and whether there are trees near the house to be saved by leaving unchanged the natural grade around them. The established first-floor elevation governs the depth of the excavation.

Ideally, the natural grade should be changed no more than is necessary to obtain surface drainage away from the house in all directions and avoid a flow of water into the basement or against the side of the house. Excavation soil frequently is used to produce such a grade. If there is extra soil not needed for this purpose, it may be utilized elsewhere on the property where it is needed, or it may be trucked away.

For best appearance and convenience, the first-floor level should not be very much above the level of the finished lawn. For a house of frame construction this would be about 19 inches, about three or four steps (Figure 12A). The finished soil level would then be at least 2 to 4 inches below the siding, which is where it should be, as soil banked against the siding causes the wood to rot.

For a house of masonry construction the soil may be built up onto the stone, brick, or other wall material. The first-floor level might be only 2 inches above the finished grade outside so that there is only a low step between the two (Figure 12B). The house thus appears to merge into its surroundings.

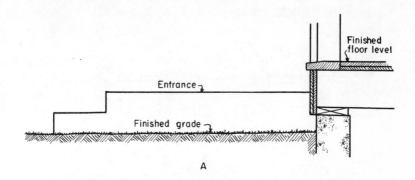

A

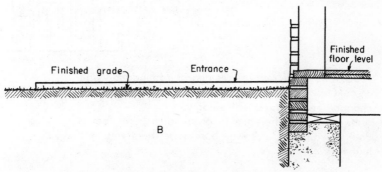

B

FIGURE 12. Determining the grade near the house.

A. Usually a house of frame (wood) construction requires a few steps between the outside grade and the first-floor level.

B. A house of masonry construction need have only one low step between the outside grade and the inside floor level.

On properties where the topography is irregular, it is necessary sometimes to have a precipitous slope at right angles to the foundation wall to give access to a basement doorway or to provide light to low windows. The difference in grade may be as much as 7 feet. Sometimes this slope is planted with ground covers, but probably it is better to build a retaining wall of stone or concrete, part of which may be covered with a vine (Figure 13, A and B).

If for some reason the house must be set higher than is ideal, allowance sometimes is made for a greater amount of fill near the foundation (Figure 14, A, B, and C).

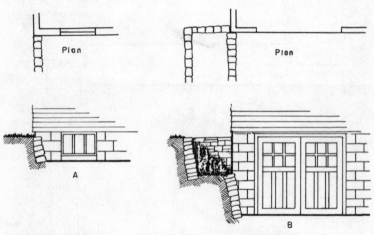

FIGURE 13. Different grades near the foundation wall.

A. Only a low retaining wall is necessary when the grade is changed near a basement window.

B. When a difference in grade of several feet is necessary, a double wall with a flower border between retains the soil at the higher level.

FIGURE 14. Grading about a house with a high foundation wall.

A. Only a narrow fill is necessary if the space is to be used for planting flowers, vines, or low-growing shrubs. If the house is placed lower with relation to the existing slope than the one indicated here, the terrace near the house would be omitted. Only a slope sufficient to carry surface water away from the house would be necessary.

B. A fill 5 or 6 feet wide is adequate for large-growing shrubs.

C. A fill 8 or more feet in width may be used for special planting and outdoor living.

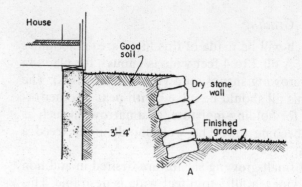

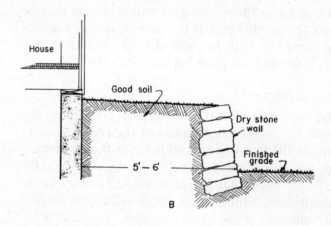

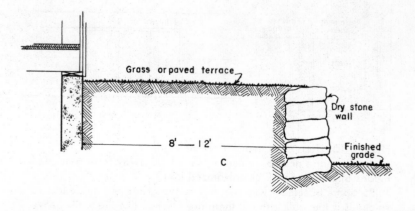

The use which will be made of this filled area determines the width of it. A fill 3 to 4 feet wide is enough for planting flowers, small-growing shrubs, and vines (Figure 14A). The soil used for this fill should be mixed with peat or other organic material for holding moisture, as a narrow fill such as this tends to become dry. The wall should not exceed a height of about 3 feet.

If large- and small-growing shrubs are desired in addition to flowers and vines, a fill 5 to 6 feet wide is desirable. This is shown in Figure 14B. If the area is increased to a width of 8 to 12 feet, it may be sown with grass seed or paved to form a terrace for outdoor living. A wider terrace may be partly paved and partly lawn. If this terrace is over 6 inches high, steps should be built in a convenient location to give access from it to the lawn level below.

BASEMENT WINDOWS

It has been suggested that the finished grade near the house should be within a few inches of the finished siding so that most of the foundation wall is covered. If basement windows or ventilators are to be below grade, a concrete retaining wall or semicircular galvanized retainer may be installed around each of these windows or ventilators (Figure 15A). If the windows are to be above grade, the general ap-

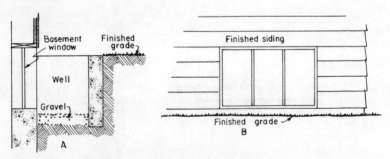

FIGURE 15. Treatment near basement windows.

A. Fill made near basement walls is held away from windows by means of concrete wall or galvanized iron.

B. Some basement windows left above grade are made less conspicuous if the walls around them are finished like the walls above.

pearance is better if some provision is made for covering the foundation wall with siding to within 2 to 4 inches of the finished grade (Figure 15B), or for painting the wall to match the color of the house.

Special Problems

ROCK LEDGES AND HIGH WATER TABLE

Sometimes unpredictable, perplexing situations arise. A high water table, a subsurface rock ledge, or some other condition makes it advisable to build the house at a higher level than was originally intended. If any such conditions are encountered, it is best to get the advice of a qualified engineer. He may be able to suggest a way to lower the water table or advise what to do about the rock ledge. Sometimes it is less expensive to dynamite into the rock so that the house may be set at the intended level than to set the house higher and have to buy fill to raise the outside grade. However, if the house must be set at a higher level for basement headroom or dry footing, the ideas suggested in Figure 14, A, B, and C, may be used to keep within reason the amount of fill needed. The available space or the way in which the higher level is to be used will indicate the best position for the wall.

DRAINAGE AND SEEPAGE

Surface runoff water may be troublesome if the land slopes downward toward the house, but the amount is much less when the ground is covered with lawn and trees than when it is bare. Where there is a considerable watershed, the amount of runoff may reach alarming proportions, particularly after a hard rain. Most of this water can be intercepted by plowing or digging a diversion ditch at the high edge of the lawn to be protected. Sometimes it is necessary to have a second diversion ditch or grass gutter graded with a smoothly rounded surface for easy mowing (Figure 16A). This will catch the water that accumulates beyond the higher ditch. The water must be channeled to a suitable outlet.

The same general principle applies to the roadside ditch

in rural places and in villages where there are no storm sewers. If there is little water running in the ditch, and this only on occasions following a heavy rain, the ditch may be no larger nor deeper than a grass gutter (Figure 16B). If greater amounts of water need to be carried, the ditch must be larger and may be left open or laid with tile of adequate size. An open ditch sometimes is lined with stone, with the wall on each side extending to the lawn level (Figure 16C). If the ditch is to be tiled, either bell-end tile or galvanized corrugated pipe may be used. Coarse sand or fine gravel is placed around the tile and filled to grade with good soil before grass seed is sown. With this arrangement an unbroken lawn extends to the roadside (Figure 16D).

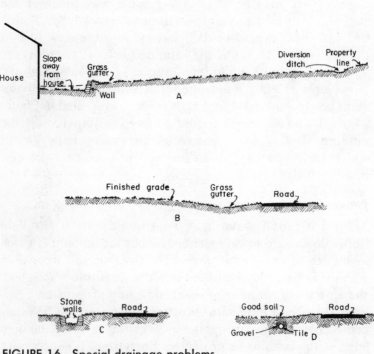

FIGURE 16. Special drainage problems.

A. Diversion ditches intercept and carry away surface water that may otherwise be troublesome.

B, C, and D. These illustrate three methods of conducting roadside surface water across a property frontage.

Seepage creates a problem on some properties when water filters down through the surface soil to an impervious layer of hardpan or heavy clay, where it flows along at this subsurface level. If its flow is toward the house or if it causes other undesirable excess moisture, a trench should be dug in a position to intercept the seepage and carry it to a suitable outlet. Dig the trench 6 or 8 inches into the impervious layer and lay agricultural drainage tile. Cover the joints with a wrapping of tar paper before covering the tile with fine gravel; then backfill the trench with soil (Figure 17).

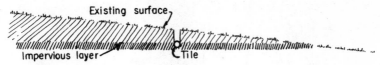

FIGURE 17. Intercepting subsurface seepage. Sometimes correctly located tile lines are necessary to carry seepage to a suitable outlet.

Tile also may be laid to drain low wet places if a suitable outlet is available.

GRADING AROUND TREES

Many valuable trees are lost by making soil cuts or fills around them before taking proper precautions. Just a few inches of fill with clay soil may cause the death of a tree. It may be killed in one season, or it may live longer. No one can say just how much soil may or must not be added. In general, it varies with the character of the soil. If a fill only 2 or 3 inches deep needs to be made, sandy soil is the best type to use as it is more porous and less harmful than clay.

When grading around a tree, remember that the main portion of the root system is contained in the soil under about half the spread of the branches but that they do extend, on a radius, a distance equal to the height of the tree or more. The lateral roots are near the surface and are more or less parallel to it. On level land these roots are perpendicular to the trunk of the tree (Figure 18A). On a slope the tree will grow in a vertical position, and the roots remain parallel to the surface of the ground, so there is an acute angle between them on one side and an obtuse angle on the other (Figure 18B).

In most cases it is not advisable to try to save young trees at much expense even though they may be good varieties. Grub them out by cutting out the crown, do the necessary grading, and at a later, proper planting season, replace them with the same or a better variety. It is probable that a larger specimen than the one you have lost can be planted for less than it would cost to save the original one.

FIGURE 18. Roots grow parallel to the surface of the ground.

Large trees of good varieties are sufficiently valuable to warrant taking all possible precautions to save them. Do not lower the grade within a radius of 15 to 20 feet of any large tree to be saved, as the roots will then be closer to the surface than the level at which they normally grow, causing them to dry out and die.

Necessary fill in the vicinity of a tree or clump of trees can be adjusted sometimes so that no new soil is placed within one-half to three-fourths of the spread of the branches. This is the area under which the major part of the root system is found. At this circumference, the fill on the high side and the original soil level on the low side can be retained by dry stone walls (Figure 19A). The amount of cut and fill determines the height of the walls. Some small roots are cut off unavoidably on the low side, but enough of the root system is retained for good growth and anchorage. This is the safest method of protecting the tree. The area under the tree

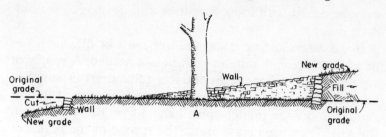

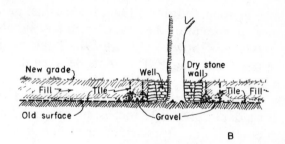

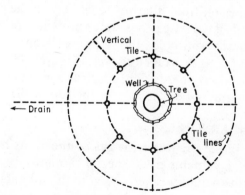

FIGURE 19. Grading around trees.

A. A fill on one side of a tree is held in place by a dry stone wall. A cut at the other side is separated from the original grade by a wall. If a cut is made on all sides of a tree, a wall is built surrounding it, forming an island of the original grade.

B. If a fill of considerable depth must be made on all sides of a tree, an open well is left around the trunk, and tile lines covered with gravel provide access for air and water to the old surface.

may be paved with loose flagstone and developed for outdoor living.

If the entire surface under the tree must be filled 6 inches or more, more elaborate preparation is needed. A supply of air and moisture for use by the tree roots must be supplied to the old surface. Drainage also must be provided. The surface under the branch spread should be forked to loosen the soil. Then broadcast under the spread of the branches 10-6-4 fertilizer, or one of about this analysis, at the rate of 3 pounds to each inch of tree-trunk diameter. Thus a tree 10 inches in diameter would receive 30 pounds of fertilizer.

Lay lines of 3-inch agricultural tile on the original grade under the complete spread of the branches in any suitable pattern, one of which is shown in Figure 19B. Slope the tile away from the tree for drainage. The joints between the tile should be wrapped with tar paper. Place field stone, gravel, broken brick, or other coarse material on the ground and over the tile for a depth of 6 to 12 inches, being careful not to move the tile out of line. A 2-inch layer of fine gravel is placed on the coarse material to be followed by a layer of straw to keep the soil from filtering down betwen the stones. Tiles are placed in a vertical position and held upright by the fill. A dry stone wall holds the soil away from the trunk of the tree and forms a protecting well (Figure 19B). If the tree is in a location where such construction would be a hazard, a grating may be placed over the top of the well.

TRENCHES NEAR TREES

If trenches for sewer, water, or gas connections need to be dug near large valuable trees, special care must be taken. Cutting big roots would weaken the growth and anchorage of the tree, causing it to decline in vigor and increasing the chances of its being tipped over during a severe storm. Small roots may be cut, as they are soon replaced by the growing tree.

Dig carefully around the roots more than 1 inch in diameter and permit them to extend through the trench into the soil on the other side (Figure 20). If some provision is made to drain the water away, a hose can be used to wash the soil from the roots. Tunnel under the large roots to the required depth. If the trench is to be left open for several days, burlap, kept wet, should be wrapped around the exposed roots.

There is little danger of roots growing into a tile line if the joints are watertight and no tiles are broken.

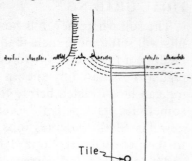

FIGURE 20. Trenches near trees. Large tree roots that extend through areas to be trenched are carefully saved by tunneling underneath them. The exposed roots are covered with wet burlap.

BACKFILL AROUND THE FOUNDATION

Some of the subsoil from the excavation may have been used for grading various parts of the property, with enough left nearby to backfill around the foundation, including any terraces to be made near the house. When the foundation wall has set thoroughly and as soon as the contractor agrees everything is ready, backfilling may be done by placing subsoil,

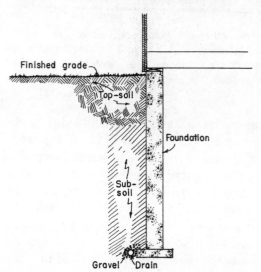

FIGURE 21. Backfill around foundation. Place good topsoil at the surface near the foundation.

containing no wood or other scrap building material, to within 2 feet of the finished grade. Topsoil is used to complete the fill ready for the foundation planting (Figure 21). It is well to get the backfill done as soon as possible to allow time for it to settle.

FINAL GRADING

The soil where new fills have been made will settle. Deep fills will settle more than shallow ones, so if the grading can be done a few months before time to sow the grass seed, irregularities caused by uneven settling or by inaccurate grading can be corrected before the topsoil is spread. Settling is sometimes hastened, if necessary, by thoroughly wetting new fills. Shallow depressions that hold water can be graded to the proper level. Look over the land from all angles in order to locate and correct the imperfections. A straight-edge and carpenter's level are useful tools to use when grading the lawn to make a proper slope for surface drainage. Tight lines between stakes often are used as a guide.

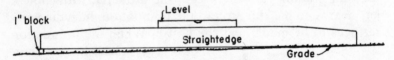

FIGURE 22. Final grading. When a 1-inch block is needed to level an 8-foot straightedge, the grade drops 1 inch in 8 feet, or about 1 per cent. This is enough for surface drainage. If a 2-inch block is needed to make the straightedge level, the slope is about 2 per cent.

When all building materials have been removed from the ground outside the house, 2 to 4 inches of topsoil (STEP 5, p. 63) is placed over all rough-graded lawn areas except under trees to be saved and where sidewalks and driveways are to be located. Allow enough depth for the type of paving construction you are to use. STEP 4 gives information on this procedure. Stones and other debris should be removed from the surface, and none should be left in the ground where it will be a nuisance when working the soil in years to come.

Driveways and Sidewalks

Driveways and sidewalks should be planned for convenience. The suggestions given here can be modified and adapted to many situations, both urban and rural. They can be used by those developing a new home and those who wish to revise the driveways and sidewalks on older places. Use the plan that most nearly meets your requirements.

Place the driveway on the service side of the house for easy access to the side entrance or kitchen doorway and for deliveries of household supplies. Unless service to both sides is needed, avoid a driveway around the house. In most situations a semicircular driveway in front is not desirable as the paved surface breaks up lawns and results in less privacy in outdoor living areas.

It is best to construct these approaches after the final grading is done but before the lawn is seeded. This provides a guide for the top of the paved surfaces, which should be flush with the finished lawn. If it must be done at a later stage, slight damage to the turf may result, but as a rule this can be remedied easily.

Wherever possible, all driveways and sidewalks should be located 6 feet or more from a building to allow for an adequate foundation planting. The larger the building, the greater should be this allowance. It usually is best for the sidewalk to meet the steps, another walk, or the driveway at a right angle.

ENTRANCE PLATFORMS AND STEPS

Platforms at doorways should be large enough to permit the screen or storm door to swing open without forcing the waiting guest into the hazardous position of stepping back, down, and around it. This means that the platform should be at least 3 or 4 feet wider and 1 or 2 feet deeper than the width of the door. Steps having 4- or 5-inch risers and 15- to 18-inch treads are more comfortable to use than higher and narrower ones. A sturdy railing at either side of the platform and steps gives added security and eliminates the danger of stepping off the sides (Figure 23).

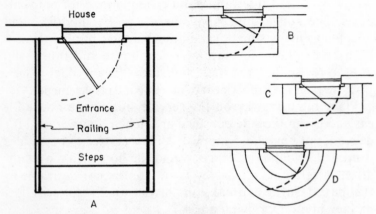

FIGURE 23. Entrance platforms and steps.

A. The entrance platform should be adequate in size for convenient use, the steps comfortable to walk up and down, and both protected by a railing.

B, C, and D illustrate poor step arrangements.

NARROW CITY AND VILLAGE LOTS

The conventional plan on narrow city and village lots calls for a garage attached to the house and facing the street. For economical and easy use of the plot, a straight driveway leads from the street directly into the garage as shown in Figure 24A. If there is enough space, it may be possible to provide an off-the-street place to park as indicated by dotted lines at the right of the driveway. Curved driveways require careful maneuvering. The owner may, in time, become accustomed to a slight curve, but guests who

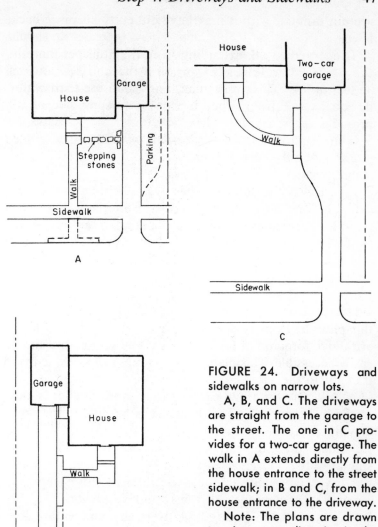

FIGURE 24. Driveways and sidewalks on narrow lots.

A, B, and C. The driveways are straight from the garage to the street. The one in C provides for a two-car garage. The walk in A extends directly from the house entrance to the street sidewalk; in B and C, from the house entrance to the driveway.

Note: The plans are drawn to give some diversity in the position of the sidewalk and driveway with relation to the house and garage. If the relation of your sidewalk and driveway is the reverse of any of these plans, turn the book so that the bottom of the page is away from you. Then hold a mirror at the bottom of the page, and the reflected image of the plan will be like yours.

are not familiar with it may have difficulty keeping off the lawn.

The straight walk extending from the house entrance to the street sidewalk is appropriate if the house is set back 35 feet or less. This position accommodates pedestrian traffic equally well from either direction. A steppingstone walk provides access from the driveway.

If street parking is the custom, the walk may be extended to and along the curb, if there is room. A 2-foot walk is sufficiently wide and saves the grass.

Figure 24B illustrates another good position for a private sidewalk for a house near the street. Here the walk extends from a platform at the base of the steps in a line parallel to the house and not less than 6 feet from it. At the other end it follows the driveway for a distance great enough to allow car passengers to step onto the walk rather than onto the grass. If desired, this walk may be extended to the street sidewalk. If not, pedestrians may use the driveway. With this plan the front lawn remains unbroken and provides an attractive foreground for the house. The service entrance is easily accessible. This plan is particularly suitable when foot travel is to the left.

A driveway for a two-car garage on a narrow lot is illustrated in Figure 24C. The driveway is parallel to the property line, but is widened on the one side to give access to the other side of the garage. The position of the sidewalk is similar to that in Figure 24B. If the garage is near the street, the driveway usually is double width for its entire length.

An arrangement for a driveway and sidewalk on a corner lot is illustrated in Figure 25A. Here the garage and main entrance to the house face the same street. The front door is near the corner of the house, a position which makes

---

FIGURE 25. Driveways and sidewalks on small corner lots.

A and B. Much of the lawn space on urban corner lots fronts on a street. This limits considerably the amount of space available for outdoor living.

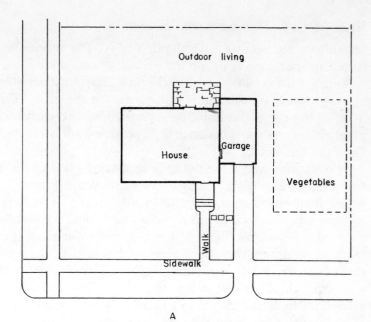

A

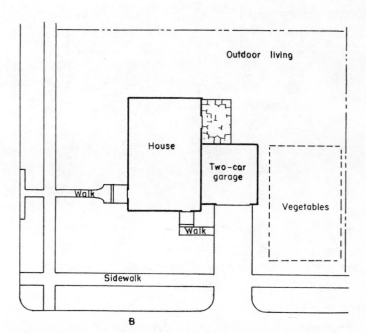

B

feasible its connection with the driveway. The service entrance to the house is inside the garage.

Another corner-lot situation (Figure 25B) illustrates the house entrance on one street, the garage on the other. The front entrance to the house is extended to the curb and parallels it for a short distance. The service walk is reached from the driveway.

In situations where the house is set back 50 feet or more from the street, the walk may curve as shown in Figure 26, A and B. The distance here is sufficiently great to have long, sweeping curves bearing in the direction most frequently traveled. As the plan illustrated in Figure 26A assumes that the walking approach to the house is from the left, the walk should curve in this direction. Steppingstones provide a walk from the driveway to the front steps. The walking approach to the house shown in Figure 26B is from the right. Here the driveway is on the same side, and they are joined for about half the distance.

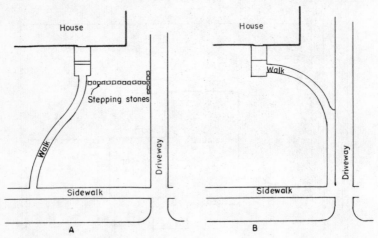

FIGURE 26. Curving sidewalks.

A and B. A curving sidewalk bears in the direction most convenient for pedestrians.

Figure 27A illustrates a Y-driveway arrangement for a narrow lot on which the garage does not face the street. The

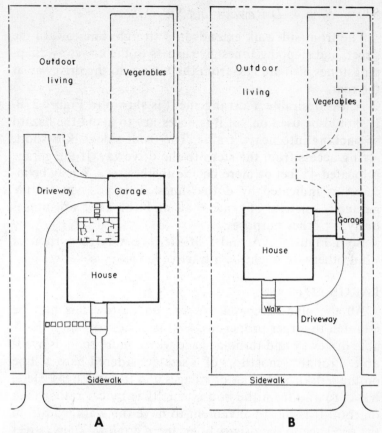

FIGURE 27. Driveway turning space on narrow lots.

A. The house must be planned especially for this garage and driveway arrangement.

B. The driveway Y in front of the house is not attractive but sometimes necessary. The alternate suggestion, made by dotted lines, is uneconomical of space and involves costly driveway construction.

necessity of backing into the street is avoided, emergency parking space is provided, and tables and chairs may be placed on the paved driveway when guests are entertained. It may also be used for some outdoor games such as tetherball. From these standpoints this arrangement is rather desirable. However, a driveway that separates the terrace from the rear lawn may be objectionable because of the interrupted view and the oil, grease spots, and dirt from car tires.

The front sidewalk extends in a straight line toward the street, and steppingstones give access to the driveway. Steppingstones also are laid from the terrace to the driveway at the rear.

A less desirable Y arrangement is shown in Figure 27B. It should be used only if it is necessary to avoid the hazard of backing into heavy traffic. The front sidewalk is short, giving access from the steps to the driveway. If the garage is located 45 feet or more behind the house, a Y may be located as indicated by dotted lines. This position for the garage is wasteful of space that might be used advantageously for other purposes.

Both Figures 27A and 27B sacrifice a large portion of what otherwise might be attractive lawn.

LARGE LOTS

All the plans prepared for use on narrow lots may be adapted to larger properties, as it is easier to plan a desirable driveway and turning space where more room is available. Probably most lots of a size considered here will be on the outskirts of cities or villages and in rural areas. Here, travel to and from the house usually is by car rather than on foot. It is most convenient to have the walk lead from the entrance to the driveway, as there are few, if any, street sidewalks in most communities such as we are now considering. Walking to the neighbors or to some special place on the grounds can be across the lawn unless the trip is frequent enough to wear a path. In this case, steppingstones may be laid.

A "Y" in the driveway requires more space than usually is visualized. The dimensions given here are ample for most cars, but it is advisable to try turning your car in the area to be sure the space is large enough. If more space is available and easier turning or more room for parking is desired, the appropriate dimensions may be increased (Figure 28).

The plan illustrated in Figure 29 is similar to the one in Figure 24B, but, because more space is available, a Y is constructed in the driveway. If additional parking space is

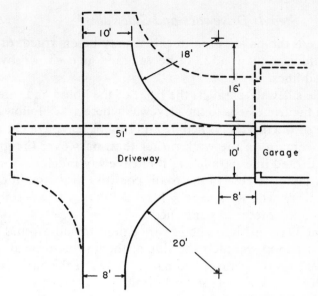

FIGURE 28. Dimensions for a driveway Y. Dotted lines show the additional space needed for a two-car garage and an alternate arrangement for backing straight out of the garage, the driveway forming a T.

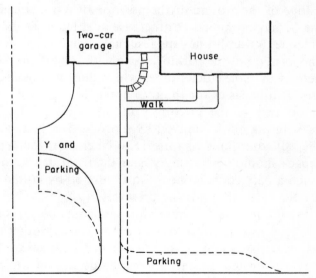

FIGURE 29. Driveway Y on a large property. The Y and parking space are located in the side lawn where they are convenient to the front entrance to the house.

desired, the paved area in the Y may be enlarged, or the shoulder of the road may be widened as is shown by the dotted lines.

The sidewalk parallels the front of the house and extends from the front steps to the driveway where a "T" follows the edge of the driveway. People entering or leaving a car may then remain on the walk rather than pass over the grass. The dotted line paralleling the driveway indicates a sidewalk giving access to the road, possibly to the mailbox in situations where there is R.F.D. delivery. Steppingstones lead to the breezeway entrance.

The plan in Figure 30 is convenient for all-around use. The driveway parallels the side of the house, turns at right angles into the garage, and has a Y toward the back. If additional parking space is desired, the driveway may be widened as indicated by the dotted lines near the garage. Steppingstones give access from the driveway to the service entrance.

If a right-angle Y is not feasible for any reason, such as the slope of the ground or the position of a tree, the shape of the Y may be spread or otherwise adapted to fit the situation. The dot-dash lines suggest such a change.

The location of the parking space with relation to the entrances of the house determines which door will be used by guests. If it is easier for them to enter through the service door because of the proximity of the parking space, the housewife may be dismayed by a procession through her kitchen. If front-door visitors are to be encouraged, a parking space should be invitingly near the front door. An idea for such a pass court is shown in Figure 30 by dotted lines where the sidewalk joins the driveway.

Although it is best to have this pass court on the side of the driveway toward the house, lack of space or other existing characteristics may make this position impractical. Then it may be located on the opposite side of the driveway. Make it long enough to park one or two cars.

It is best to have the pass court in a level or nearly level place. Sometimes, however, there is a slope in the ground

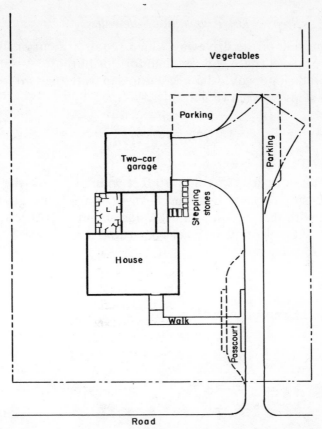

FIGURE 30. Several ideas for turning and parking on a large property. One is represented by full lines, another by a dot-dash line, and others by dotted lines.

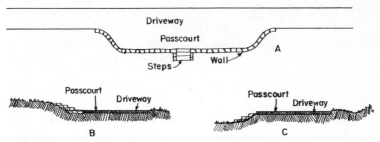

FIGURE 31. Details of pass court. The pass court is made most easily on level land, but sloping ground can be utilized by grading suitably and building a wall and steps. Cross section B shows a slope upward toward the house, and C a slope downward toward the house.

at the side of the driveway which requires a cut or fill to make a level space wide enough for this purpose. A wall or planted slope would be needed to separate the two levels with steps between (Figure 31).

Construction

DRIVEWAYS

Make the driveway 8 or 10 feet wide and have the finished surface level with the lawn or, on sloping ground, level with the shoulder on each side (Figure 32). The three general types of all-weather construction are stone, blacktop, and concrete.

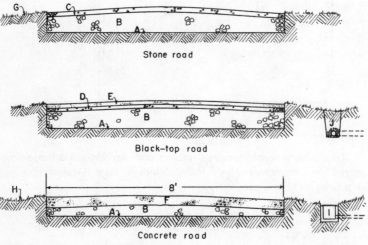

Stone road

Black–top road

Concrete road

FIGURE 32. Road construction details. These construction details were obtained from the Building and Grounds Department, Cornell University.

In any of these types of construction, grade the roadbed (A) to easy slopes on a solid foundation by excavating to a depth of 10 inches for a stone road, 12 inches for a blacktop, and 9½ inches for concrete. Then put a layer of coarse stone in the bottom of the excavation (B) and roll or otherwise compact it. This layer should be 8 inches deep for stone and black-top roads and 4 inches deep for concrete.

For a stone road, put a 2-inch layer of fine crushed stone (from ¼ to 1 inch in size) on the surface and roll it (C). To maintain this road, fill the surface holes and hollows with fine crushed stone and roll the road firmly. Keep a crown in the center.

For a black-top road, put a 2-inch layer of fine crushed stone (D) on the base, keep a 2-inch crown, and roll the road. Put a layer of asphalt mix (E) 2 inches deep on the surface, using a mix that will not become soft and sticky in hot weather. Roll to a smooth surface. Asphalt mix is sold under a variety of trade names.

For a concrete road make the side forms 5½ inches high and place between them No. 3 6x6-inch highway wire. Pour concrete (1-2-3½ mix) between the forms (F), embedding the wire. Crown the surface at the center and smooth with a wood-float finish. Make the expansion joints 50 feet apart.

Four types of grading with drainage construction are illustrated. Select the type appropriate for your situation. If the natural slope of the ground permits, keep a gentle pitch downward from the road on both sides. The road should be higher than the adjacent grades so no water will stand on the surface (G). If there is a slight incline, make shallow, smoothly rounded grass gutters (H) to carry the surface water to a suitable outlet. In low, wet places, install concrete catch basins (I) with tile leading to a suitable outlet. Sometimes a ditch with a tile at its base (J) and covered with gravel will carry excess water away satisfactorily.

SIDEWALKS

Make the main walk, the one leading to the guest entrance, 3½ feet or more in width. It may be made of concrete, brick, concrete faced with stone or brick, large flagstone with grass growing in the joints (Figure 33C), or any black-top construction that will not become soft and sticky in hot weather. Make the surface of the walk flush with the lawn.

Sidewalk construction need not be so heavy as that for a driveway. The base for the concrete or asphalt walk need be only 4 inches deep and may be of gravel, cinders, or sand. Put 4 inches of concrete (1-2-3½ mix) on top of this and smooth it with a wood-float finish. Put expansion joints 50 feet apart and make creases 5 feet apart with a joining tool.

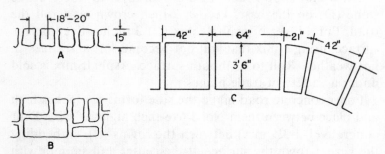

FIGURE 33. Details for stone walks.
  A. Steppingstone walk. Space the stones so that you step easily from one stone to the next.
  B. Crannied-stone walk.
  C. Flagstone walk.

For an asphalt walk, put 2 inches of asphalt mix on top of the 4-inch base and roll it thoroughly. Be sure to use a material that will not get soft and sticky in hot weather.

Flagstone walks may be laid on 2 or 3 inches of sand or cinders. The excavation for this type of walk need be only deep enough to permit the surface of the stone to be flush with the surface of the lawn. No part of the walk should be lower than the adjacent grade as this would allow water to stand on the surface. Sometimes, on sloping ground, one edge of the walk is made from ¼ to ½ inch lower than the opposite edge to permit surface drainage.

Most concrete and asphalt work is best done by a contractor.

SERVICE WALKS

Extend the service walks from the side or rear entrance of the house to the driveway, garage, vegetable garden, or other frequented part of the property.

Make these walks from 2 to 2½ feet wide. Although the plans show all service walks made with steppingstones, they may be made with brick or other suitable material. They may be made of solid construction, as suggested for the main walk, but usually steppingstones, set in the ground or on a sand cushion with the top surface level with the lawn, are satisfactory. The steppingstone walk and crannied-stone walk (Figure 33, A and B), are less conspicuous than a walk of solid construction and, therefore, are better for these minor walks. Each stone should be smooth on the surface with no dimension less than 12 inches. Small stones quickly become grown over with grass.

Four or five steppingstones placed in a frequented, narrow path avoid a bare place being worn in the grass.

Lawns

The processes described in this STEP can be used to make a new lawn or make over an old one. Information is given on lawn maintenance, including weed control.

Lawn Making

SOIL SAMPLES, TESTS, AND FERTILIZERS

Soil samples taken from your property should be obtained from a depth of 2 to 3 inches. On large properties several are taken from each area, thoroughly mixed together, and 1 pint taken from the mixture. On average-sized home properties, take one from the front, one from each side, one from the rear lawn, one from the vegetable garden, and one from each special planting area. On narrow home sites, one from the front lawn and one from the back is enough. One pint of soil is a suitable amount for each sample.

Put each sample in a separate paper carton and label it clearly "front lawn," "side lawn," "back lawn," or "vegetable garden," and take or mail it to your county agricultural agent or the agronomy department of your State College of Agriculture for examination and test. In an accompanying letter give some basic information, such as, "the area from which this sample was taken will be used for a lawn—vegetable garden—shrub border—planting roses—planting rhododendrons"—or any other use you plan to make of this soil. State the depth from which you have taken the samples. Ask for appropriate tests and for recommendations as to the amounts and kinds of seed and fertilizer to use, whether or not the soil needs organic matter, ground limestone, or sulfur.

Without much doubt you will be advised to broadcast about 30 to 40 pounds of a mixed fertilizer on each 1,000 square feet of surface. A common fertilizer recommended for this purpose is 5-10-5. These figures represent the percentages of nitrogen, phosphorus, and potash contained in the mixture. In other mixtures these figures are different, but the order—nitrogen, phosphorus, and potash—always remains the same. These are the elements most often lacking.

Probably you will be told that the soil you sent has a certain pH value, probably some number between 4.5 and 8.5. The numbers refer to a standard scale measuring acidity and alkalinity, sometimes called "sour" and "sweet." The neutral point is pH 7. Numbers lower than 7 indicate the extent of acidity, and those higher than 7, alkalinity (Figure 34). Usually ground limestone is recommended to decrease acidity or increase alkalinity, and sulfur or aluminum sulphate to increase acidity or decrease alkalinity.

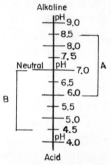

FIGURE 34. The acid-alkaline scale.

A. Kentucky bluegrass and most plants will do well in this range.

B. Fescues, creeping bentgrasses, and other acid-soil plants will do in this range.

Most soils are deficient in organic matter, and the form most often available in your community may be recommended. Those most used include peat, composted soil, commercial humus, sawdust, ground corncobs, spent mushroom soil, and barnyard manure.

All the materials recommended may be broadcast over the surface of the ground and mixed into the soil in one operation.

If the recommendations based on the results of your soil test differ from those given here, use those made for your specific situation, not these general ones. However, if you have not had a soil test, those given here may be used for most situations with satisfactory results.

TOPSOIL

Even though the existing topsoil has been saved carefully, it is frequently necessary to obtain additional amounts
to use on the lawn and for other plantings. For many years
the recommended practice has been to place a 3- to 4-inch
layer of topsoil over the rough grade.

Unfortunately, no specifications are available describing
good topsoil, probably because it varies widely in quality.
Many homeowners pay high prices for soil that is little better than that which they have on their property. Probably
the best way to be sure you are getting good quality soil is
to buy it from a reliable person or have someone who is
qualified advise you. Have the topsoil tested so that you will
be able to supply, in recommended amounts, fertilizers and
soil amendments such as organic matter, ground limestone,
or sulfur.

Good topsoil frequently is obtained from swamps or
from the surface of a productive farm field. It should have
a high percentage of organic matter and be of medium texture, a mixture containing a little more clay than sand. The
organic matter, sand, and clay content can be estimated by
its color and by "feel." It is dark, nearly black, like decomposed or partly decomposed leaves and twigs. A soil having
good texture will crumble when moist and, when wet, does
not pack tightly like a snowball. Clay, when wet, packs sol-
idly. Rub a pinch of soil between your thumb and fore-
finger. Clay soil is made up of very small particles and is
smooth and sticky. If there is some sand in the soil, these
larger particles feel gritty. Texture is far more important
than fertility, as a mixed fertilizer can be added easily to
provide adequate amounts of nitrogen, phosphorus, and
potash.

PREPARING THE SOIL FOR SEEDING

If the suggestions given in STEP 3 have been followed, the
ground has been graded to slope away from the house in all
directions to obtain surface drainage, and drain tile laid

where necessary. The topsoil has been moved from all areas where the existing grade needed to be changed; the rough grading has been done; phosphorus and potash have been mixed into the subsoil. Stones and other debris left on the surface have been removed. The available topsoil has been spread over the surface and graded to an even slope.

Seldom do two individuals follow the same exact process in preparing the soil for seeding a lawn, but most of them obtain a satisfactory turf. The rapidity with which a new lawn becomes established and the quality of the turf in years to come vary somewhat with the thoroughness of preparation. In general, the more ideal the preparation, the better the results; but very good lawns have been produced on clay soils considered far from ideal. Described in order of preference, first, second, and third, the different methods might be listed this way:

1. As little as 1 inch of topsoil may be used, but 4 inches will produce better and more lasting results. Broadcast a fertilizer of about 10-8-6 analysis over the entire surface at the rate of 30 pounds to each 1,000 square feet of lawn. This is mixed into the surface when it is raked to grade.

2. If no topsoil is available, spread a 2- to 4-inch layer of organic material such as peat, composted soil, commercial humus, sawdust, ground corncobs, spent mushroom soil, or barnyard manure. Any of these may be substituted for topsoil to improve the water-holding capacity of sandy soils or to lighten clay. Rotted barnyard manure contains many weed seeds that may be troublesome later. Peat, sawdust, ground corncobs, or other undecomposed organic matter deplete the supply of nitrogen in the soil. For this reason, if they are used, a greater amount of fertilizer, about 50 pounds of 10-8-6, is broadcast over each 1,000 square feet of surface. The organic material and fertilizer is then mixed with the top 3 or 4 inches of soil by forking or with a rotary tiller.

3. Sometimes neither topsoil nor organic matter is available. Although it is not generally recommended, practical experience and some experimental evidence indicates that

good lawns can be made on clayey subsoil if it is fertilized heavily and cultivated with a machine such as a rotary tiller. In addition to the 30 pounds of 0-10-10 mixed into the subsoil previously, broadcast about 25 pounds of 10-8-6 and mix it into the top 3 or 4 inches of soil.

The new commercial soil conditioners may prove to be valuable as a substitute for organic matter in improving clay soils, but they have not yet been tested sufficiently for one to be certain of results.

If the soil is almost entirely of sand, use the method described in (1) or (2).

Whether you have used topsoil, a substitute for topsoil, or have prepared the subsoil as the base for your lawn, you are now ready to smooth the surface to the proper slope by raking. The final raking before seeding should be done when the soil is quite dry. Alternate rolling and raking is advisable. Rolling compacts the surface and makes imperfections in the grade more obvious. These imperfections can be corrected by pushing and pulling the soil from the high spots into the low places with a garden rake. This, at the same time, loosens the surface to form a good seedbed.

TIME OF YEAR TO SEED

Fall is the preferred time for seeding a lawn, and if preparations are made early in the season, one may avoid a last-minute rush. All preliminary work should be done before the first of September, at about the 41st Parallel, which extends across southern New York, northern Ohio, Indiana, and Illinois, central Iowa, and Nebraska. For each 5 degrees of latitude north of this, you should seed about two weeks earlier, and for each 5 degrees south of the 41st Parallel, about two weeks later.

August is a good time to prepare the surface for seeding, as this is apt to be a dry period with little danger of being delayed by wet soils. For locations near the 41st Parallel, if the grading is finished by the middle of August, weed seeds left near the surface will germinate before September 1. These weeds can be hoed or otherwise cultivated out of existence before the grass seed is sown; thus the new lawn will have few weeds in it. Grass will appear before cold weather, and the lawn will be well established, ready to grow into a more dense turf at the first sign of spring.

The second-best time to sow grass seed is early in the spring, about the middle of April near the 41st Parallel. For each week of delay after this date, the chance of reasonable success becomes progressively poorer as natural rainfall diminishes. The later the date, the more artificial watering will be required to produce equivalent results.

LAWN GRASSES

The lawn grasses most used today are the same ones that have been used for many years. However, new strains are now available in small quantities, and other new ones are being developed and tested in many parts of the country. Your State College of Agriculture or Experiment Station can give you up-to-date information on the new developments in your area.

KENTUCKY BLUEGRASS is used at the rate of 3 pounds to each 1,000 square feet of surface. It is the most popular lawn grass throughout the East and Middle West, where it grows natively, but does not do well in tropical and semi-tropical climates. This grass produces a dense turf and is best adapted to a loamy soil and sunny locations, although it will do well in heavy clay, in the shade of houses, or under a tree of open framework. It does not do well under closely planted trees nor trees having a dense branching habit and surface roots. Norway maple has these characteristics. Kentucky bluegrass is best when mowed about 1½ inches high. It turns brown in dry summer weather but recovers its fresh green color a day or two after a good rain or after adequate artificial watering.

MERION BLUEGRASS is a new strain that shows considerable promise and is available in ever-increasing quantities. It seems to withstand dry periods well and may be mowed lower than Kentucky bluegrass. If sown alone in good soil, 1 pound of this seed is enough to use on each 1,000 square feet. In less favorable conditions, use it at twice this rate. If used with other seeds, at least 30 per cent of the mixture should be Merion bluegrass.

WILD WHITE CLOVER, when added to Kentucky bluegrass, is used at the rate of 2 ounces to each 1,000 square feet of area. One of its main values rests in its ability to remain green through extended dry periods. For this reason the appearance of a bluegrass lawn is improved by the addition of this clover seed. This clover is valuable also for its contribution of nitrogen to the soil, one of the major fertilizers needed by grasses and other plants. Used alone or in too great abundance with Kentucky bluegrass, it does not produce a good turf. It is open, soft, slippery, and does not wear well under heavy use but recuperates rapidly. If you decide to use clover in your seed mixture, be sure to use a wild white clover such as Kent or New York, not white Dutch clover.

On each 1,000 square feet of lawn, you should use 3 pounds of Kentucky bluegrass mixed with 2 ounces of wild white clover.

CHEWINGS FESCUE and CREEPING RED FESCUE are used at the rate of 6 pounds to each 1,000 square feet. These lawn grasses are tolerant of adverse growing conditions. They have a creeping growth habit but do bunch somewhat. They grow well in dry soils, such as sandy and gravelly soils, acid soils, and in the shade of dense trees. They also grow well in full sunlight. They will be more successful on steep slopes than will Kentucky bluegrass. Fescues have a finer leaf blade than does Kentucky bluegrass and produce a fine-textured, light blue-green lawn, one that will stand up under rough usage. The leaf blades have a wiry toughness but can be cut without difficulty if mowed often with a sharp, well-adjusted mower. When it becomes long and dense, it is somewhat difficult to mow.

There is a new strain called Illahee fescue. It also has a creeping habit of growth and is preferred by some to the creeping red fescue.

BENTGRASSES are those most often seen on golf putting greens as they make a beautiful, fine-textured turf and with proper care are tolerant of close clipping. Bentgrasses are sometimes seen on home properties, but they require more care than most homeowners wish to spend on them. They are susceptible to diseases and require frequent watering, fertilizing, and mowing. If some bentgrass is desired in a home lawn, a strain of colonial bent, such as Astoria or New Zealand, is the best kind to use. It blends well with Kentucky bluegrass. Mix 4 ounces of colonial bent with 3 pounds of Kentucky bluegrass for each 1,000 square feet of lawn.

Polycross bentgrass is a new strain that shows considerable promise. It has been developed for use on golf putting greens but may find its place on the lawn of a homeowner who desires a superior type of turf.

BERMUDAGRASS and ZOYSIA are two lawn grasses used mostly in the South, where they provide a cover throughout the year. The old varieties are at their best during the winter season. In the dryness of summer they become brown unless they are watered heavily and frequently. These grasses are being studied, and new and better strains are gradually becoming available, some that are better than the existing kinds for the deep South and some that successfully combine with other grasses for use in the North. Lawns of bermudagrass and zoysia are made by setting plugs of sod or planting stolons in evenly spaced rows rather than by sowing seed.

Among the new strains that appear to have special merit are U3 bermudagrass and zoysia 52.

TEMPORARY LAWNS

Probably REDTOP and RYEGRASS are the two temporary grasses most often used in lawn seed mixtures. Sometimes they are called a "nurse crop" because they germinate quickly and form a green cover from one to two weeks earlier than bluegrass, fescue, or bentgrass. If they are used at all, the amount should be kept down to 10 per cent or less of the whole. Redtop is a rather coarse-textured grass, and it is believed that more than 10 per cent will produce an inferior turf. It is not tolerant of regular mowing and will disappear in two or three years. Both Italian ryegrass, which is an annual, and the perennial kinds are coarse in texture and usually should be omitted from seed mixtures. However, they frequently are used to cover bare ground with a sward when the soil is prepared too late in the spring for seeding a permanent lawn and too early for fall sowing.

SEED MIXTURES

It is doubtful if there is any advantage in buying a packaged lawn-seed mixture containing four or more different kinds of seed. Certainly there is financial disadvantage in buying a seed mixture containing a high percentage of undesirable grasses, temporary grasses, weeds, foreign matter, and seeds showing, by test, a low germination count. Cheap seed is the most expensive kind to buy. Only a small amount of good seed is needed, and an extra fifty cents for each pound will not seriously affect the total cost. Even though a packaged mixture containing a high percentage of three or four different kinds of good lawn grasses is used, those most tolerant of the existing conditions will thrive and in a few years crowd out the others. No seed mixture should contain less than 60 to 75 per cent of good perennial grasses. Each package must state on the label the kind of seeds contained therein and a record of the germination test of each kind.

Pennywise and resultwise it is best to use the seed or seeds best adapted to the existing conditions of climate, soil, sun, and shade. The separate kinds can be purchased from and good seed store, a farmer's cooperative, or a feed and grain dealer.

SEEDING

If two or more kinds of seed are being used, they should be mixed together thoroughly before sowing.

Seeding is most accurately done with a mechanical device that can be set to distribute the seed at the recommended rate. This would be 3 pounds of Kentucky bluegrass or 6 pounds of fescue for each 1,000 square feet if the seed is sown in one operation. However, a more even distribution is obtained if it is done in two operations, sowing half the seed as the machine is pulled in one direction and the other half as it is pulled at right angles to the first sowing.

In either case, to ensure complete coverage, use stakes and strings to divide the lawn into as large units as is practical, keeping the sides parallel if possible (Figure 35). On a

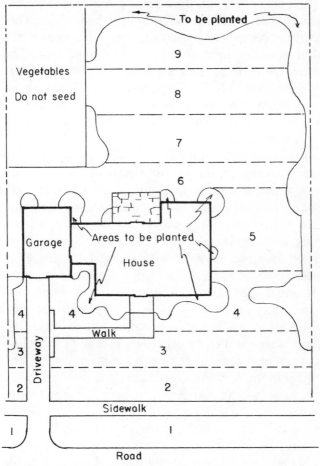

FIGURE 35. To ensure complete coverage with grass seed, an entire home property can be divided into sections, using stakes and strings for the dividing lines. Do not sow grass seed in the areas to be planted.

calm day operate the machine in slightly overlapping rows, being sure that all edges and corners are covered. Overseeding at the ends of rows is avoided if the machine is shut off while turning. Do not let the hopper run out of seed. The best place to replenish the supply is at the end of the row. Any small areas not reached with the machine may be seeded by hand.

Home gardeners can do a good job of sowing grass seed by hand if they follow a rather simple procedure. The main difficulty encountered is that of being able to sow evenly a small amount of seed on a relatively large area. This can be overcome by increasing the bulk to be broadcast. If Kentucky bluegrass is to be sown, weigh out 3 pounds of seed for each 1,000 square feet of surface to be covered. Thoroughly mix this seed with fine sand to increase the volume about ten times.

Follow the same directions given for sowing with a mechanical seeder. Mark off the lawn with stakes and strings, wait for a calm day, and divide the seed and sand in two equal portions. Then, walking slowly, sow one portion in one direction, the second portion at right angles to the first, overlapping slightly and making sure all lawn surfaces are covered. Sow only those parts where a lawn is desired.

The entire seeded area, whether hand- or machine-sown, is then lightly raked to provide adequate contact between the soil and seed. Care must be taken not to bunch the seed in some places and leave others bare. The best tool for this job is a wooden rake, as the teeth are blunt and will not dig deeply into the soil. An iron rake may be used if care is taken to use it lightly so as not to bury the seed too deep to germinate.

At this time, if the soil is quite dry, the seeded and raked areas may be rolled as is frequently recommended. However, do not use a roller on wet soil, as the roller will pick it up along with some seed, redistributing unevenly the seed you have so carefully broadcast. Rolling after the fertilizer has been mixed in has compacted the soil sufficiently to draw capillary water to the surface. Raking after seeding has established contact between the seed and the soil. Adequate moisture for germination is still needed. If natural rainfall does not keep the surface moist, water lightly and frequently with a fine spray at least once a day. Be careful not to wash the seed as this will leave bare spots. Alternate wetting and drying of the soil may destroy the seed; once the soil has become wet, therefore, be sure it does not dry out.

If you have used redtop or perennial ryegrass mixed with your permanent perennial grass seed, some green color will show in about a week. Kentucky bluegrass, fescue, and bentgrass will appear in about two weeks. Cold weather or dry soil retards germination. An average of four or five weeks is required to obtain a turf sufficiently dense to use for outdoor living.

New grass should be mowed when it is about 2 inches high. The blades of the lawn mower should be set 1½ inches high or more if they can be adjusted to this height. Unfortunately, some hand lawn mowers cannot be set this high. Mow as often as is necessary to keep the length of the clippings ½ to ¾ of an inch. Longer clippings may mat down and smother the new grass.

SODDING

If you are in a special hurry to obtain a complete lawn or only a special, conspicuous portion of it, this may be accomplished by sodding. When sod is to be laid, the prepared surface should be the same as for a lawn but about 1½ inches below the finished grade to allow for the depth of the sod. A lawn made in this way is expensive, but immediate results are obtained at any time of the spring, summer, or fall.

Some nurserymen and landscape contractors maintain large areas of turf from which they cut sod of uniform depth and width. Sometimes good sod is obtained from a well-kept pasture. About 1½ inches of soil depth is taken with the grass. The length and width of each strip may vary, but they usually are about 3 feet long and 12 to 14 inches wide. These strips of sod are laid on the graded soil, side by side, end to end, with the edges firmed snugly together. The end joints are staggered. After the sod is laid, any joints that do not fit closely are filled with fine topsoil. The new lawn is then watered thoroughly and rolled with a heavy roller. If the sodding is done in the summer, watering should be frequent and thorough, especially in dry weather. If the grass begins to turn brown, watering should be done more often and more thoroughly.

STEEP SLOPES

Making a good lawn on a steep slope is difficult, because any rain heavier than a light sprinkle washes the soil, including the seed, down to the foot of the slope. Maintaining a lawn on a steep slope is just as much of a problem. Rain or water from a hose flows over the surface too fast to penetrate the soil. As a result, more frequent watering and fertilization is necessary. If you should be fortunate enough to obtain a dense turf, it is difficult to mow in any direction —lengthwise, up, or down.

There are two good ways to deal with a steep slope. One is to plant it with low-growing shrubs and ground covers; the other is to build a dry stone wall and plant it as a wall garden. These two methods are described in STEP 9, pp. 198–200.

If you still prefer grass on an embankment, the surest method of obtaining it is by sodding, as has just been described. Wooden pegs driven through the sod into the soil will prevent the sod from slipping.

A less expensive way to obtain a turf on such a slope is to seed it. One of the creeping fescues described under lawn grasses, is the best to use as they are tolerant of dry soil. After seeding, erosion can be diminished by a 2-inch covering of loose, clean straw, strips of burlap, or other open fabric. When the grass is established, the straw may be raked off. Burlap may be left to decompose.

Lawn Maintenance

MOWING

Probably the most common and persistent mistake home-owners make in the maintenance of their lawns is cutting the grass too short. Lawn-mower blades sometimes are set so low that they actually scrape the earth in places where small mounds are encountered. Grass will not tolerate such abuse. Most lawn grasses, including bluegrass and fescue, should be cut at least 1½ inches high. This makes them more thrifty and dense enough to crowd out many weeds. Bentgrasses are tolerant of closer mowing, as short as ½ inch.

In order to adjust the lawn mower for height of cut, the roller is raised or lowered to the proper position as determined by the measured height of the cutting bar from the ground (Figure 36). Most hand lawn mowers should be set

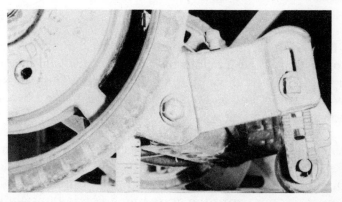

FIGURE 36. Adjust the lawn mower. Check the cutting height of the lawn-mower blades.

as high as they can be adjusted. This means that the roller is secured at the lowest position possible. Put the bolts in the highest holes in the two roller brackets and slide them to the bottom of the slots in the mower side frames. Tighten the bolts firmly. Check the cutting height by placing the mower on a smooth surface, such as a sidewalk, and measuring the vertical distance from the sidewalk to the edge of the cutting bar.

During the season of rapid growth, such as late spring and early fall, when moisture and temperature conditions are ideal for growth, the lawn should be mowed more often than during dry weather. Gauge the period between mowings by the growth of the grass, not by the number of days. Allow the grass to grow from ½ to 1 inch so the clippings are about that length.

The clippings should be left on the lawn. As they decompose, they add to the layer of organic matter and return some fertility to the soil. The only occasion on which the clippings should be raked off is that when the lawn has been neglected. Then the clippings are so long that they mat over the grass and, when dried, give a brown cast to the lawn. Occasionally, when the clippings are desired for a mulch in a flower or vegetable garden, they may be raked off and used for this purpose.

By mowing around in a counterclockwise direction, most mowers throw the clippings toward the inside, and the next trip around cuts them into smaller pieces. This tends to avoid matting, and as the small clippings dry and become brown, discoloration will be less obvious.

There is some advantage in mowing around a square rather than back and forth in consecutive rows. The wheel of the lawn mower packs a strip of uncut grass which does not immediately recover to its upright position. Mowing around a square gives the grass time to spring upright before the next trip. Thus it does not remain packed until too late to be cut on the return trip, and ridges of grass are avoided.

FERTILIZING

New lawns that have been fertilized properly before being seeded need not be fertilized again for about a year. Thereafter, one application of a mixed fertilizer, such as a

10-8-6, broadcast in the early spring at the rate of 20 to 30 pounds to each 1,000 square feet, is enough for most lawns. Those growing on infertile soil may require a second application, this one to be broadcast early in the fall and at the same rate. Lawns containing some clover and growing on heavy soil may not need to be fertilized for several years, as these soils contain and retain nutrients for long periods of time. Also, the clover will continually supply the soil with the ever-important element, nitrogen.

Probably the appearance and growth of the grass is the best indication as to whether or not fertilizers are needed. If the turf is dense, growing thriftily, and is a good dark green color, there probably is no need to stimulate more growth. Thin turf, poor growth, and yellow-green color all point toward lack of fertility in the soil.

Fertilizers should be applied evenly to avoid spottiness or streakiness in the lawn. Even distribution is obtained with an inexpensive mechanical spreader, but a little practice enables most people to do a creditable job by hand. It should be broadcast when the grass is dry, so that the granules will fall down between the blades of grass to the ground. Fertilize just before a rain, or water the ground with a hose after application. Either dilutes the fertilizer so it does not injure the grass. Placing the fertilizer on moist grass and soil provides only slight dilution, and the grass and roots may be seriously burned.

WATERING

Lawn grasses fortunately have amazing recuperative ability and survive extended periods of dry weather. They turn brown and may appear to be completely dead. Two or three days after a thorough watering they will be green again. Brown lawns are not so attractive as green lawns, but if you can tolerate a few weeks of this discoloration, you do not need to water.

Watering a lawn adequately with a hose or sprinkler system during periods of drought will maintain a green lawn throughout the summer. Leave the sprinkler in the same place for two or three hours so that the water will penetrate several inches into the soil. Covering all the lawn once a week in this manner usually is enough. One part of the lawn may be done on one day, another part the next, and so on until the entire lawn is covered.

Frequent light watering during dry weather is detrimental to lawn grasses as it induces shallow rooting. Plants with shallow roots may be damaged during periods of drought.

ROLLING

The type of roller containing a water tank is best suited for use on home lawns, as the weight is easily adjusted with the amount of water put in it. In areas where the soil is subject to frost action, rolling is done early in the spring, just as the frost is coming out of the ground. The roots of grass and clover that have been heaved out are thus pressed back into place. Rolling at this time smooths the lawn more effectively than after the soil has settled.

Rolling the lawn at other seasons is not recommended.

SMOOTHING ROUGH LAWNS

Established lawns made on poor soils sometimes are too rough for convenient use or easy mowing. They may be smoothed by broadcasting a dressing of good topsoil that is free of stones. This may be obtained from a productive vegetable garden, cultivated farm field, low bottom land near a stream or swamp, or from the woods. It should be high in organic matter.

This topsoil is leveled into the low places by dragging a rubber or metal door mat or a plank over the lawn. Go over the entire area twice, the second time at right angles to the first. On a small lawn the topsoil can be leveled into the low places with the back of an iron garden rake.

Places where fills of ¼ to ½ inch have been made need not be reseeded, as the grass from the lawn soon comes through. Greater fills may need to be sown with the kind of seed adapted to the situation.

Large bare spots in a lawn should be scratched with an

iron garden rake to loosen the surface before sowing the seed.

RENOVATING OLD LAWNS

Lawns that need to be completely done over are treated in various ways, depending upon existing conditions. If the ground is very rough, if there are no large trees on the lawn, and if bare soil is not objectionable for a month to six weeks, the old lawn may be plowed and kept cultivated until late August, when it can be graded and seeded as described for making a new lawn. Plowing sod under is not recommended unless there is ample time for the sod to decompose. If the process is hurried, the ground settles unevenly and results in a lawn almost as rough as it was originally.

If there are large trees on the lawn, the roots make plowing difficult, if not impossible. In this case the old turf can be cut with a disk harrow if care is taken not to cut deeply within the spread of the branches of the trees. After the ground is thoroughly cultivated, it should be graded to an even slope, raked, and seeded.

WEED CONTROL

Many weeds are avoided if the new lawn is prepared and sown in the fall, if chemical fertilizers are used instead of barnyard manure, and if cultivation immediately precedes sowing with a good grade of seed.

Many types of weeds are eliminated automatically with proper lawn maintenance. Fertilizing the grass and mowing it at a height of 1½ inches encourages the growth of a turf so dense that many weeds are crowded out.

In spite of all early precautions, established lawns become infested with weeds of various sorts. In days gone by, a weed-free lawn was something to behold. It was a sure sign that the owner or his gardener had spent many hours digging weeds by hand. Hand weeding is still carried out effectively and probably will always be a recommended practice for certain weeds. If weeds are eradicated before they produce ripened seeds, this source of reinfestation is eliminated.

A few years ago a dramatic discovery was made, and home gardeners now have at their disposal a chemical that kills some of the broad-leaved lawn weeds such as dandelion and plantain. It selects these unwanted lawn weeds as its victim and does not damage the grass. This chemical is 2,4-dichlorophenoxyacetic acid and is popularly known as 2,4-D. It is made and packaged by several different chemical companies, each selling it under a different trade name. However, the label on the package describes the contents and gives recommendations for its use. Follow these instructions, as they have been proven effective by accurate tests.

A number of different contrivances are available for applying lawn weed killers. One consists of a glass bottle or metal container into which a concentrated solution of 2,4-D is poured. The cover for this container fits tightly and is equipped with a spray nozzle and a threaded opening for screwing onto the end of a garden hose. The suction provided by the running of water through the nozzle draws the 2,4-D into the water stream and mixes the two together before they are applied to the weeds. Although these proportioners are inexpensive and satisfactory for small lawns, the tiny aperture through which the concentrate is drawn sometimes becomes plugged. It is then necessary to clear it. Before this difficulty is observed, a considerable area of lawn may unknowingly have been sprayed with clear water or an ineffectively dilute solution of 2,4-D. Also, the amount of concentrate drawn from the container varies with the fluctuations of water pressure, and thus some too-dilute and some too-concentrated solutions are applied.

Probably the best equipment for applying lawn weed killers is a 2- to 4-gallon compressed air sprayer. The pressure is pumped by hand. A short hose with wand-type connection to the nozzle makes it possible to apply the spray at close range without stooping. It provides a comfortable working height and minimizes the danger of damaging other plants. The air pressure of these sprayers can be kept reasonably steady by frequent pumping, and the concentration of the 2,4-D applied is constant.

Regardless of the type of applicator you decide upon, it is best to use it for weed killers only. Identify it conspicuously with red paint. You may use different types of weed killers in it, but do not use it to apply insecticides or fungicides because you may seriously injure or kill some plants you value highly. Have a separate sprayer for pesticides.

Wait for a calm day to spray the weeds because even a mild breeze may carry the mist a considerable distance. Some plants, such as tomatoes and squash, are highly susceptible to very dilute concentrations. 2,4-D kills dandelions and plantain at any time during the summer, from the time they appear in the spring through October. Badly infested lawns should be given complete coverage. In order to do this efficiently it is necessary to hold the nozzle about 2 feet away from the surface of the lawn. Once the existing weeds have been eliminated, the worst of your lawn-weed troubles are over, but weed seeds will be blown and carried in, and new specimens will appear from time to time, sometimes in considerable abundance. When the majority of the weeds have been eliminated, "spot spraying" may be done on individual dandelions and plantain as they appear. In this way the lawn can be kept relatively free of these pests. When "spot spraying," hold the nozzle down close to the weed so there is less danger of the mist's being blown onto other nearby plants.

There are other lawn weeds such as chickweed, in variety, on which 2,4-D is not always effective. For chickweed and other broad-leaved weeds, if the first application is not effective, try again with a solution about 1½ times stronger. Two or more applications may be needed. Be still more careful of the mist's being carried to other plants.

Do not expect to see these treated weeds wilt and disappear immediately, as 2,4-D does not act swiftly. However, within forty-eight hours an effectively treated plant begins to respond. The leaves become brittle and curl and twist into distorted shapes. In two or three weeks the weeds will completely disappear, and the entire plant will be dead.

Another weed killer, called 2,4,5-T, is effective on a greater variety of broad-leaved weeds, including chickweed. In addition, it kills a number of broad-leaved woody plants. Highways, railroads, and electric power companies are using 2,4,5-T and other chemical herbicides to kill plants along the right of way. Scientific experiments have proved repeatedly that neither 2,4-D nor 2,4,5-T are toxic to humans or any form of animal life.

Crabgrass is another troublesome lawn weed. It is an annual plant, produces seeds prolifically, and spreads over large areas of lawn in two or three years unless it is observed and controlled before it becomes established. Dig or pull out each plant you discover and burn it. Do not let the seeds mature, as they are the source of next year's crop. Crabgrass is an aggressive grower during late July and August, and severe infestations crowd out the desirable lawn grasses.

Several weed killers have been used experimentally on crabgrass, and two of them have given good results. The seeds of this weed germinate early in June, and in the early stages a water-soluble phenyl mercury compound is effective. One of these is popularly known as PMAS, which may be applied in liquid form or as a powder. Follow accurately the directions on the container. The great advantage of using this herbicide early is that the plants are killed while young, before the seed has set, and the greatest source of next year's infestation is eliminated. It may be necessary to repeat treatment the following season to combat plants started from seeds brought in by birds or those produced by plants which survived the current year's spraying.

The phenyl mercury compounds are most effective on crabgrass at the seedling stage, but good results have been obtained on mature plants. However, potassium cyanate is most effective on old plants. This chemical is sprayed on during late July and August. Do not be disturbed if this material discolors the grass, because its normal color soon returns.

Much research work is being done with chemical weed killers, not only for lawns but for private and public rights of way, and in the maintenance of farm crops. If you have a special problem along this line, you can always get reliable, up-to-date information from your State Experiment Station, State College of Agriculture, or County Extension Service.

MOSS IN THE LAWN

Moss in the lawn is more often an indication of low fertility than of acid (sour) soil. Lime should not be used unless a soil test indicates that it is needed.

The moss should be raked out and 10-8-6 fertilizer broadcast over the affected area at the rate of 30 pounds to each 1,000 square feet. The surface soil is then loosened with an iron garden rake, and the areas sown with the kind of lawn seed best suited to the situation, as described earlier in this STEP. Annual fertilization thereafter stimulates dense turf and discourages the reappearance of moss.

Planting and Care
of Woody Ornamentals

This description of good procedure in planting, transplanting, and maintenance of woody ornamentals is intended to help all home gardeners.

Planting Woody Ornamentals

NURSERY-GROWN PLANTS

All trees, shrubs, and evergreens grown in nurseries, if they have been properly cared for, have been transplanted or root-pruned and top-pruned at least two or three times before they are ready for market. In the process of root pruning and transplanting, the long roots are cut off, a procedure which stimulates a growth of feeding roots in a mass directly underneath the plant. This makes digging, packing, and planting much easier, and plants become established more quickly when they are set out. Nursery plants usually are better shaped than native trees and shrubs from fields and woods. The tops have been pruned for a desirable head, while many of the native plants require careful pruning to obtain a well-formed plant. Usually this training must be done gradually from year to year, cutting out the ill-shaped and unnecessary wood to encourage the branches that will ultimately fill in the open spaces and form a strong structural framework. Some plants naturally grow in a dense, compact form and need to be thinned by removing some of the branches that seriously crowd others.

82

SURVIVAL

The failure of newly set plants to survive is apt to be caused by a lack of care in planting. Each plant should be set at the proper depth with good soil firmed completely around all the roots. Other causes of failure include roots seriously broken or dried before planting, too much water, lack of water, particularly during the first growing season, insufficient top pruning, or failure to mulch. If plants are carefully planted and cared for, it is not unusual to have complete success with a fairly large order. Seldom will the loss be greater than 10 per cent.

CARE OF PLANTS RECEIVED

Plants that cannot be set as soon as they are received from the nursery should be properly stored. If they are to be planted within a day or two after they are received, they should be left in the package. Wet them with a hose or dip them in water and store them in a cool, shaded place. If planting is to be delayed more than two days, they should be unpacked and heeled into the ground by digging a trench, placing the roots in the bottom, and covering them with soil (Figure 37). If the roots are dry, they should be immersed in water for an hour or two before they are heeled in. The soil that has been firmed around the roots should be kept moist. They may be stored over winter in this man-

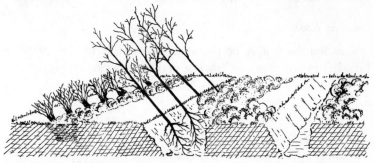

FIGURE 37. Heeling in. Plants may be stored safely with the roots covered with soil, kept moist.

ner if necessary, but it is best to plant them in their permanent positions as soon as possible.

SEASON TO PLANT

Hardy Trees, Shrubs, and Vines

Experimental evidence on the best season to transplant woody ornamental plants is varied and confusing. It changes from season to season, from one locality to another, and with the different species of plants, some being transplanted successfully either in the fall or spring, others being transplanted more successfully in the spring.

Most hardy trees, shrubs, and vines, if they have been freshly dug, packaged, and planted within an hour or two after they are received, will survive equally well whether planted in the spring or fall, providing the roots have not been exposed to drying sun and winds. Spring planting probably is somewhat safer than fall planting. It has been fairly well established that root growth will not occur when the soil temperature is below 40° to 45°F. At Ithaca, New York, the soil temperature at the 12- to 18-inch depth is below 40° to 45°F. from about October 15 to May 1. This includes all of the fall planting season, from the time the leaves begin to turn color until the ground is frozen. It also includes most of the spring planting season, from the time the frost is out of the ground and the soil is dry enough to be workable until growth starts. This means that the roots of a fall-planted tree, shrub, or vine remain dormant until the soil becomes warm in the spring.

Garden Roses

Garden roses may be planted successfully in the spring or fall. In severe climates, spring planting is preferable.

Evergreens

Broad-leaved evergreens, such as laurel and rhododendron, are planted successfully either in the fall or the spring, but early spring probably is the safer time.

Narrow-leaved evergreens, such as pine, spruce, juniper,

yew, and the like, are best planted early in the spring. Early fall planting usually is successful also. Fall planting usually begins about August 15 in central New York, depending upon the season, and lasts for four or five weeks. The spring planting season begins as soon as the frost is out of the ground and continues until growth starts.

Summer Planting

Some nurseries now sell and plant evergreen shrubs throughout the summer and guarantee them. Such plants are stored with a ball of earth which is wrapped with burlap and packed in wet peat or in loose ground which is kept moist. Sometimes they are planted in special containers, such as heavy paper or clay pots. The plants thus remain in good growing condition until they are planted. Transportation and planting does not disturb the root system to a marked degree, and, with a little extra care in watering, the plants do well.

The same is being done with flowering shrubs, perennials, and garden roses. Large trees are being moved with success in midsummer when the trees are in full leaf. Although this practice is comparatively new, several nurseries have carried on the operation with success. The main consideration in the survival of these plants seems to be in giving them enough moisture.

SOIL PREPARATION

Deciduous Trees, Shrubs, Vines, and All Alkaline-soil Plants

Often the soil obtained from the excavation has been put on the surface of the ground surrounding the house. This subsoil needs to be improved with organic matter such as peat or well-rotted barnyard manure before it is suitable for growing plants. On a farm the manure is available in quantity, and in the city one can get peat. Of the two materials, peat is the better. It retains a larger amount of moisture than does manure and is free of weed seeds. However, either of these materials can be used to advantage by adding about one-fourth, by volume, to three-fourths of soil. In a shrub-

bery bed a 2- to 3-inch layer can be spread over the area
and forked into the top 8 to 12 inches of soil. To prepare
the soil for a specimen plant, such as a shade tree, a single
hole is dug large enough to hold the plant, and the soil thus
obtained is mixed with one-fourth that amount of wet peat.
Wet peat mixes much better with the soil than does dry
peat, and the result in plant growth will be better. No fertilizers are mixed with the planting soil.

Acid-soil Plants

Acid-soil plants, such as rhododendrons, blueberries,
mountain andromeda, laurel, and the like, require special
soil conditions—a moist soil that is acid in reaction and a
situation protected from drying winds. A soil containing
large amounts of organic matter is favorable. No attempt
should be made to set these acid-soil plants in a place that
is underlaid with limestone or any strongly alkaline soil, as
it will be almost impossible to keep it acid enough for
thrifty growth. Soil that is slightly acid or slightly alkaline
in reaction may be changed to the proper acidity by mixing
with it powdered sulfur in the following amounts:

Acidity at start	*Sulfur to 100 square feet*
Medium acid (pH 5.5 to 6.0)	2 pounds
Slightly acid (pH 6.0 to 7.0)	4 pounds
Slightly alkaline (pH 7.0 to 7.5)	7 pounds
Strongly alkaline (pH 7.5 to 8.0)	Unsuitable for use

A pH value of 4.0 to 5.0 is ideal for most acid-soil plants,
but they will do well in soil that is neutral in reaction if the
organic content is high. As pH 7.0 is the neutral point,
pH 5.0 is two points on the acid side. Sulfur may be added
year after year if a test of the soil indicates that a more acid
soil is required for the best growth of the plants.

Another method is to keep a permanent mulch underneath the plants. This mulch may be acid peat, oak leaves,
pine needles, tan bark, or well-decayed sawdust. The mulch
is applied in the fall, left through the winter, lightly forked

into the soil in the spring, and a new mulch put on immediately.

A bed made to receive a planting of acid-soil plants may be composed of acid woods dirt that contains a large amount of organic matter. If this is not available, a satisfactory bed can be prepared with equal parts of acid garden loam, acid sand, and acid peat. These materials are mixed together before any planting is done.

SETTING THE PLANT

Bare-rooted Plants

Plants that are delivered with bare roots, such as deciduous shrubs and small trees, should be planted at once. Before the plants are unpacked, dig a hole large enough to allow the roots to be spread out completely.

A plant should be set at the same level as it was growing in its previous location. In heavy clay, the plant may be set a little high; in sandy soil or garden loam, it may be a little deeper. Good soil, free from sod, stones, and large lumps, should be packed firmly around the roots. If any subsoil, such as heavy clay, is obtained in the process of digging the hole, this should be spread on top, not placed around the roots. The first tamping is done effectively with a pick or shovel handle or any small tamping tool which helps to fill air pockets. When the hole is full, press the soil down firmly with your feet.

If the soil has good natural drainage, a concave surface should be left around the base of each plant so that water will drain toward the roots rather than off to the side. In heavy clay soil, the hole dug to receive the plant forms a tight cup. The natural drainage of the soil may be tested by pouring water in the hole until it is 2 or 3 inches deep. If the water soaks in, drainage is adequate, and the surface may be left in a concave shape. If the water fails to soak in for about an hour, mound the soil slightly around the plant.

After a medium- or large-sized tree is planted, it is securely fastened with guy wires to keep it from swaying in the wind, as swaying would loosen the roots and cause the tree to lean. Rubber hose, screw eyes, or wood slats are used to secure the wires to the tree (Figure 38). These protect the trunk from being girdled. Very little, if any, fertilizer is used to stimulate growth on newly set plants. It is most important that they become established with a new root system before top growth is forced.

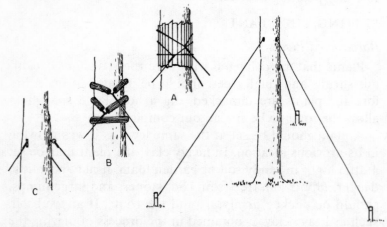

FIGURE 38. Guying a newly planted tree. Protect the trunk from injury with wood slats (A), short pieces of rubber hose (B), or screw eyes (C) to which the wires are secured.

Plants with Ball of Earth

Some plants, such as medium-sized trees 3 to 6 inches in trunk diameter, and evergreen shrubs, are dug with a ball of earth on the roots and wrapped in burlap. Plant these as soon as delivered. Dig a hole large enough to have a clearance of 6 to 12 inches all around the ball of earth (Figure 39) and 2 to 3 inches deeper than the height of the ball. For best results, mix the soil for the backfill with wet peat. From 2 to 3 inches of this soil should be shoveled into the bottom of the hole before the plant, with the burlap still around the ball of earth, is set in the hole. Then pack 2 to 3 inches of prepared soil around the sides. Cut the burlap loose and fold it back on this shallow layer of earth. Care must be taken not to break the ball. Fill the hole half full of good soil, and water the plant thoroughly. After the water has soaked in, the hole is filled with just enough firmed soil to leave a saucer-shaped surface around the base of the plant.

Homeowners who are without shade in sunny places can obtain it quickly by planting large trees. Moving large trees is rather costly and is a specialized work not to be attempted

FIGURE 39. Method of setting plant with ball of earth. Leave the burlap around the ball until the plant is in place; then do not try to remove it, but only fold it back.

by most homeowners, but most nurserymen are equipped to handle trees up to 6 inches in diameter. Professional arborists are equipped to move trees of any size up to 18 inches in diameter. A few arborists can move much larger trees for short distances. Although such trees will survive, they are slow to become reestablished, and they remain about the same size for several years. A 6-inch tree, if it is dug, moved, and planted correctly, will become established much more quickly and, year by year, will gain in size on the larger tree.

Watering

After planting, a thorough watering is necessary to settle the soil firmly around the roots and temporarily provide ample moisture. A moist soil facilitates root penetration. The ground should not be allowed to dry out, at least during the first growing season. If natural rainfall is not enough to keep the ground moist, artificial watering should be substituted. With most plants, overwatering is as injurious as underwatering, particularly in heavy clay soil. Many plants will not tolerate an excess of water.

Mulching

After planting, a mulch of some material such as peat, sawdust, leaves, pine needles, or other easily available organic material should be spread over the bed to a depth of from 2 to 3 inches. If planting is done in the fall, the mulch should be left on the surface of the bed through the winter. This mulch prevents the frost from going to its usual depth and decreases the amount of destructive alternate thawing and freezing in the spring and fall. In the spring, this protecting mulch may be worked into the soil with a spading fork, but care must be taken not to spade deep enough to injure the roots. In spring planting, the mulch may be applied as it was for fall planting and left on the surface of the ground through the summer before it is worked into the soil. Manure is objectionable because of its odor and because of the weed seeds it contains.

PRUNING NEWLY SET PLANTS

Deciduous Shrubs

Small bare-root shrubs that have only a few branches, as well as plants to be used for a clipped hedge, should be trimmed by reducing each stem to about one-third to one-half its length. Make each cut about ¼ inch above a bud (Figure 40, C and D) and leave the stems unequal in length. If possible, leave the longest stems in the center of the plant, the shorter ones toward the outside (Figure 40A).

Larger and more fully branched shrubs are reduced in size in about the same proportion, one-third to one-half, with the pruning done to produce a well-shaped plant. Branches that are crowding or rubbing others are removed, the cut usually being made flush with the branch from which it is growing (Figure 40, C and D). Misshapen and broken branches are cut off. If correcting faulty structure does not remove a sufficient amount of the top, some of the longest lateral branches may be shortened. Occasionally an entire branch is removed (Figure 40B).

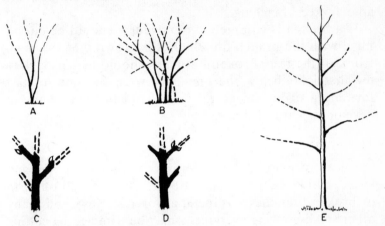

FIGURE 40. Pruning newly set plants.
- A. Sparsely branched shrub.
- B. Densely branched shrub.
- C. Detail pruning. Shrub with alternate branching.
- D. Detail pruning. Shrub with opposite branching.
- E. Sparsely branched tree.

Vines

Newly set vines are trimmed in the same proportion and in the same manner as sparsely branched shrubs.

Deciduous Trees

Deciduous trees are trimmed by merely thinning out the head of the tree. Crowding branches are eliminated. Other faulty structures are corrected by cutting out interfering branches and eliminating narrow crotches if this is possible without ruining the shape of the tree. Narrow crotches are not so strong as are wide ones.

Pruning sparsely branched small trees at the time of planting is confined to cutting back each of the lateral branches about one-half their length (Figure 40E). Make each cut about ¼ inch above a bud or flush with the branch from which it is growing, as illustrated in Figure 40, C and D. Do not cut off the leader, as this would induce two or more side branches to curve upward, making an undesirable, forked branching.

If a branch is completely removed, it should be cut off flush with the branch on which it is growing or the main trunk of the tree. Broken branches should be cut back to the first joint below the break. Now is the time to start forming a strong structural framework in the tree and to develop its natural shape.

Evergreens

Recently planted tree evergreens, such as pines and spruces, are seldom pruned, if ever, except to cut off dead or broken branches. Junipers, arborvitae, yew, and many other small-growing evergreens may be trimmed by cutting off the ends of lateral branches. This trimming forces a dense growth.

Transplanting

RENOVATING ESTABLISHED AND
OVERGROWN PLANTINGS

If you have acquired property on which the plantings do not appeal to you, you may wish to change them to give a more pleasing result. Sometimes established plantings have become overcrowded. In either case, it is best to revise the planting. The more desirable plants are left where they are to develop in a natural shape or are moved to a different location if they are to be utilized elsewhere. Sometimes these extra plants are large and, when transplanted to a more appropriate place, produce a mature effect immediately.

TRANSPLANTING SHRUBS, EVERGREENS, VINES, AND TREES

Many homeowners are fearful of attempting to transplant growing woody ornamentals, believing that the result will not be successful. Some plants are more tolerant of rough treatment than others, but most woody ornamentals have amazing recuperative ability. Keep in mind that when a plant is moved, some of the roots are severed or broken. The broken ends should be cut off with pruning shears or a sharp knife. The disturbance and decrease of actual absorbing surface of the root system is balanced by pruning some branches to decrease the foliage surface of deciduous plants as described on page 90. Deciduous plants are those that drop their leaves in winter.

First decide whether or not each plant to be moved is worth saving at all. If it is not in a healthy growing condition, is misshapen, or is infested with insects or diseases, it is not worth saving. The section "Removal of Unwanted Plants," on page 113, describes how to remove them. If it is in a healthy growing condition, is only slightly misshapen, and is not infested with pests, the plant is worth saving. The STEPS "Foundation Plantings" and "Border Plantings" may give helpful ideas on where to use it. If you are going to use it, prepare an adequate-sized hole at the new location before you remove the plant (Figure 41A). Then the roots will not be exposed long enough to be seriously dried.

The size of the hole to be dug is regulated by the size of the plant to be moved. This is described under the next heading, "Size of Ball of Earth." The sides of the hole should be vertical, and the bottom should be flat, not cup-shaped. Transplant during the dormant season, fall or spring, and on a day when the humidity is high.

Size of Ball of Earth

The size of the ball of earth to be taken will vary with the size of the plant. One-half the spread of the branches is a

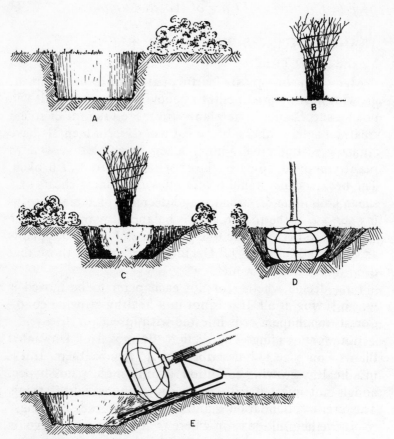

FIGURE 41. Transplanting trees and shrubs.

A. First dig a hole ample in size and with vertical sides in the location where the plant is to be set.

B. Tie the branches of the shrub or tree.

C. Leave a ball of earth around the roots.

D. In light soils, wrap the ball of earth with burlap tied with rope.

E. Large shrubs and trees taken with a ball of earth are heavy, and power equipment is needed to move them.

good rule to follow for most shrubs, whether evergreen or deciduous.

A small vine may require a ball 12 to 18 inches in diameter, while a large one may need one 2 to 3 feet across.

Trees, both evergreen and deciduous, should be moved

with a ball 1 foot in diameter to each 1 inch of tree-trunk diameter measured at a point 1 foot above the surface of the ground. For example, a tree 5 inches in diameter would require a 5-foot ball of earth. The size of the ball and the place of measurement applies to both large and small trees.

Digging the Plant

Before starting to dig the plant, whether it be vine, shrub, or tree, tie the branches together by winding a heavy cord or light rope around them (Figure 41B). Force the branches together as much as possible without breaking them. This keeps the top of the plant out of your way while digging and protects the branches from breaking.

Moving a plant is done most safely with a ball of earth because the roots contained therein are not disturbed and therefore lose little of their ability to absorb water and nutrients. Plants growing in clay or clay-loam soil may be moved with a ball of earth more easily because of the adhesive qualities of clay. Those growing in sandy or gravelly soil are more difficult to move with a ball of earth because the soil falls away from the roots as the plant is dug. Even though the work is done carefully, many of the fine feeding roots are lost. This loss of feeding power can be balanced by digging a greater proportion of the root system. This is easily done in light soils.

To obtain a ball of earth on the roots, a long-handled shovel or a spade is used to dig around the plant. Remove the loose soil and cut the ball of earth to size (Figure 41C). Cut under the plant as far as can be reached and loosen the bottom of the ball by tipping the plant. The undercut is made at a depth of 12 to 18 inches, depending upon the size of the plant.

In sandy or gravelly soil a compact ball of earth can be obtained only by wrapping it with burlap or canvas as the plant is dug. To hold a large ball securely, the covering is bound on with rope (Figure 41D).

If no attempt is to be made to get a ball of earth on the roots, it is best to get a larger root system. This is done by digging a trench farther back from the plant and loosening the soil from the roots with an iron bar or a pick. Work toward the crown of the plant, alternately loosening the soil, combing out the roots, and shoveling out the soil, always being careful not to injure the roots. As the roots are exposed, cover them with wet burlap unless a rainy day is chosen for the work. This method is used in either heavy or light soil when it is desirable to decrease the size of the ball of earth on a large plant. The weight to be moved can thus be decreased considerably.

Another method of protecting the roots from drying while the plant is moved is to puddle the soil in the hole so the roots will be covered with mud. Covering with wet burlap will supplement this protection.

Transplanting Large Trees

Most homeowners will not want to attempt to transplant a shade tree larger than 4 or 5 inches in diameter (Figure 41E), even though they have power equipment available. A tree this size will give some shade immediately, and it will become established more quickly than will a larger tree. A shade tree smaller than 1½ inches in diameter is hardly worth bothering with.

Do not try to move to level ground a tree that is growing on a steep slope. A tree trunk grows vertically, and the roots parallel, more or less, the surface of the ground (Figure 18, page 40). A tree growing on a slope has roots extending at an oblique angle to the trunk, and if this tree is planted on level ground, the roots are too shallow on one side and too deep on the other.

Moving the Plants

Small plants are light and not difficult to move. If there is danger of breaking the ball of earth, they should be handled carefully by carrying them on a canvas or burlap. Somewhat larger plants can be carried in a wheelbarrow or garden cart. Large shrubs and small trees with a ball of earth are very heavy. They can be moved short distances on planks or on a stoneboat and rollers. Sometimes large shrubs or trees are moved greater distances with a tractor equipped with a power lift. When this method is used, be sure to wrap with burlap and protect with wood splints any part of the shrub or tree that may become damaged by the lift. A considerable amount of bark may be stripped off if this protection is not provided.

Planting, pruning, and guying have been described previously in this STEP.

Native Plants

In most parts of the United States, certain varieties of native ornamental shrubs and trees grow in abundance. Some of them are protected by state law. A few plants of those that are not protected may be transplanted to form a part of the home landscape. However, each person contemplating such planting should keep in mind the natural beauty of these plants and should refrain from taking those that grow infrequently in the neighborhood. These same varieties of plants are available at nurseries, and one should balance the commercial price against the labor involved in finding the plant, digging it, and packing it, and the cost of transportation. If you decide to attempt it, do not make the mistake of carelessly protecting the plant, tying it to the outside of the car and driving home with the roots exposed. The roots will be hopelessly dried, and the plant will be lost to its native position and to you.

Maintenance of Woody Ornamentals

CULTIVATION

Shrub Borders

Newly planted shrub borders require only hoeing to eliminate weeds. As the plants mature in size, they become so dense that few weeds grow beneath them, and the amount of cultivation necessary is reduced to a minimum. However, in later years, seeds of shrubs and trees carried by wind or otherwise deposited on the bare ground underneath the shrubs germinate and produce seedling plants. It is much easier physically to eliminate these small plants with a garden hoe than to dig and chop them out several years later. Also, it is easier mentally for one who is sentimental about plants to eliminate seedlings than to destroy large plants.

Specimen Plants

Plants, such as trees or large shrubs, growing in the lawn as individual specimens, usually are grown with the grass extending up to the base of the plant. Some persons prefer to have a bare circle of ground around them. The bare area needs only to be kept free of weeds.

MULCHES

A mulch is a layer of organic material spread on the ground from 2 to 3 inches deep. Experiments indicate that some of the best materials are peat, straw, leaves, sawdust, pine needles, ground corncobs, buckwheat hulls, and excelsior. Some of these materials, such as sawdust and ground corncobs, if they are fresh, deplete the nitrogen level in the soil, and it is necessary to use additional amounts of a nitrogen fertilizer, such as ammonium nitrate. This may be used at the rate of 110 pounds to each one ton of mulching material.

Newly set hardy plants should be protected with a mulch, particularly during the first winter, and tender plants should be protected with a mulch every winter.

Much may be said about the use of a permanent mulch, that is, having a mulch on the shrubbery bed the year around. Summer mulch discourages the growth of weeds and helps to retain moisture, but its continued use encourages a growth of fibrous or feeding roots near the surface of the soil. This is not a desirable condition because these surface roots wither during hot dry periods. However, most plants have enough deep roots to supply ample water and nutrients during these dry periods. Deeper rooting is encouraged by continued cultivation.

WATERING

Newly planted woody ornamentals should be watered during the first growing season as often as is necessary to keep the soil moist. After the trees, shrubs, and vines have become established, they will not need to be watered artificially except in abnormally dry weather. Then watering with a hose may be resorted to if the plants show a definite need for it as indicated by wilting leaves. A thorough soaking once a week is better than a light watering each day. The sprinkler may be left in the same place for an hour or two. This gives the water an opportunity to soak into the ground for some depth rather than to remain on the surface where it is taken up by the sun.

FERTILIZERS

Inorganic commercial fertilizers are the most common types used today. They are sold in dry form and are available in various mixtures containing nitrogen, phosphorus, and potash, the three elements most often deficient in soils. Although each of these elements has a number of specific functions, nitrogen is particularly associated with the growth of the aboveground parts of plants. Easily soluble in water, it seeps through the soil to considerable depths. Phosphorus is mainly associated with root growth and, in the form most often used, is not easily soluble in water. Therefore it does not penetrate the soil either laterally or in depth to a noticeable degree. Potash is associated with a number of less specific plant functions, such as cell growth and the color of the leaves, flowers, and fruit. It is not easily soluble in water.

A 5-10-5 fertilizer contains 5 per cent of nitrogen, 10 per cent of phosphorus, and 5 per cent of potash. For general use, a fertilizer of about this analysis is broadcast at the rate of 20 to 30 pounds to each 1,000 square feet of area. A 10-20-10 fertilizer contains the same proportion of each element, but it is twice as strong as a 5-10-5 and would, therefore, be used at half the rate, or 10 to 15 pounds to each 1,000 square feet.

Woody ornamentals that are not growing thriftily can be improved by using a high nitrogen fertilizer, such as a 10-8-6, at the rate of 15 to 20 pounds to each 1,000 square feet. The higher percentage of nitrogen in the mixture stimulates top growth.

The usual practice is to apply these dry fertilizers to the soil, either broadcast on the surface or mixed into the soil by plowing or cultivation. Liquid fertilizers are being used experimentally and, to a lesser degree, in practice. Urea, an organic form of nitrogen, has been used successfully as a spray on the leaves of trees to correct a nitrogen deficiency. The nitrogen is absorbed into the leaves, and the plant responds more rapidly than with dry fertilizers applied to the soil. However, soil application has a more lasting effect.

Experiments being conducted on the use of liquid fertilizers containing more easily soluble materials may affect future practices.

Although nitrogen, phosphorus, and potash are considered the major fertilizer elements needed in most soils, detailed studies of plant growth indicate that a number of minor elements are necessary in small amounts in order to produce healthy plants. Included are iron, zinc, manganese, magnesium, and several others. Plants growing in soils deficient in any one of these elements will exhibit rather specific color symptoms, usually in the leaves. Plant scientists can identify many of them on sight and can recommend corrective treatment.

If plants are getting adequate moisture and are free from fungus and insects, an abnormal leaf color or stunted growth probably is due to malnutrition. If application of a fertilizer, such as a 10-8-6, does not correct the condition, it is time to consult a plant scientist.

The extent to which fertilizers are applied for established plants depends upon the fertility of the soil in which they are growing. It is best to keep plants in a healthy growing condition by annual fertilization as they are then more resistant to insect and disease attack. If plants are making good growth and have good foliage color, the soil in which they are growing probably is fertile enough, and more fertilizers need not be added.

Shrubs, Evergreen and Deciduous

Application of fertilizers, whether it be to an individual plant or a shrubbery bed, may be made in the spring about the time the buds begin to break. A late fall application is satisfactory if it is made after all growth has stopped for that season. Early fall fertilization sometimes forces new tender growth that may not survive the winter. If additional fertilizer is required, it may be applied in midsummer and should be followed by a thorough watering.

Trees, Evergreen and Deciduous

Trees need to be fertilized only when they are not making good annual growth. If growth is not normal, it is advisable to fertilize annually to keep the trees in a healthy growing condition.

A tree that is weak from malnutrition is more subject to attack by insects and diseases than is a healthy tree. Even though a strongly growing tree is exposed to attack by its enemies, the damage done will be overcome more easily and more rapidly if the tree is well nourished. Several methods are used to fertilize trees, and experiments are now going on to test these and the type of fertilizer that is most effective. The fertilizer may be broadcast either in the dry or liquid form by using the crowbar method or by the aerofertilizer method. The aerofertilizer method is used by professional arborists and requires special equipment. The fertilizer is dispersed through the ground with air or water pressure. Either the crowbar method or the broadcasting method may be used by anyone. The crowbar method is done by driving holes in the ground from 12 to 15 inches deep with an iron bar and pouring a small amount of fertilizer, about 2/3 cup, into each hole, which is then filled with water. The holes should be approximately 3 feet apart and should include all the area under the tree within a diameter of from 10 to 20 feet greater than the spread of the branches.

Some evidence indicates that the broadcasting method is fully as effective as the crowbar method, and it surely is much easier. The fertilizer is simply broadcast evenly over the same area as for other methods. The amount of fertilizer to use depends upon the size of the tree—1 pound of fertilizer for each inch of trunk diameter for small trees up to 3 inches in diameter, 2 pounds for trees 3 to 10 inches in diameter, and 3 pounds of fertilizer to the inch for trees more than 10 inches in diameter. A 10-8-6 fertilizer is suitable.

Experiments indicate that many of the feeding roots of American elm growing in a heavy clay soil extend from 4 to 20 inches deep to a distance approximately equal to the height of the tree. Those growing in sandy soil probably are deeper rooting. If this rooting character is true for other shade trees, a more effective result would be obtained by using the fertilizer over a greater diameter than the spread of the branches.

Acid-soil Plants

Acid-soil plants, such as rhododendron, laurel, and leucothoe, may be fertilized with cottonseed meal (about 5-2-2 analysis). This is a slowly available organic fertilizer and is acid in reaction. It may be applied at the rate of 4 pounds to 100 square feet of bed surface when the ground is bare, after the old mulch is cultivated into the soil and before the new mulch is applied.

Inorganic fertilizers, such as a 10-8-6, also are used on acid-soil plants. It is best to use ammonium sulphate, which is acid in reaction, for the nitrogen portion of this mixture.

PRUNING

Deciduous Shrubs

The pruning done at the time of planting is all that is necessary on most shrubs for at least two or three years. Do not prune at all for this length of time, or longer, unless it is necessary to correct minor faulty branching missed in the original pruning or to remove broken, diseased, or deadwood. Thereafter, the amount of pruning necessary will be kept to a minimum if the plants have been selected wisely for each situation, particularly with regard to their mature size.

From the standpoint of favorable growth, vigor, ease of doing the work, and precaution against winter injury, deciduous shrubs are pruned most favorably late in the dormant season, late winter or early spring. Heavy summer pruning usually should be avoided because it has a dwarfing effect on the plants, but when a plant is slightly outgrowing its position, pruning in the summer may help to keep it more nearly the proper size. During the dormant season, when deciduous shrubs are bare of leaves, every faulty detail of the branching is seen easily and can be corrected. Late summer or early fall pruning is hazardous because, in addition to having a dwarfing effect on the plant, it may result in a considerable amount of winter injury.

Except for diseased plants and those affected by insects, the principal aftercare of most hardy deciduous shrubs consists of pruning and fertilization. The function of the shrubs and their location on the property determines the amount and character of pruning to be done each year. Most shrubs in a home planting should be kept in a normal shape, either individually or as a group. Dense shrub forms are best to use where mass effects are desired, such as some place near the base of the house or a border planting separating one lawn area from another, giving privacy from an adjacent property or screening an undesirable view. Tree-form shrubs are used as accent plants either near the base of the house or in a border planting, sometimes where they will frame a desirable view. They may also be used to give shade to a small area.

Form of the Plant

Shrubs that naturally grow with many branches from the base (shrub form) and have been neglected for several years need special care in pruning. Gradual replacement of old branches by new ones should be the rule. This is accomplished by cutting off a few of the oldest branches as near the ground as possible (Figure 42A), which will probably force a growth of some new branches from the base of the shrub. The following year a few more of the oldest branches may be cut off. This practice may be continued until all the oldest branches have been removed and new ones have taken their place. Sometimes, if cutting old branches is overdone at any one time, long, straight shoots are produced.

FIGURE 42. Form of the plant.
   A. The shrub form grows with many stems from the base.
   B. The semitree form, or clump, grows with few stems from the base.
   C. The tree form grows with a single trunk.

These should be cut off either at a point flush with the mother branch, leaving only the normal new growth, or flush with the outside head of the shrub. These "sucker shoots" may be cut off at any time of year. Some shrubs may be very dense on one side and not in other parts of the head. Then it may be necessary to remove a few branches from these crowded places. Each stem to be removed should be cut flush with the branch from which it arises or at a place ⅛ to ¼ inch above a bud (Figure 40, C and D).

Many shrub-form plants, if they have become ill-shaped, may be cut off just above the ground in late winter or early spring and allowed to grow up from the base.

Some shrubs, such as buddelja and snowhill hydrangea

make a full growth and flower in one season. These plants may die to the ground during the dormant season in localities where the winters are severe. The roots remain alive, and new shoots grow from them in the spring. Such shrubs may be cut to the ground either in the fall or in the spring. When growth begins, any stems that may have survived the winter are easily identified and the deadwood is then removed. The old stems are more sturdy than the succulent new growth, and the large flowers are held more nearly upright.

Shrubs that normally grow in semitree or tree form, such as shrub althea, panicle hydrangea, nannyberry, and Japanese lilac, are pruned in the head of the plant. Densely branching portions are thinned; interfering or rubbing branches and diseased or broken branches are removed (Figure 42, B and C). Each cut should be made just above a bud or flush with the branch from which it is growing (Figure 40, C and D).

Sometimes it is preferable to have these tree-form plants growing in shrub form, in which case one or two of the large branches may be cut off near the ground. Usually this forces several new shoots to grow from the base. In some cases such pruning is more successful with young plants than with old ones, and it is best to leave some of the old branches on each plant until new ones have started to grow from the base. After the new branches have become established, the others may be removed. Severe pruning of this kind is best done early in the spring.

Maximum Flower Production

If light pruning is done annually or once every two years to correct minor faulty structure and to remove diseased wood or broken branches, there will be no extensive loss of flowers or fruit even though the work is done during late winter or early spring. If no more than one-half the growing points (Figure 43) are removed, an ample display of flowers will be produced. Shrubs that have been neglected for several years may need to be pruned heavily. This should be done late in the dormant period even though most of the flowers will be sacrificed for the following year.

Most early-flowering plants bloom from buds formed on last summer's twigs. Examples of this group are forsythia, deutzia, Vanhoutte spirea, lilac, and the like. Such plants should be lightly pruned from one to two weeks after they bloom in order to have the maximum number of flowers annually. This is called summer pruning, although the actual time of performing the work may be in May or June, soon after the plants are through flowering. If this pruning is delayed until the following dormant season and some of last summer's twigs are then removed, there will be a considerable loss of bloom until the plant has had a year to grow new twigs. Plants of this group, as well as most others, produce their flowers on the young wood.

FIGURE 43. Growing points. The growing points elongate into new stems; some produce flowers.

Late-flowering plants produce new twigs in the spring, and on this new wood the flowers appear late in the summer. Examples of this group are peegee hydrangea, shrub althea, Anthony Waterer spirea, and rugosa rose. Such plants are best pruned in the early spring for least loss of flower buds and least damage to the plants.

The flowering period of a few shrubs can be prolonged, or a second crop of flowers produced, by cutting off those that have gone by. Shrubs in this group are buddelia, rugosa rose, weigela, and Anthony Waterer spirea.

Some shrubs, such as lilacs and azaleas, tend to have alternate seasons of prolific flower production. A satisfactory number of flowers can be produced annually if the faded flower heads are cut off and the shrubs are fertilized each year. The strength that would normally be used for maturing the seeds is conserved for the production of flower buds that will open during the succeeding season's bloom.

Desirable Fruit

The plants that are particularly desirable in the landscape scheme because of their fruit, such as viburnums (in variety), dogwoods (in variety), winterberry, Japanese barberry, hawthorns (in variety), and privet (in variety), may also be valuable because of their flowers. The flowers are produced from buds that have been formed on the preceding year's twig growth, and the fruit succeeds the flower just as is true with the edible fruits. If all the flowering branches, which are also the ones which produce the fruit, are cut off as soon as they bloom, no fruit will be produced. With this group of shrubs, light pruning should be practiced soon after the flowers disappear. This pruning should be done in a similar way to that described on page 104—that is, by removing a few of the oldest branches at the ground and by thinning the top branches where the stems are too crowded. The method is the same, but the amount of pruning varies. The fruiting shrubs should not be pruned so heavily as the flowering types. The shrubs should merely be opened up to allow the light to reach the center of the plant. Usually this thinning shows much of the fruit that would otherwise be concealed by the dense foliage.

Showy Stem Coloration

Shrubs that have showy-colored stems produce their most brilliant color on new wood. For this reason heavy pruning should be resorted to every year. The method of pruning is the same as for other plants, but more pruning is done. Plants that come in this group are some of the dogwoods such as redstemmed dogwood, yellowtwigged dogwood, silky dogwood, and some other shrubs such as kerria, forsythia, and some of the low-growing shrub roses. Plants in this group that also have showy flowers should be pruned so as to leave some of the two- and three-year-old wood.

Pruning to Shape

Pruning done to maintain or modify the shape of a plant varies considerably, depending upon the desired effect. Special consideration must be given to each individual when a modification of the normal shape is desired. If the normal shape of a plant is pyramidal and this form must be accentuated, the lateral branches should be trimmed back to an inside bud or branch (Figure 44A). If, on the other hand, a broader plant is desired, the lateral branches may be trimmed back to an outside bud (Figure 44B). Cutting to an outside bud accents the horizontal or stratified growing habit of a shrub, and cutting to an inside bud minimizes this effect.

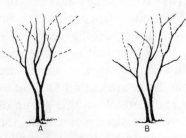

FIGURE 44. Pruning to modify normal shape.

A. Pruning to an inside bud results in a narrower plant.

B. Pruning to an outside bud results in a wider plant.

Other instances of modified form in plants are espalier fruit trees and some shrubs, such as forsythia, used as vines. The espalier fruit trees are trimmed to produce a shape similar to a five- or seven-branched candlestick, and the branches are tied to a trellis. This may form an enclosure to a flower garden, a screen for a service area, or a vine effect at the side of a building. A shrub trimmed as a vine may be used near the house or on a porch where most vines would be too heavy, too dense, or too large. This practice requires some special pruning. All of the stems except two or three at the base are cut off. These two or three stems are supported on a trellis or wire, as are other vines.

Trimmed hedges should be used sparingly and judiciously on most home properties. They are likely to be entirely out of keeping as a border for walks and boundaries of the front lawn. This arrangement sometimes appears neat and tidy if it is well kept, but it requires considerable work in trimming. Hedges are useful as border plantings especially where it is necessary or desirable to conserve space as described in STEP 9 on Border Plantings. Formal gardens may be enclosed appropriately with clipped hedges, or such hedges may be properly used as a background for small architectural features in a flower garden.

When hedge plants are set, they are trimmed as illustrated in Figure 40A. Usually this forces branches to develop near the base of the plant and induces dense branching along the stems. Trimming during succeeding years is done on the lateral branches only, until the hedge has reached the desired height. Then the entire hedge is trimmed with hand or power-driven hedge shears.

A clipped hedge should be trimmed in June. This removes most of the current season's growth, and unless the plants are very thrifty, they need no more trimming for the rest of the summer. Hedge plants that grow more rapidly than usual may need to be trimmed three or more times a year (early May, late June, and late July) if they are to be kept neat. The hedge should be narrower at the top than at the bottom (Figure 45). A hedge 2 feet in height should be from 3 to 4 inches narrower at the top than at the bottom. Shaping the hedge in this form should be started about the second season after planting, and should be maintained year after year until the hedge has obtained the desired height. This form enables the sun to strike the sides from the top to the bottom and helps to maintain a dense growth close to the ground.

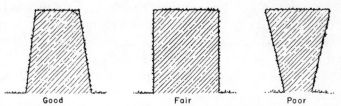

Good   Fair   Poor

FIGURE 45. Shapes of trimmed hedges. A well-trimmed hedge is wide at the bottom and narrower at the top, where it may be either flat or rounded. Those shaped square may be satisfactory, but those trimmed wide at the top and narrow at the bottom seldom have dense foliage to the ground.

Vines

After vines have become established, little trimming, if any, is done. Sometimes overcrowded portions are thinned, and the dead or diseased branches are removed. Occasionally, a large branch is cut at the base and completely removed. As with shrubs, vines are trimmed one to two weeks after they have flowered if maximum flower production is desired.

Because of the density of most vines and because of their tenacious character, it is more difficult to remove pruned branches than it is with shrubs. Twining stems cling to each other and to fences and trellises that support them. Clinging vines hold fast to their supporting walls. In either case short lengths need to be cut and each one freed in succession.

Deciduous Trees

The general practices described for pruning tree-form shrubs and newly planted trees are followed when pruning large shade trees. However, large trees require more pruning because of their increased size, greater number of branches, and because they are more subject to storm damage. This is a job only for physically strong and nimble individuals who are not affected by climbing to considerable heights. Tree trimming is no job for the weakhearted.

Broken branches are either completely removed or cut off just above the first joint below the break. Narrow crotches in the main branching of the tree are eliminated if it is possible to do so without ruining the shape of the tree. Narrow crotches are not so strong as wide ones. The poorer of two rubbing branches is removed in part or as a whole. Densely branching areas are thinned.

All cuts are made about ¼ inch above a bud or flush with the branch or trunk from which the one to be removed is growing. Never leave a stub end (Figure 46A). Large branches should be removed by making three saw cuts (Figure 46B). This avoids splitting down the trunk of the tree and provides a flush cut for better appearance and quicker healing. The possibility of decay organisms entering the tree is decreased. There is evidence to indicate that a wound heals more quickly if it is not allowed to dry out. As soon as possible after the wound is made, shade it with burlap. Keep the wound moist by wetting the burlap.

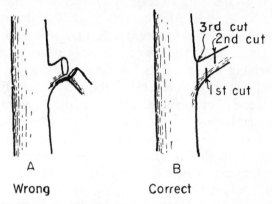

A — Wrong

B — Correct

FIGURE 46. Trimming large tree branches.

A. This wrong way to remove a branch frequently results in serious damage. Before the top cut is completed, the branch breaks downward, tearing off large areas of bark and live wood tissue.

B. Each large branch to be removed should be removed in three operations. First cut from the bottom, then from above and beyond the first cut, and then remove the stub with a cut flush with the trunk. The branch may have to be supported with a rope while the undercut is being made. Trees damaged during severe storms can be repaired by removing branches in this way.

General tree pruning is done during the late winter or very early spring. During the early spring cambium growth is most active, and the wound heals much more quickly than if it is done at other times of the year. However, such trimming may be done at almost any time of year without damage to the tree if proper precaution is taken to paint all wounds ¾ inch or more in diameter. There are several tree-wound dressing materials available. Emulsified asphalt is also a good wound dressing.

Trees that are of value because of their flowers, such as

hawthorns and flowering dogwood, should be pruned after the bloom is past if annual full benefit of the flowers is to be obtained.

Extensive tree surgery by the amateur is not recommended. Qualified arborists are available to do any necessary type of tree work. They are equipped with modern tools and safety devices. Although this profession has received some adverse publicity because of a few poorly trained and unqualified men who have preyed on uninformed homeowners, it is developed on high standards of business ethics and ability. The better-known arborists belong to the National Shade Tree Conference, various state arborists' associations and certified tree-expert societies. Their credentials are available.

It is possible that some homeowners will want to gouge out rotted and diseased wood in a tree and to paint the exposed surface with a fungicide, such as bordeaux paste or copper sulphate (1 ounce to 1 gallon), and to cover this surface with emulsified asphalt or a dark-colored linseed-oil paint. The cambium layer, those cells between the bark and the solid wood, should be covered with orange shellac before the other materials are applied. Orange shellac will not injure the growing tissue to any noticeable extent. Some bracing of weak crotches may be done if care is taken not to girdle the branches that are to be braced. Screw hooks may be placed in the two branches to be strengthened and a cable secured between them. This usually saves a weak crotch from splitting.

Narrow-leaved Evergreens

Necessary pruning of narrow-leaved evergreens can be done at any time of the year except during the spring growing season or the hot dry periods of summer. The best time is early in the spring before growth has started, but this work may be done in October when growth has ceased. Those suitable to use in Christmas decorations may be pruned early in December if desired.

Evergreen trees, such as pines and spruces, should not be

trimmed at all except to cut out dead or diseased wood. If the tree has developed more than one leader, cut out all except the largest and most erect. If desired, a dense growth can be forced on these trees by cutting off the ends of the lateral branches. The same is true of evergreens such as arborvitae, juniper, yew, and retinospora.

Do not mistake the natural browning of evergreen needles in the fall for some disease. Evergreens have some leaf drop each year, but most of the needles remain green and stay on the plant.

Shrub-form narrow-leaved evergreens, such as Pfitzer juniper and Japanese yew, usually grow to a considerable width, and over a period of years, absorb a larger space than was intended. They can be kept informal in character and their width decreased by cutting off their side branches irregularly in a staggered fashion. More should be cut off some branches than others. However, if a formal-shaped plant is suitable, the side branches may be cut off evenly.

REMOVAL OF UNWANTED SHRUBS AND TREES

Old plantings that have become crowded or badly overgrown sometimes require rather drastic treatment. This crowded condition may be caused by setting shrubs too close together in the original planting or by the production of new plants from seed or by layering. Layering occurs when a low branch remains in contact with the ground long enough to take root and produce new shoots.

Many home gardeners quake at the idea of destroying any plants, but the removal of the poorest ones in a crowded situation makes room for the better ones to mature in their characteristic form. Likewise, those that have overgrown their space extensively might better be removed and replaced with a plant more suitable in mature size. This procedure is no more expensive than maintaining the overgrown plant for several years. It is up to each individual to decide whether or not the plant to be removed is sufficiently ill-shaped and in poor enough condition to be destroyed.

To remove unwanted shrubs and trees, dig around the base of them near the crown and, as the roots are encountered, cut them off. The process of digging and cutting is continued until the plant is loose and can be removed (Figure 47). If the stems are simply cut off flush with the ground, many new shoots may grow from the crown. Cutting off the roots and removing the crown will kill most plants, but a few will be persistent enough to send up new shoots from the roots that have been left in the soil. These roots will have to be removed or treated with an herbicide. When plant-killing chemicals are used, care must be taken not to damage nearby plants.

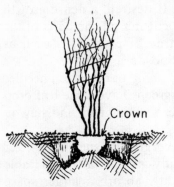

Crown

FIGURE 47. Removing a plant to be destroyed. Tie the branches and dig close to the crown, cutting off all roots as they are encountered.

GIRDLING ROOTS

A phase of pruning frequently overlooked is that of cutting out girdling roots. Sometimes these offenders are visible at the base of the tree; at other times they are below the surface of the ground, and it is necessary to remove some soil from near the crown of the tree to find them.

This condition begins in a rather unalarming fashion as a small root grows over another lateral root. As both increase in size they press against each other, restricting circulation of water and nutrients from the soil to the top of the tree. The tree, gradually but obviously, decreases in vigor as the situation becomes progressively more severe, especially when several girdling roots occur on one tree. The sooner these offenders are found and removed, the better. The smaller of each pair of girdling roots should be cut out with pruning shears or chisel and mallet. Care must be taken not to damage the root to be saved. The cut surface of the remaining root should be painted with asphalt paint.

SIDEWALK DAMAGE BY TREE ROOTS

Trees that have been planted too close to sidewalks sometimes cause damage. As the shallow lateral roots gain in size, they exert pressure from underneath, forcing one or more sections of the sidewalk out of line. The best insurance against this situation is to avoid planting trees closer to a sidewalk than 4 or 5 feet.

If there is any indication that such damage will occur, the offending roots should be cut off. All wounds should be coated with asphalt paint. If no large roots need to be cut, there will be no serious damage to the tree; but if large roots are severed, considerable damage may be done in decreased circulation and weaker anchorage. The tree should be pruned to decrease about one-quarter of the foliage surface. This balances somewhat the loss of absorbing root surface and decreases the leverage exerted by a high wind; thus the tree is less likely to be tipped over.

If a sidewalk has been badly damaged by large roots, there are a few alternate courses of action. If the tree is in poor condition because of broken branches or decay or if it is an undesirable variety, it should be removed. If the tree is worth saving and the roots are too large and too numerous to be cut off safely, the sidewalk should be repaired or rebuilt above or beyond the offending roots.

STUMP REMOVAL

Tree stumps in a lawn sometimes are rightly a source of concern to homeowners. There is no easy way to remove them. Various chemicals have been suggested, some of which are said to hasten decay, others to make the wood more inflammable. Several of these chemicals have been tested, and none of them has proved entirely satisfactory.

If the stump is not too large, it is best to remove it by digging it out as described on page 114. Power machinery may be used to help if care is taken not to damage nearby walks, drives, or plant material. If it is too large to remove in that way, cut it off flush with the ground and remove most of the wood with a power-driven chisel or large drill or leave it to decompose. Sometimes a shallow, smoothly curving layer of soil is placed over the lowcut stump and seeded with lawn grass. Seldom, if ever, is it advisable to make a flower bed around the stump or attempt to adorn it in any other fashion.

Tree Plantings for Roadsides and Home Lawns

This is a guide to the selection and location of street and shade trees for new plantings and for the revision of old plantings. It presents some of the public relations and legal aspects involved.

PLANTING FOR PRESENT AND FUTURE

Street and roadside trees were recognized by our fore-fathers as indispensable to our city, village, and country roadsides. The comfort and beauty we enjoy from these trees is due to the forethought of such men. Many of those who planted small seedlings surely knew that their children would benefit even more than they.

Present-day observation of their work makes us realize that they chose wisely from the varieties available and planted them skillfully. Some of them, however, planted these trees too closely together—an easy mistake to make, as 10 to 20 feet between small seedlings appears to be more than adequate. Years later, when we see how crowded and misshapen these trees become, we realize that a spacing of 40 to 50 feet would have been better. Probably more of these trees would be alive today if wider spacings had been used in the original plantings.

We of this generation are planting not only for our comfort and pleasure but for those of future generations as well. Because we have available newly obtained scientific infor-

mation, we may be able to do a better job; but there is no
assurance that what we do today will last longer. We cannot predict what insect or disease will attack our trees in the
future, but we do have improved equipment and the benefit
of years of experience of trained professional arborists.

Street and Roadside Trees

The homeowner of today should know something about
the problems involved in planning new public plantings and
maintaining old ones. An appreciation of these factors will
bring about better understanding and more cooperation.

Street trees in villages and cities, and roadside trees in
rural areas, are located on public land within the boundaries of the highway and, therefore, fall into the same cate-
gory as trees growing in a public park. They are under the
jurisdiction of an organization known as the "Park Board,"
"Shade Tree Commission," or some other significant name.
The members are qualified, public-spirited citizens who
serve usually without salary. They are responsible for order-
ing the planting and maintenance of all public lands. The
"City Forester," "City Arborist," "Park Superintendent," or
"Highway Superintendent," and his staff of helpers carry out
the orders and regulations set forth by the governing body.

In some communities the homeowner is responsible for
planting his frontage on the roadside. This is not the ideal
procedure, as personal preference frequently results in a
hodgepodge of trees, selected and spaced according to the
whim of each individual. No homeowner should do any
street tree planting or maintenance on existing roadside
trees without the approval of the public official in charge.

For the best in ultimate effect, each citizen should co-
operate fully with the qualified organization and individuals
in charge to carry out the planned arrangement throughout
the street, even though the recommended plantings are not
in accord with his own ideas. The trees specified will have
been selected with regard to mature size, good appearance,
likely number of years of usefulness, adaptability to exist-

ing growing conditions, resistance to insect and disease attack, and resistance to storm damage. Those trees will have been avoided which have shallow root systems that may damage sidewalks, or which have deep, strong root systems that frequently clog sewers. Some varieties are prohibited for use both on public and private land.

Certain species and varieties of trees may be assigned to each street, and only that kind may be planted. This provides uniform appearance, and maintenance economies are effected in the spraying program and autumn-leaf cleanup. Each species may require its individual spraying program, and the date of leaf drop varies. Sometimes, however, two or three harmonious species are chosen for use on each street. Then, if one of them is stricken by a new and unexpected fatal attack by insects or disease, the others probably would be spared, and the street would not be entirely devoid of shade. Some professional men prefer to accept this precaution even though the trees selected require more frequent spraying and two or three sessions of raking fallen leaves.

SYMMETRICAL ARRANGEMENT

The position of each tree to be planted is decided only after careful study of the situation. Spacing between trees is determined by the mature size and shape of each variety and the area of soil available for root growth. Experience has taught us that sugar maples are best planted 40 to 50 feet apart, and red oak and American elm, 60 to 75 feet apart. These large-growing trees are ideal for wide streets where they may be planted in a box pattern (Figure 48A). On slightly narrower streets these trees may be set in a staggered pattern (Figure 48B). Symmetrical arrangements of this kind are good for straight or only slightly curving streets. Common practice is to provide at least 8 feet of planting space between the sidewalk and curb, with the trees set midway between. Wide sidewalks, narrow planting spaces, and wide pavements leave little space for water and air to penetrate the ground where they are needed for root growth. Wherever possible, large trees should not be planted under electric-power or telephone lines.

Narrow streets sometimes are planted with low-growing trees or trees that grow narrow and upright in shape. Flowering dogwood, flowering crab, amur maple, and star magnolia are examples of the low-growing trees. They should be set at least 12 feet away from a sidewalk, 20 feet away from a driveway, and 35 feet away from a street intersection. Columnar forms of sugar maple, Norway maple, red maple, and ginkgo are examples of the upright types. A proper

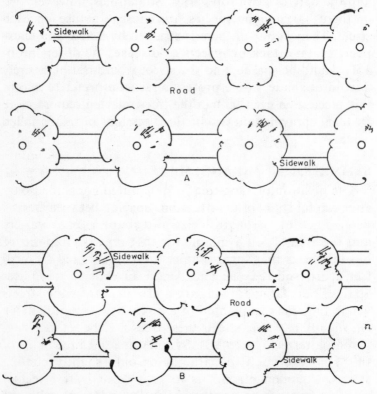

FIGURE 48. Symmetrical arrangements for street trees.

A. The box pattern is suitable for streets 60 feet or more in width.

B. A staggered pattern is good for streets 50 feet or less in width.

spacing between these trees is 15 to 25 feet. Trees of columnar form may be closer to the sidewalks and about the same
distance away from driveways and street intersections as
small trees.

Who pays for the planting and maintenance of these roadside trees? Usually the work is paid for with funds appropri-
ated from the general taxes or by direct assessment against
the owner on whose street frontage the work is done. Street
trees are an asset to the community as a whole and to the
individual property owner.

INFORMAL AND NATURALISTIC ARRANGEMENT

The use of large-growing street trees may not be practical
where there is limited space between the sidewalk and curb
or if there are overhead wires. In this case low-growing ones
are preferable. The large-growing trees may be planted in
the front lawn of each private property, where they belong
to the owner of the land. Each individual may then select
the variety of tree and its position on his land so long as it
conforms to the local regulations. He should also consider
the planting on adjacent properties as suggested later in this
STEP. Although this arrangement lacks symmetry, there
need be no sacrifice in beauty. This planting is informal in
character and especially adapted to curving streets, but may
be used on straight streets (Figure 49, A and B).

Occasionally residential subdivisions are carved out of
natural woodlands. Most often they are planned with curving streets, which are in character with the naturalistic
planting. Few, if any, trees are added, as the existing ones
are adequate. Both the informal and naturalistic plantings
are suited to rural and suburban settings.

GOOD PUBLIC RELATIONS

Citizens rarely raise serious objections to obviously bene-
ficial work done by public employees to street trees, roadside trees, and those in public parks. Watering newly planted
trees during dry periods is praised. Spraying trees for insect
and disease control is accepted as a necessary precaution

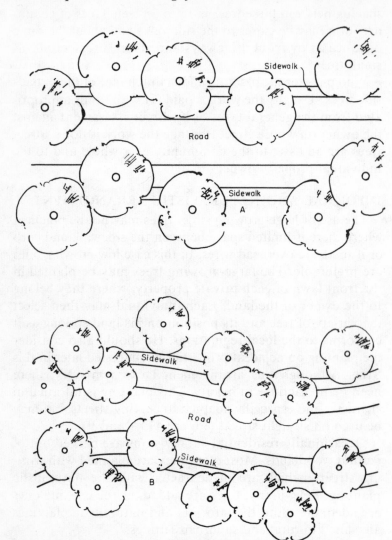

FIGURE 49. Informal and naturalistic arrangement of street trees.

A. In this informal arrangement the trees are nearly evenly spaced but are not planted in a straight line. Sometimes small-growing trees are planted under electric wires.

B. In this naturalistic arrangement both large- and small-growing trees may be used—not planted in straight rows or equal distances apart.

even if an unexpected gust of wind carries some of the spray onto newly cleaned windows. Heavy pruning of large trees brings forth raised eyebrows and a few minor explosions until the reason for the work is carefully and diplomatically explained. Sometimes electric power companies have their men do extensive but judicious pruning to clear the lines in an effort to maintain uninterrupted service. Such pruning frequently is done by tree-expert companies who have contracted with the electric power companies. This ensures good consideration for the beauty of the trees and effective clearance for the wires. The public resentment and reverberations initiated by the removal of a tree, large or small, is strong, long, and loud. In one respect this is gratifying, since it shows the strong sentiment our people have for trees. However, this sentiment should be directed from trees in general to the better varieties, to the most healthy and shapely specimens, to those that are not endangering life and property, and to those that are in keeping with a long-time, over-all street-tree-planting plan. The men responsible for this plan and for the fulfillment of it have a high degree of respect for the best trees for each situation. After careful study of each individual case some trees may be condemned to removal.

Trees planted many years ago may have been set too closely together. At their present size they are now or soon will be competing for space, both aboveground and in the soil. If none of them is removed, all of them will decline in vigor and become continually more misshapen. Some will die. If the poorer trees are removed before too much damage has been done, those that remain will improve in every respect.

Fast-growing trees have brittle wood and often are broken in severe storms. Large trees, even though they may be the best varieties for the area, may be weakened seriously by decay and insect or disease attack; they are thereby subject to storm damage. It is not uncommon for such trees to be uprooted or to have large branches broken by heavy rain and wind storms. If these trees are on public property, the damage caused may be a public responsibility; on private property they may be the responsibility of the owner. It is safest to remove these trees and avoid being accused of negligence.

Experience has shown that the root systems of some trees are particularly troublesome in sewers and drains. There probably is a local ordinance against the planting of these varieties, but those that were planted before the ordinance became effective have to be eliminated before they cause extensive trouble. Favorable results have been obtained in clearing roots from sewers by flushing copper sulphate down any of the household plumbing fixtures. Five pounds of this chemical is used monthly for three or four treatments, after which time improvement should be noticed. When the sewer is clear use a 1-pound treatment every three months. This has been done without damage to the aboveground parts of the tree.

More difficult to explain, because the reasons are less obvious, is the removal of reasonably good trees that do not conform to the over-all planting plan. Usually such trees are left until there is a practical and concrete reason for their removal. All new plantings will conform to the general scheme.

Shade Trees for the Home Lawn

Shade trees, properly placed with relation to your home and its surroundings, bring both pleasure and comfort. Plant only a few good shade trees and place them where they are most needed. Mistakes made in the selection and placement of your shade trees are difficult and costly to correct, especially after these plants have grown to a considerable size.

Homeowners whose property is not blessed with good shade trees are anxious to obtain adequate shade as soon as possible. They want the trees that grow fastest. Unfortunately, the fast-growing trees are not good ones, as they have brittle wood that breaks easily in storms. They also have strong root systems that invade drain tiles and sewers and compete strongly with the lawn, flowers, shrubs, and vegetables for moisture and nutrients. A better practice is to plant a desirable tree even though it may be a little slower to mature. Many good shade trees are reasonably rapid in growth if they are planted in good soil, are provided with ample moisture, and are fertilized annually.

If it is of prime importance to obtain shade quickly, the best way is to plant a large size of a desirable variety. For most purposes, trees 1½ to 2 inches in diameter are good sizes to plant; those 4 to 6 inches will give a fair amount of shade the first season and will not be excessively expensive. Larger trees are available at a cost proportional to their size.

Those who will remove trees when necessary may like the alternate idea of planting one or two fast-growing trees to give temporary shade while the more desirable ones are maturing in their permanent positions. This procedure is recommended only for those who will eliminate unhesitatingly the temporary trees as soon as they begin to crowd the permanent ones. If this plan is followed, the desirable varieties should be planted where they are to remain, and the temporary trees should be placed 15 to 20 feet from them.

Fixing the position of trees accurately is a most important job. When planning the location of large-growing trees, always keep in mind their most important functions—to shade the house and outdoor living areas, to frame the house or to provide a background for it, to frame a good view or screen an undesirable one. Remember that large trees tend to dwarf a small house. Consider the existing trees on your property, if any, the roadside planting, and those near your other boundary lines. Work toward a spacing of 40 feet or more. This ideal spacing may not always be practicable, as a new tree may need to be set closer than 40 feet to an existing tree.

SHADE WHERE NEEDED

The first requirement is to provide shade where and when it is desired. Afternoon and evening—the more leisurely time of day for most people—is apt to be spent in the living room, on the outdoor terrace or porch, or perhaps in the picnic area. If these are so located that the afternoon and early-evening sun is too bright and hot, a shade tree planted to the west or southwest of these places will provide more comfort.

Your dining room and kitchen are used at intervals during the day. The position of the windows in these rooms and the compass direction they face determine the general location of a tree that will provide shade. Bedroom windows may need shade from the early-morning or early-evening sunlight.

Deciduous trees, those that drop their leaves in winter, usually are preferred in situations near the house when winter sunlight is needed. Evergreens would shade the house both in winter and summer. Existing trees in the neighborhood may influence your choice of the kind to use. Those with odd growth habits, such as weeping mulberry and bungei catalpa, are not suitable for most places.

USES OF TREES

The number of large-growing trees that can be used on a small property probably is limited to the few that are to shade the house. If you have large lawn areas, you may need a few more. If so, locate them near the borders of the lawn in positions where they will frame a good view, screen an undesirable view, or give some privacy to an outdoor living area. In general, place the trees at unequal distances and not in straight lines. This will give an informal character to the planting. However, in formal settings, it sometimes is best to plant the trees symmetrically, equidistant from the corners of the house. A few trees in the lawn provide perspective to the view, thus giving the illusion of spaciousness.

Plant neither trees nor shrubs in lawns that are to be used for games or near a flower or vegetable garden. You may, however, plant trees near the sides or ends of play areas where they will not interfere with the games. A play space for small children might be shaded by a tree. As children develop, their interests and activities change, so the over-all plan should be flexible enough to meet their various needs. The baby, whose sandbox requires little space with some shade, soon becomes an active child who wants the space necessary for football or croquet. The STEP "Outdoor Recreation" elaborates on this problem.

SPACING AND DISTANCE FROM THE HOUSE

No hard and fast rules can be given for the spacing between trees. From three to five trees might be planted in one hole, as is done sometimes with birches to obtain a naturalistic effect. Except for special-purpose planting of this kind, large-growing shade trees should be spaced 40 feet or more apart.

If existing shade trees on the lawn or street are closer together than 40 feet, it would be well for you to consider removing some of them. Remove the poorest trees—those that are poorly shaped, diseased, seriously rotted, or broken. Usually, it is better to have a few good shade trees than a lot of poor ones. Crowded trees soon become poor trees because the heads become misshapen, the roots compete for nutrients, and the soil is rapidly depleted of moisture and fertility. Not only are the trees weakened, but the lawn, shrubs, flowers, and vegetables nearby are stunted.

A large-growing shade tree may be planted as near as 15 feet to the house or any other building. For new plantings, 15 feet could be taken as a minimum distance. If a large tree is already growing near a building, the condition and shape of the tree will determine whether or not it should be removed. If it has become weakened by decay or if a large branch extends over the house, a storm might break the tree and cause considerable damage. Such a tree is a hazard and should be removed.

After the general location of each shade tree is determined, the position may be made more exact by holding an 8- to 10-foot stake, such as a fish pole, in the proposed location. Visualize the pole as having side branches and study its position from all viewpoints, from inside the house looking out of the windows and from the outside looking back toward the house. Shift the pole a few feet this way or that until it seems to meet the requirements. Keep in mind that each tree should be located where it will shade the desired part of the house and grounds and, at the same time, frame the view of the house from outside or form a background. It should not block the view of the house unless there is an architectural defect that needs to be screened. When the precise place for each tree is determined, drive a stake into the ground to mark it.

Smaller stakes can be driven into the ground in a circle 30 feet in diameter around each tree stake. This will outline the branch spread of a semimature shade tree and may lead to a decision that you should have fewer trees than you originally planned. It is much easier to shift the position of

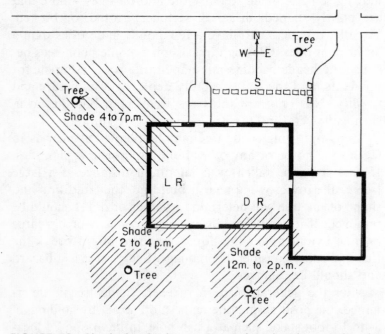

FIGURE 50. Shade for the home. Trees placed with regard to the compass direction and the time of day shade is needed will provide more comfortable living. The main function of the tree in the upper-right corner is to frame the house from that side.

a few stakes than it is to move a tree after it has been planted. The shade indicated in Figures 50, 51, and 52 is approximate. It will vary from season to season, from one geographic location to another.

SMALL-GROWING TREES

Small-growing trees sometimes are used near a house or in a border planting in a manner described in STEPS 8 and 9.

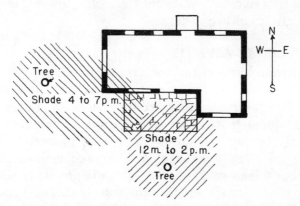

FIGURE 51. Shade for the terrace. Trees planted south and west of an outdoor terrace will shade it at the time of day it is used most often.

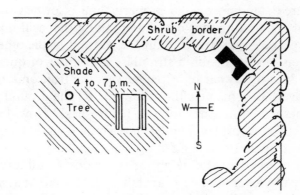

FIGURE 52. Shade for the picnic area. A tree located west of the picnic area will provide shade for an outdoor evening meal.

They may be used singly or in groups in the lawn where they will frame the view of a small house, a distant landscape, or screen a small unsightly area. They are used effectively in a shrub border where some extra height will break the monotony or in a position where they will provide a transition in size from a large tree to a shrub planting. They are well used where they will shade a garden seat or narrow garden path. When planted in groups in a lawn or in a wide border, small trees are spaced irregularly from 6 to 15 feet apart. In a narrow border they are often used singly or in small groups of two or three.

SOME LEGAL ASPECTS

Many questions of tree ownership and damage caused by trees have been tried in court. A review of some of these cases brings forth some interesting decisions. In general, it is considered that a tree whose trunk is entirely on one property belongs to the owner of that property. This includes any fruit produced on a branch overhanging his neighbor's land or roots that extend into it. It seems to make no difference whether the fruit is still on the tree or has fallen to the ground. The neighbor may cut off any bothersome branches that extend over his lot or roots that penetrate his land, but the wood obtained therefrom belongs to the owner of the tree.

A tree standing on the property line is owned by both neighbors, and neither may do anything that will injure or destroy the entire tree without the consent of the other.

Decisions of this kind stimulate a number of questions. How does the owner of a tree harvest the fruit on a branch that overhangs his neighbor's land or on the ground below that branch without risking suit for trespass? How does the neighbor mow his lawn under the overhanging branch without destroying the fallen fruit?

Let us say that the neighbor is seriously and adversely affected by overhanging branches and by roots that extend into his land. He cuts them off near the property line and, to play safe, leaves an extra foot on each branch and root.

This is his legal right, and he gives the wood to the owner of the tree. So many of the branches and so much of the root system is removed that the tree is either badly injured or dies, or its anchorage is weakened so that a strong windstorm tips the tree over onto the owner's house. Who is held responsible?

Rather than be bothered with all of these legal technicalities, it probably will be best to plant your trees sufficiently far from your property line so that no serious difficulties will arise. If there is an existing tree on or near the property line and causing trouble, talk over the problem with your neighbor. The chances are that he is a rather good fellow and that a reasonable decision can be reached.

Large Trees that Grow 40 Feet or More in Height

The trees listed here are hardy in most of the northeastern quarter of the United States, south through Tennessee, and west to the foothills of the Rocky Mountains. Those classified as "tender" may not survive the winters of the coldest parts of this area. In the warmer portions more plants could be added. Only the most important characteristics of each tree are given. Lower-growing trees are listed on pages 279 to 284.

Lists of trees for other parts of the country may be obtained from your state college of agriculture or from local nurserymen.

Deciduous Trees

BOX-ELDER: *Acer negundo* [a'-sir nee-gun'-doe]
Remarks: Rapid in growth, weak wood, frequently broken during severe storms, strong root system; may clog drain tile.

NORWAY MAPLE: *Acer platanoides* [a'-sir plah-tan-oh-eye'-des]
Leaves: Large, yellow in autumn.
Flowers: Yellow, produced abundantly before the leaves.
Remarks: Dense shade, shallow roots, difficult to maintain a good lawn or other plant growth under the branch spread.
RED NORWAY MAPLE: *Acer platanoides rubrum* [roo'-brum], has

red leaves throughout summer. SCHWEDLER MAPLE: *Acer platanoides schwedleri* [schwed'-ler-eye], has red leaves in the
spring, turning green later. Both have undesirable characteristics of Norway maple.

RED MAPLE: *Acer rubrum* [a'-sir roo'-brum]
Leaves: Usually red in autumn, sometimes yellow.
Flowers: Small, red, produced abundantly before the leaves.
Remarks: Light shade, fairly rapid in growth, sometimes dam-
aged in storms.

SILVER MAPLE: *Acer saccharinum* [a'-sir sak-car-eye'-num]
Leaves: Usually yellow in autumn, sometimes red.
Remarks: Rapid in growth, weak wood, frequently broken dur-
ing storms, strong root system, may clog drain tile.

SUGAR MAPLE: *Acer saccharum* [a'-sir sak'-car-um]
Leaves: Orange, crimson, and yellow in autumn.
Remarks: One of finest street and shade trees, medium in
growth rate.

HORSE-CHESTNUT: *Aesculus hippocastanum*
[aes'-cuh-lus hip-poe-cas'-tay-num]
Leaves: Large, brown in autumn.
Flowers: Showy, white clusters in May.
Remarks: Red- and yellow-flowering varieties available; fruit
litters lawn; double-flowering variety, *baumannii*
(bow'-man-ee-eye), produces no fruit.

TREE OF HEAVEN: *Ailanthus altissima* [eye-lan'-thus
al-tiss'-ih-mah]
Remarks: Many undesirable characteristics, tolerant of adverse
growing conditions, satisfactory in cities where most trees
succumb.

BIRCHES: Often killed by borers, yellow leaves in autumn.

CHERRY OR SWEET BIRCH: *Betula lenta* [bet'-u-lah len'-tah]
Bark: Reddish brown; cherrylike lenticels.
Remarks: Does well in moist locations.

PAPER OR CANOE BIRCH: *Betula papyrifera* [bet'-u-lah
pay-per-if'-er-ah]
Bark: White.

Remarks: One of best white-barked birches, does well in moist locations, resistant to borers.

EUROPEAN WHITE BIRCH: *Betula pendula* [bet'-u-lah pen'-du-lah]
Bark: White.
Remarks: Drooping habit of growth.

GRAY BIRCH: *Betula populifolia* [bet'-u-lah pop-u-lih-foe'-lee-ah]
Bark: Brown when young, white when older.
Remarks: Does well in sandy soils, frequently grows in naturalistic clumps.

SHAGBARK HICKORY: *Carya ovata* [kay'-ree-uh oh-vay'-tuh]
Leaves: Yellow to brown in autumn.
Fruit: Edible nut.
Bark: Scales off in curving pieces.
Remarks: Strong wood, irregular growth, long-lasting, picturesque; nuts litter the lawn. Grafted varieties produce better nuts.

WESTERN CATALPA: *Catalpa speciosa* [cah-tal'-pah spee-see-oh'-sah]
Leaves: Large, coarse texture, yellowish in autumn.
Flowers: Showy, white clusters in mid-June.
Fruit: Pods litter the lawn.
Remarks: Petals and large leaves litter the lawn.

AMERICAN BEECH: *Fagus grandifolia* [fay'-gus gran-dih-foe'-lee-ah]
Leaves: Glossy, russet-brown in autumn.
Bark: Smooth, light gray.
Remarks: Fine specimen for large lawn, low branches make area 30 to 40 feet in diameter under the tree bare and inaccessible.

EUROPEAN BEECH: *Fagus sylvatica* [fay'-gus sill-vah'-tee-kuh]
Remarks: Like American beech but somewhat tender. Purple-leaf form, cut-leaf form, and narrow, upright form available.

WHITE ASH: *Fraxinus americana* [frax'-ih-nus ah-mair-ih-kay'-nah]
Leaves: Purplish in autumn.
Fruit: Winged seed, produces new trees all too abundantly.

Remarks: Relatively rapid in growth, rather resistant to storm damage.

MAIDENHAIR TREE: *Ginkgo biloba* [gink′-go bil′-oh-bah]
Leaves: Interesting fan shape, clear yellow in autumn.
Fruit: Litters the lawn, messy, ill-smelling. Use *only staminate flowering trees* which do not bear fruit.
Remarks: Frequently ill-shaped as young tree, older trees dense, well-formed.

HONEY LOCUST: *Gleditsia triacanthos* [glah-deet′-see-ah try-ah-can′-thos]
Leaves: Small leaflets, light shade, yellow in early autumn.
Fruit: Seed pods litter the lawn.
Remarks: Good street or shade tree on large lawn; sharp thorns may need to be cut off, or use thornless variety *inermis*.

BLACK WALNUT: *Juglans nigra* [ju′-glans ny′-grah]
Leaves: Brown in autumn.
Fruit: Edible nut, grafted varieties preferred.
Remarks: Rugged tree, valuable for making furniture and other wood products, large trees disappearing from American landscape. Roots apparently release toxic substance, sometimes harmful to growth of tomatoes, alfalfa, and some broadleaved evergreens.

EUROPEAN LARCH: *Larix decidua* [lay′-rix dee-cid′-u-ah]
Leaves: Needlelike, beautiful green in spring, yellow in autumn.
Remarks: Sometimes mistaken for evergreen. Grows well in dry locations.

AMERICAN LARCH OR TAMARACK: *Larix laricina* [lay′-rix lay-rih′-see-nah]
Leaves: Same as for European larch.
Remarks: Grows well in moist locations.

SWEET GUM: *Liquidambar styraciflua* [liquid-am′-bar sty-rah-sih′-flu-ah]
Leaves: Deeply lobed, star-shaped, brilliant red in autumn.
Remarks: Beautiful tree, difficult to transplant successfully, tender.

TULIP-TREE: *Liriodendron tulipifera* [leer-ee-oh-den′-dron too-lih-pif′-er-ah]

Leaves: Large, yellow in autumn.

Flowers: Large, greenish yellow with orange at base, mostly concealed by leaves.

Remarks: Occasionally broken during severe storms.

CUCUMBER-TREE: *Magnolia acuminata* [mag-no′-lee-ah ah-cue-mah-nay′-tah]

Leaves: Large, greenish in autumn.

Flowers: Large, greenish, but not showy as oriental varieties.

Remarks: Large tree, hardy, grows natively in Eastern half of United States except in deep South.

APPLE: *Malus sylvestris* [may′-lus sill-ves′-tris]

Flowers: Showy, white, or light pink.

Remarks: Good shade, sometimes picturesque, litters the lawn with fruit, requires frequent spraying to produce good fruit.

TUPELO, SOURGUM: *Nyssa sylvatica* [niss′-ah sill-vah′-tee-kuh]

Leaves: Brilliant red in autumn.

Remarks: Irregular branching, picturesque, native as far north as Maine, hard to transplant successfully.

BUTTONWOOD, SYCAMORE: *Platanus occidentalis* [plah′-tah-nus ox-sih-den-tay′-liss]

Leaves: Large, brown in autumn.

Bark: Showy blotches of light gray, brown, and dark gray.

Remarks: Grows in wet places, picturesque branching, litters the lawn with dead twigs, subject to storm damage.

WHITE POPLAR: *Populus alba* [pop′-u-lus al′-bah]

Leaves: Maple-shaped, white underneath.

Remarks: Too many faults to list; may be against city ordinance to use.

CAROLINA POPLAR: *Populus canadensis* [pop′-u-lus can-ah-den′-sis]

Remarks: Same as white poplar.

WILD BLACK CHERRY: *Prunus serotina* [pru′-nus see-roe′-tih-nah]

Leaves: Dark red in autumn.

Remarks: Wood valuable for furniture and other wood products; large trees disappearing from the American landscape.

OAKS: The oaks are considered to be among the best of our street and shade trees. They have attractive, brilliant-red to dark-red autumn color, are sturdy trees, resistant to storm damage. They are most successfully transplanted in the spring.

All oaks, especially the red and black oaks, are susceptible to a fatal wilt disease most prevalent in the Middle West but observed as far east as western Pennsylvania. Even in those areas they may be used with relative safety if planted at least 75 feet from other oaks.

WHITE OAK: *Quercus alba* [kwer'-cus al'-bah]
Leaves: Deep lobes, rounded tips.
Remarks: Sturdy tree, slow-growing, lasting beauty and shade.

RED OAK: *Quercus borealis maxima (rubra)* [kwer'-cus bow-ree-a'-lis max'-ih-mah]
Leaves: Pointed lobes.
Remarks: Medium in growth rate.

SCARLET OAK: *Quercus coccinea* [kwer'-cus cox-cin'-ee-ah]
Leaves: Deeply lobed, pointed tips.
Remarks: Medium in growth rate.

PIN OAK: *Quercus palustris* [kwer'-cus pa-lus'-tris]
Leaves: Deeply lobed, pointed tips.
Remarks: Medium in growth rate.

BLACK LOCUST: *Robinia pseudoacacia* [roe-bin'-ih-ah soo-doe-ah-kay'-sha]
Leaves: Small leaflets, yellowish in autumn.
Flowers: White in early June, fragrant.
Remarks: Irregular growth, picturesque, susceptible to borer and leaf-miner attack; when weakened, breaks easily in storms; litters lawn with branches and seed pods.

YELLOW WILLOW: *Salix alba vitellina* [say'-lix al'-bah vie-tell-eye'-nah]
Remarks: Not good tree, sometimes used on large lawns and in wet soil, rapid-growing, breaks easily in storms, large root system, clogs nearby drains.

WISCONSIN WEEPING WILLOW: *Salix blanda* [say'-lix blan'-dah]
Remarks: Drooping habit of growth; use in same way as yellow willow; has same undesirable characteristics.

BASSWOOD, AMERICAN LINDEN: *Tilia americana* [till'-ee-ah
  ah-mair-ih-can'-ah]
Leaves: Large, coarse texture, yellow in autumn.
Flowers: White in early July, fragrant.
Remarks: Neither dense nor shapely.

SMALL-LEAVED LINDEN: *Tilia cordata* [till'-ee-ah kor-day'-tah]
Leaves: Small, yellow in autumn.
Flowers: White in early July, fragrant.
Remarks: Good for small lawns and narrow streets.

AMERICAN ELM: *Ulmus americana* [ull'-mus ah-mair-ih-can'-nah]
Leaves: Yellow in autumn.
Remarks: One of most effective trees for wide streets. Dutch
  elm disease and phloem necrosis are now being somewhat
  controlled.

DWARF SIBERIAN ELM: *Ulmus pumila* [ull'-mus pu'-mih-lah]
Leaves: Yellow in autumn.
Remarks: Rapid-growing, breaks easily in storms, undesirable.

Pyramidal Deciduous Trees

Until quite recently, LOMBARDY POPLAR, *Populus nigra
italica,* was the only tree with narrow, upright growth used
extensively in ornamental plantings. Now much better
varieties are available in ever-increasing quantity. They are
excellent for use along narrow streets and in border plantings where accents are needed. The species are described in
the listing of large trees. Those most often used are:

COLUMNAR NORWAY MAPLE: *Acer platanoides columnare*
  [co-lum-nay'-ree]
COLUMNAR RED MAPLE: *Acer rubrum columnare* [co-lum-nay'-ree]
PYRAMIDAL SUGAR MAPLE: *Acer saccharum monumentale*
  [mon-u-men-tay'-lee]
PYRAMIDAL BEECH: *Fagus sylvatica fastigiata* [fas-tih-gee-a'-tah]
SENTRY GINKGO: *Ginkgo biloba fastigiata* [fas-tih-gee-a'-tah]

Narrow-leaved Evergreen Trees

FIR: The three firs listed here are among the best of several
  varieties available. They grow in a wide-base, pyramid form
  and may be maintained satisfactorily as a tall clipped hedge.

BALSAM FIR: *Abies balsamea* [a'-bees bahl-say'-mee-ah]
Remarks: One of the best for Christmas tree, retains needles two or three weeks after brought indoors.

WHITE FIR: *Abies concolor* [a'-bees kon'-color]
Leaves: Light bluish green.
Remarks: Good for windbreak.

VEITCH FIR: *Abies veitchii* [a'-bees veetch'-ee-eye]
Leaves: White on lower side, dark green above, striking in appearance.
Remarks: Bright in color, better tree than COLORADO BLUE SPRUCE.

SPRUCE: Only two of the most often used are listed here.

NORWAY SPRUCE: *Picea abies* [pie'-see-ah a'-bees]
Remarks: Most often used for windbreak, in good soil relatively rapid growth, in poor soil growth retarded, branching sparse, and effectiveness lost.

COLORADO BLUE SPRUCE: *Picea pungens glauca* [pie'-see-ah pun'-gens glau'-kah]
Leaves: Bright blue, grafted varieties more showy.
Remarks: Often improperly used; bright color draws undue attention to themselves, detracting from surroundings.

PINES: Only five of the many varieties of pines are listed here. They are best used on large properties, in border plantings, or as specimens in a large lawn. Some, such as Jack or Scotch pine, may be used in naturalistic clumps.

JACK PINE: *Pinus banksiana* [pie'-nus bank-see-a'-nah]
Leaves: Two in bundle, stiff, twisted.
Remarks: Irregular, curving branching habit, picturesque.

AUSTRIAN PINE: *Pinus nigra austriaca* [pie'-nus ny'-gra aus-try'-ah-cah]
Leaves: Two in bundle, stiff, sharp-pointed.
Remarks: Round outline, dark-colored bark, deeply ridged.

RED PINE: *Pinus resinosa* [pie'-nus rez-in-oh'-sah]
Leaves: Two in bundle, long, soft, and sharp-pointed.
Remarks: Very good tree, rough, scaly bark, exposed inner surface red-brown in color.

WHITE PINE: *Pinus strobus* [pie'-nus stroh'-bus]

Leaves: Five in bundle, soft and slender.

Remarks: Soft texture, dense, successful as tall clipped hedge, subject to white-pine blister rust and attack by pine weevil.

SCOTCH PINE: *Pinus sylvestris* [pie'-nus sill-ves'-tris]

Leaves: Two in bundle, short, twisted.

Remarks: Striking bright orange-colored bark when mature, picturesque.

DOUGLAS FIR: *Pseudotsuga taxifolia* [soo-doe-tsoo'-gah tax-ih-foe'-lee-ah]

Remarks: Pyramidal form, graceful habit of growth, good for large clipped hedges.

CANADA HEMLOCK: *Tsuga canadensis* [tsoo'-gah can-ah-den'-sis]

Remarks: Fine tree, soft texture, excellent for tall clipped hedge.

  CAROLINA HEMLOCK: Tsuga caroliniana [care-oh-line-ih-an'-ah], native of South but hardy in North.

Foundation Plantings
about the House

The information given in this STEP may be used for planning new plantings or revising old ones. The ideas may be used suitably for houses either in urban or rural situations.

The type of foundation planting for any home is subject to individual differences of opinion; what one person likes another disapproves. The taste of the individual should dictate his own preference.

Some persons believe that no plantings should be placed near the house. There is merit to this opinion, particularly if the house is architecturally well designed and is in a setting of spacious tree-shaded lawns. Other persons believe that many shrubs are needed, particularly about the house not well designed and with a high foundation wall visible above the soil line. For most situations, a medium between the two extremes may be best.

Probably there is better reason for more planting around the base of a house that has a high foundation wall exposed above the soil line than there is around a house that has low foundation walls. Also a house that has poor architectural lines may need large masses of plants to screen these imperfections. A large-growing shade tree placed 15 to 20 feet from the corner of a house minimizes rather effectively the high appearance of a house that is narrow and upright. Plants with a horizontal branching habit help, as do structural devices such as window boxes, window blinds, and two-tone painting. Horizontal lines diminish the apparent height, while narrow, upright plant forms or structural design increase the visual height.

CHOICE OF PLANTS

Some homeowners want all of the front planting and perhaps more to be entirely of evergreens so that they will have green foliage in winter. Others want deciduous, flowering shrubs because they like the informal effect and the flower color in summer. To obtain both effects, you may plant a combination of evergreens and flowering shrubs. In suitable locations you may plant broad-leaved evergreens such as mountain-laurel and rhododendron. These have green leaves in winter and flower in summer.

In areas where winters are severe, the matter of protecting plants from snowslides from the roof is a problem. Plants set under the slope of the roof may be badly damaged by an avalanche. If these plants are evergreen and they are covered with snow, the winter effect is lost. Sometimes they are protected from damage with a wrapping of burlap or by a wooden shelter. In either case they are hidden from view by the protective covering, and, except from memory, no one would know that evergreens are planted there.

Winding a rope tightly around the branches to hold them closely together is an effective and reasonably inconspicuous method of protecting shrubs, especially those that are upright in growth. The rope may be tied to a screw hook in the wall to keep the plants from bending over with the weight of snow. This may draw them temporarily into a somewhat unnatural shape, but their winter value as evergreens is not lost.

Some late-flowering shrubs such as buddelja, snowhill hydrangea, Anthony Waterer spirea, and peonies may be used under a roof where snowslides occur, as they may be cut to the ground in the fall. The roots live throughout the winter, send up new shoots in the spring, and produce flowers during the summer. Remember that the house should be the focal center of the picture. All foundation plantings should be designed to improve this picture and should not be so massive that they cover it or so bright in color that they detract from it.

In Relation to the Design of the House

Whether the house is traditional or modern in design, large-growing shrubs and trees are suitable for use around a two-story structure, and low-growing shrubs and low-growing trees near a one-story building. In all situations the character and design of the house should influence the choice of plants. The setting for a house is most appropriately created by the use of plant material prevalent during the period which the house represents. Early American homes appear at their best with such familiar plants as sweetautumn clematis, trumpet honeysuckle, English ivy, periwinkle, flowering almond, coralberry, snowberry, snowhill hydrangea, sweet-shrub, kerria, flowering quince, bayberry, azaleas, weigela, summersweet, forsythia, flowering currant, Harison's yellow rose, bridalwreath, lilac, mockorange, bush honeysuckle, flowering dogwood, sugar maple, red oak, and many others.

Select a few different kinds of shrubs for your plantings, to produce some succession of bloom and different flower colors during the spring and summer. Too many different varieties produce a confused effect. A small house requires proportionately fewer varieties than a large one. Consider the color of your house, and select plants whose flowers will show to good advantage against it. The yellow flowers of forsythia and Harison's yellow rose are not so effective near a house painted yellow as they are near a white or red house, but they will repeat satisfactorily the color of yellow trim. It is inappropriate to use rugosa rose near a house painted red or near one constructed of red brick, but shrubs with white or yellow flowers are excellent against brick. Highly colored plants, red- and yellow-leaved varieties, and those with variegated foliage should be used with great restraint.

Planting under Wide Eaves

Planting under wide, overhanging eaves is not a serious problem. Many plants will grow satisfactorily without being exposed to direct sunlight, so the choice of plants for such situations is quite varied. Of greatest importance is an adequate supply of moisture. Preparing the planting soil with large amounts of organic material such as peat, keeping a mulch under the plants throughout the year, and watering the soil with a hose before it becomes dry will keep the plants growing thriftily. The organic material in the soil and the mulch will conserve moisture, and only infrequent artificial watering will be necessary.

In Relation to Mature Size

Select each plant for its intended position with regard to its mature size. After the size requirement is met, the selection of the plant you use in each place is a matter of personal choice. You will be happier with your own selection than with that of someone else.

It makes considerable difference in the ultimate appearance whether a plant grows to be 3, 5, 8, or 15 feet or more in height. It is not wise to use a plant that will mature at 8 feet in a position where a dwarf plant would be more suitable. You would need to prune the large shrub severely to keep it down to a proper size for that location. Severe pruning ruins the natural shape of a shrub and usually eliminates flower production.

Most persons buy young plants because they are less expensive than mature ones of the same variety. Space these small plants to allow for several years' growth. A new planting of this kind may be disappointing to the homeowner because of the sparse appearance, which can, however, be minimized by planting annuals or perennials between the shrubs. Each succeeding year the area you devote to flowers decreases in size as the shrubs become larger, until the permanent plants absorb the space intended for them.

Of the other ways to obtain an immediate effect, probably the best is to purchase nearly mature sizes of suitable kinds of plants. These large plants are considerably more expensive than small ones of the same kind. The choice of whether you use large or small sizes will be governed by your ability to wait happily for the plants to mature or to pay for large plants.

Another method, and probably the least practical one, is to follow the old advice to "plant thick and thin quick." This involves the use of several small plants in the same area that one plant will occupy after a few years' growth. You get a fairly good immediate effect, but the procedure is impractical because some of these plants will have to be removed and possibly discarded. Although each plant is relatively inexpensive, the total spent for several small ones sometimes is as much as or more than the amount one would spend on a single large plant that would fill the same space. Another argument against the close planting of small-sized

shrubs has a human element as its background. Each succeeding year the plants with their annual growth become more and more crowded and

FIGURE 53. This is a poor planting of evergreen trees such as spruce, pine, fir, or hemlock. The picture at the top is representative of a new planting, the one in the center is the same planting as it will appear about three years later, and the one at the bottom shows what it will be fifteen years later.

misshapen. Regardless of this, most persons refuse to remove the plants, although they are rapidly becoming detrimental to the rest of the group. To leave all the original plants in the group always results in a planting that needs to be replaced sooner or later. The crowding of these plants causes each to lose its characteristic shape and individuality.

Old plantings that have been made incorrectly should be managed differently, depending upon how seriously out of line they are or will become in a few years.

FIGURE 54. This is a poor planting of one variety of medium- to tall-growing shrub as it appears when newly planted (top), three years later (center), and ten years later (bottom).

Three types of incorrect plantings are illustrated in Figures 53, 54, and 55. Shrubs that are only slightly large for their positions may be modified in size by removing some of the older branches at the base. If, however, any of the shrubs, whether evergreen or deciduous, are decidedly too large for their positions, it is best to remove them. A new and lower-growing plant should replace the tall one. In this way old plantings that have been incorrectly made can be revised to approach, if not duplicate, the new plantings described in this STEP. If the old plant is still well shaped and in good condition, it may be transplanted to a more suitable position, such as the corner of a building, a large wall space, or a border planting. Such a plant, especially an evergreen not in good

FIGURE 55. This is a poor planting using different kinds of plants and tall-growing shrubs screening the window. The picture at the top shows a new planting, the one at the center shows how it will look three years later, and the one at the bottom how it will look ten years later. The saw-tooth effect occurs when a low-growing shrub is alternated with a tall-growing one.

condition, might better be discarded. Old deciduous, ill-shaped plants usually can be brought back to well-shaped plants by cutting them back severely. This forces new shoots to come up from the base.

The illustrations of old plantings in Figures 53, 54, and 55 show how excessive growth soon outdistances the pruning shears. A planting of poorly chosen evergreens is illustrated in Figure 53. In a few years they become crowded and too tall. A single row of one medium-to-tall-growing variety is shown in Figure 54. It becomes monotonous in appearance both in flower and in foliage. All the plants grow to the same height, the foliage is the same, the flower color is the same, and they all bloom at once. Tall-growing plants have been used mistakenly too close to the windows in Figure 55.

Developing Foundation Planting Details

Reading this entire STEP before you proceed further will help you to work in a logical and effective way to develop a foundation planting plan suited to your own home. It will tell you what to look for as you begin the second stage—

that of studying your own house from every angle until you have clearly in mind the general effect you wish to create and what architectural features need to be emphasized or minimized. Such factors as the size of the house, its over-all length, width, and height, the amount of foundation wall exposed above the soil line, the position of windows in relation to one another, to doorways, and to the corners of the house, and the location of sidewalks and driveway are important details to observe.

Next you are ready to work from the blueprints from which your house was built, from fairly accurate scale drawings, or from enlarged photographs of each of the four sides of your house. Make a tracing of one of them from which to work. On these drawings include all windows, doorways, porches, and other features.

First plan each area separately—entrances, corners, and the various wall sections. Choose from the sectional plans (Figures 56 through 62) those plantings best suited to your house. For example, you may have a doorway near one of the corners. Plantings for such a doorway are shown in Figure 56, D and E.

If your home presents other problems, the ideas given here for similar situations may be adapted. Sketch roughly on your tracing paper the foliage masses that represent the effect you wish to obtain.

The numbers used for each planting in Figures 56 through 62 refer to the size group in the plant list that begins on page 253. Considering the exposure with regard to sun or shade, choose suitable plants from the proper size group, either evergreens or flowering shrubs. Select the shrub that you know and like, or if you prefer, get something that you do not know. Refer to a reliable book or nursery catalogue for a description and illustration of less familiar plants. A still better procedure is to go to a nearby nursery, ask to see the plants that you are interested in, and learn about their characteristics. Obtain complete information about the plants, including their mature size, the color of the flowers and fruits, and the time of year each is effective.

Plants to be used under windows are selected with regard

to the height of the window sill from the ground, regardless of whether it is a one- or two-story house. In most situations it is best to choose one that will mature 18 inches or more below the window sill.

Some parts of your house plan may be the reverse of the similar plan shown here. For example, the door in Figure 56D is at the right front corner of the house, while yours may be at the left. If this is the case, turn this book so that the top of the page is toward you, and hold a mirror at the bottom. The reflected image will reverse the plan so that it resembles your situation.

ENTRANCE PLANTINGS

Entrance plantings as illustrated in Figures 56 to 59 should give a feeling of easy access to the house. This feeling is obtained by using low-growing plants at the side of the steps. Tall plants in this position frequently encroach on the entrance, making access uninviting and difficult.

All the plantings illustrated in Figures 56 to 61 are for one- or one-and-a-half-story houses with a low foundation wall showing above the soil line. Taller houses and those with high foundation walls should be planted with some taller-growing shrubs than those indicated here, as illustrated and described in Figures 62, D and F, 64, 65, and 66.

A simple doorway planting in a situation where the windows are spaced approximately equidistant from the door is illustrated in Figure 56A. The door may or need not be spaced in the center of the front wall of the house. A shrub from size group 3, page 259, such as the dwarf Japanese yew, could be selected for this planting. As indicated in the spacing information in the plant lists, this plant should be set about 2 feet from the foundation and 3 feet from the entrance platform.

A similar situation is illustrated in Figure 56B, but one window is near the entrance and the other farther away. A vine is used against the larger wall space, and a plant selected from size group 3 is placed on each side of the entrance platform.

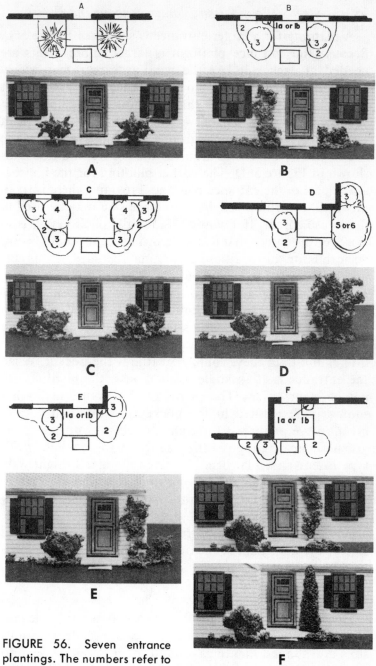

FIGURE 56. Seven entrance plantings. The numbers refer to the plant size groups.

A planting for a larger entrance is shown in Figure 56C. Because the entrance platform is larger, more plants are needed at each side. As the windows are rather widely spaced, a plant from size group 4 is selected for the corner between the entrance and the front wall of the house. If a window is closer to the doorway, so that a 4- to 5-foot plant would grow over it, use one from size group 3 for this place.

Frequently doorways are near the corner of a house, as shown in Figure 56D. The corner planting for the house is also a part of the entrance planting. Providing there is room in width, a shrub of medium to large size may be used at the house corner. If a window, sidewalk, or driveway is so close to this corner that a large-growing shrub would be undesirable for this position, a vine may be used at this corner, as indicated in Figure 56E.

If your house plans call for an entrance platform extending farther to one side of the door than to the other side, an open pocket will sometimes simplify the entrance planting problem (Figure 56F). Such arrangements are often more interesting than they would be without the pocket. When the entrance is at an angle of the house, the planting will not be symmetrical. The plan and the picture at the left show a vine planted in the pocket. An alternate idea is given in the picture at the right showing an upright evergreen occupying the planting space in the pocket. If this type of entrance platform is located along a straight wall, the pocket will enable the owner to do a symmetrical planting, as in Figure 56A. If windows are located above any planting spaces, the plants should be selected from size group 3. A larger-growing shrub or a vine may be set at one side of the door than at the other side if a larger wall space is located there.

PLANTING AROUND TERRACES

Paved terraces are often constructed along one side of a house, usually at the side or rear. They are made in various sizes and shapes. Plantings around them should be kept to a minimum. If the terrace is completely paved along the sides abutting the house foundation, no planting can be done unless boxes are provided. Some forethought here will pay dividends in appearance and pleasure. Open pockets may be left within the area of the terrace in positions where plantings would be effective (Figures 56F and 57, A, B, and C). Use the same types of plants suggested in other parts of this STEP for similar situations with regard to doors, windows, and wall spaces.

Figure 57A shows two pockets, one on either side of the door. Low-growing plants may be used here, and, in addition, a vine might be planted and trained to the wall above. The planting at the corner of the house is done the same way as for similar corners. In situations where more privacy is desired from one direction or another, add a few more medium-sized shrubs or a vine-covered trellis to the corner planting.

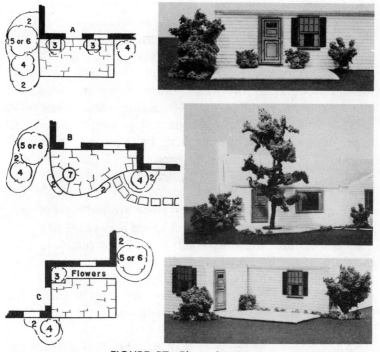

FIGURE 57. Planted terraces.

At the other end of the terrace a single shrub is used, its size largely governed by whether or not there is a window directly above. If this terrace does not extend to a corner of the house, the planting suggested at the right end would be duplicated on the left.

Figure 57B shows a terrace with a curving margin. An opening 3 or 4 feet in diameter is made in a position where the shade from a small-growing tree would be welcome. In this planting a few ground covers are used at the edge of the terrace. In some situations the screen planting indicated gives the desired privacy.

Figure 57C shows a terrace located in an angle of the house. The planting pocket here is long and narrow, possibly 2 feet wide, with a wider pocket at the corner. The wider pocket is for a shrub, and the narrow one for flowers.

Planting pockets of this kind should be provided with an ample supply of good soil, the depth of which varies from 1 foot for flowers to 30 inches for a small-growing tree.

Little planting is done at the sides of a terrace. If these sides are flush with the lawn, the grass may extend to the paved surface. When the terrace is above the adjacent lawn and a masonry wall is used to support it, a low planting may be done along the wall. A supporting dry stone wall may be planted in the manner of a wall garden, as described in STEP 9, page 198. In case the soil is simply sloped between the two levels, the resulting bank should be planted to ground covers, not sown to grass.

PLANTING BREEZEWAYS

A limited amount of planting is done around most breezeways. Frequently part of the wall space is devoted to an entrance, and there are only small areas to be planted. Also, the floor of the breezeway usually is about one step above the ground. Obviously, only low-growing shrubs can suitably be used here. A small-growing vine may be supported by a trellis in a position where it will break the view from the front into the rear yard.

Sometimes a low fence or wall suitably designed for the house is used to enclose a small, intimate flower garden in the area between the house and the garage (Figure 58A). Sometimes it extends in front of the house to enclose the front doorway (Figure 58B).

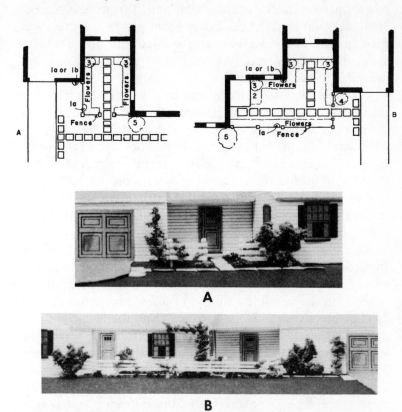

FIGURE 58. Two small flower gardens at entrance.

PLANTING AROUND LARGE PORCHES

Since many fine old homes have large porches, this section is devoted to suggestions suitable for planting them. Illustrated here are porches that have an open, spindle railing. Proportionately larger-growing shrubs than those indicated in these plans should be used near porches with a solid-wall railing and those with a higher foundation wall.

All of the plantings illustrated in Figure 59 are much the same in principle as in Figure 56. Each one is simply adjusted to correspond to the position of the entrance. The position of the vine might be changed in any of these plans. The main purpose of a vine growing on a porch is to shade or give privacy to the portion where the furniture is placed. Near very large porches, a tree-form shrub sometimes is used instead of a vine. This arrangement not only provides shade and privacy but gives interesting variation in the appearance of the planting.

A simple planting for an entrance in the center of the front porch is shown in Figure 59A. If the entrance is slightly to one side or the other, the group 3 plants (page 259) would be placed in the same position with relation to the steps. If this porch faces either north or south, a vine at the west would shade it from the afternoon sun but would not give privacy from the front. Shrubs from group 3 are set at the corners of the porch, and taller-growing shrubs are placed at the house corners.

An entrance near the corner of the porch is illustrated in Figure 59B. The porch corner and the entrance plantings are combined. Three group 3 shrubs adequately fill the space with the possible addition of a few plants from group 2. The vine gives shade and privacy from the front.

A planting that may be done in a situation where the steps extend off the end of the porch is indicated in Figure 59C. A vine and one shrub from group 3 or a tall-growing shrub is placed at the house corner. At the other side of the steps three group 3 plants form the entrance and porch-corner planting. The steps here extend off the right end of the porch. If your steps extend off the left end, reverse the planting plan.

A type of house where the porch occupies only one side of the front is illustrated in Figure 59D. The planting here is similar to the others, with a shrub from size group 3 at each side of the entrance, one from group 4 where the porch joins the house front, and a still taller-growing one at the house corner. If the house has a wood siding, use a vine from the 1a list (page 253); if of masonry construction, use one from the 1b list. If no vine is desired use only a shrub from group 4.

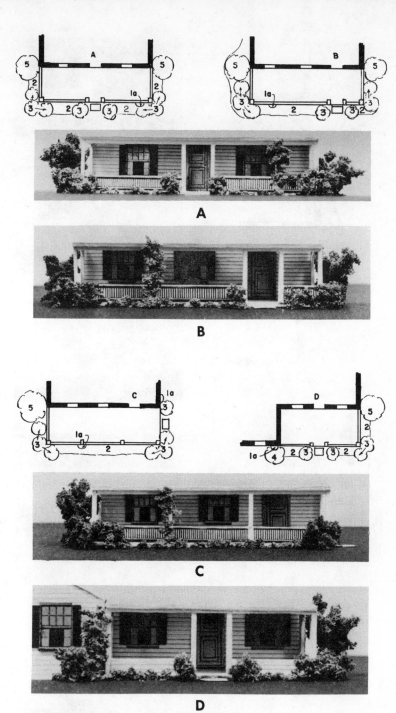

FIGURE 59. Four plantings for large porches.

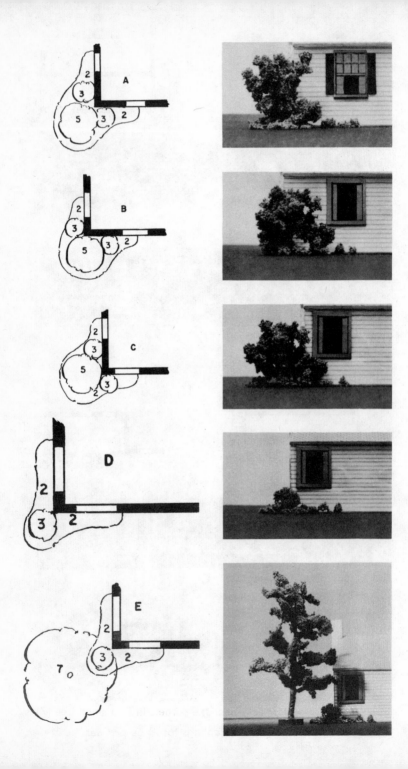

CORNER PLANTINGS

A simple corner planting of three shrubs and some ground covers is shown in Figure 60A. In this plan both windows are shown a considerable distance from the corner, and the tall shrub is placed in a position diagonally from the corner. In this location it will not grow up in front of either window.

In Figure 60B, the window on the side wall is near the corner, while the window on the other wall is several feet away. The large shrub is, therefore, placed on a line with the side wall which brings it approximately halfway between the two windows. Lower-growing plants are placed under the windows. This type of planting is used also in situations where the house is relatively low and long. Placing the shrub inside the corner decreases the apparent length of the house.

The reverse condition is illustrated in Figure 60C. The front window is near the corner, and the side window is several feet away. Again the large plant is placed in a position where it will not grow in front of either window. This type of planting, with the tall shrub placed outside the corner may be used to increase the apparent length of the house with a narrow front wall. In any of these corner plantings, if space is limited, one of the small shrubs may have to be omitted.

The illustrations in Figure 60, D and E, show both windows near the corner. Situations of this kind may be managed by planting a tall tree-form shrub or a small tree in a position that will shade these windows somewhat and break the view into the house from outside but will not cut out an excessive amount of light (Figure 60E). If shade on these windows is no consideration, a low-growing shrub may be

FIGURE 60. Some corner plantings. Note the position of the shrub in relation to the windows. In A, with windows 4' or more from corner, the large shrub is placed diagonally from corner. In C, the large shrub (5) is placed around the corner from the nearest window. D illustrates windows at or very near the corner. In E, a small tree (7) is used.

used, as shown in Figure 60D. Some persons prefer to have no planting at all at a corner such as this.

Inside Corners

The plans in Figure 61 show two plantings suitable at an inside corner. The size of the angle in the house and the position of the windows determine the number and size of the plants to use. If the inside corner is small, the planting may be combined with a nearby outside-corner planting, as illustrated in Figure 60.

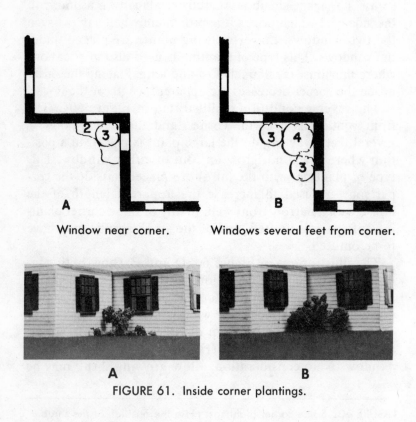

Window near corner.   Windows several feet from corner.

A   B

FIGURE 61. Inside corner plantings.

WALL PLANTINGS

The six illustrations of wall plantings shown in Figure 62 represent situations found in most homes. Your home may have some variation of one or more of these conditions, and you may need to make changes to correspond with the positions of the windows and the size and shape of the chimney.

A suitable planting for a wall space between windows that are several feet apart is shown in Figure 62A. This planting probably is somewhat more interesting than a symmetrical one in which a shrub is placed halfway between the two windows. The low-growing plants set underneath the windows may be woody ground covers, annuals, or perennials. Such plants also may be used along a foundation wall between the shrubs.

The same window arrangement is shown in Figure 62B, but the space in width is restricted by the nearness of a sidewalk, driveway, or property line. Here you can use a vine which will give foliage height without requiring several feet in width.

A planting for a wall with a large window is illustrated in Figure 62C. The same type of planting is used in places where two or more windows are too close together to warrant planting tall shrubs between them. If this window or group of windows is on a sunny side of the house and light shade is desired, a small tree or tree-form shrub is a good choice for planting beside the window and near to it. Consider the direction from which the sunlight comes, and set the plant on the proper side of the window to give the desired shade. Such a planting is interesting and has a utilitarian value. If desired, a lower-growing shrub may be used beside the window instead of the tall one.

Large picture windows sometimes are placed on a front or side wall of a house in locations where the view into the house from the street or from the neighbor's is as good as, or better than, the view from inside the house. When this is the case, planting a vine, small-growing tree, or tree-form shrub will keep the view advantage from within the house. Regardless of which of these plants is used for this purpose, it should not be allowed to become very dense. Cut off enough stems and branches to thin the plant sufficiently to obtain a lacy foliage effect in front of the window. If a vine

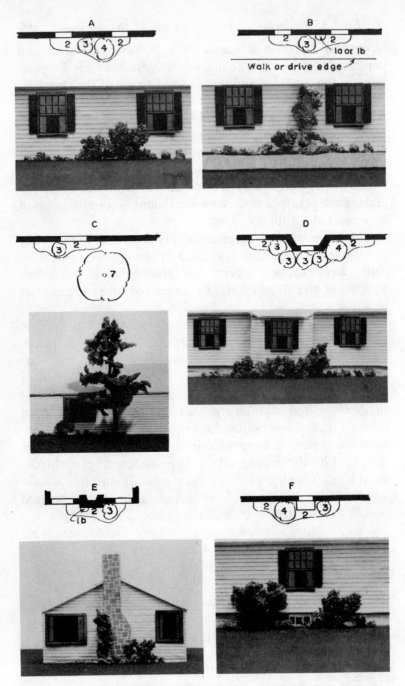

FIGURE 62. Some wall plantings.

is used, a heavy wire or light cable is a good inconspicuous type of support (Figure 63B).

Low-growing shrubs may be planted beneath bay windows, as shown in Figure 62D. This planting not only improves the appearance of the wall space but hides the open area underneath the bay. A taller-growing shrub may be used beside the window, even taller than illustrated in this plan if some shade is desired. The planting would be the same whether the bay has right-angle or acute-angle sides.

A chimney planting with a vine selected from group 1b is shown in Figure 62E. A shrub placed at one corner of the chimney adds to the interest of the planting. If the chimney is small, only large enough to contain one flue, it may be best to use a tall-growing shrub and not a vine.

A planting on each side of a basement window areaway is illustrated in Figure 62F. If preferred, the shrubs on each side could be selected from the same size group; but the less symmetrical planting probably is more interesting. Ground covers planted in front of the areaway will not block the light.

High foundation walls sometimes have basement windows entirely above grade. In this case ground covers may be used in front of the windows. If light is needed, plant dwarf shrubs on either side of the window but not directly in front of it. The shrub on either side may be tied back when it is necessary to open the window to put fuel or other materials into the basement.

Either one- or two-story houses with low foundation walls require little or no planting under windows. Sometimes the lawn is maintained up to the wall; at other times ground covers or other low-growing plants are used there. Occasionally annual or perennial flowers are used in such locations, but, if so, those with bright-colored flowers or foliage should be avoided as they attract too much attention to themselves, thus detracting from the rest of the picture. The same applies to houses that have high foundation walls. In addition, dwarf shrubs or clinging vines may be used to cover these walls.

USE OF VINES

Vines used to ornament the walls and porches of homes should be selected with regard to the type of construction and the space they are to occupy. Twining vines (group 1a) should be used on homes with wood siding and may be used on masonry (stone or brick) construction if proper support is provided. Clinging vines (group 1b) are more often used on stone or brick. Bittersweet, wisteria, and Boston ivy cover large spaces, while vines such as clematis, trumpet honeysuckle, and akebia are not so rank in growth and are better used to cover small areas. Vines that have thorns, such as climbing roses, may be troublesome when used near doorways or other passageways. They are better used on a fence or trellis at the edge of a lawn, or enclosing a flower garden.

Most clinging vines do not require artificial support, as they attach themselves to a wall. Sometimes heavy clinging vines such as bigleaf wintercreeper and trumpetcreeper, need extra support. A loose strap or one of the commercial vine-holding devices fastened to the wall and around the stem usually keeps them secure.

Twining vines must have a trellis or some other support. Most trellis designs should be simple and planned for the place they are to occupy, as twining vines assume the shape of the support provided for them. Some situations require only a rectangular shape. Occasionally two vines are used, one on either side of a window or doorway, with overhead support, so that the window or doorway is entirely framed with the two vines.

A trellis on one side and over a doorway is shown in Figure 63A. The same might be done for a window. Two-by-six supports are bolted to the wall, and the wood trellis is screwed into them. When it is time to paint, the screws can be removed and the trellis and vine placed over on the ground while the painting is done and replaced when the paint is dry.

A cable support with metal screw hooks inserted in the

wall is shown in Figure 63B. Light rust-resistant cable is used; thimble eyelets are placed at the ends and over the hooks. Cross wires are twisted, soldered, or spot-welded into the vertical cables. This is an inconspicuous method of vine support, and the hooks and cables can be arranged in various interesting patterns. The wires can be unhooked and placed on the ground when painting is to be done.

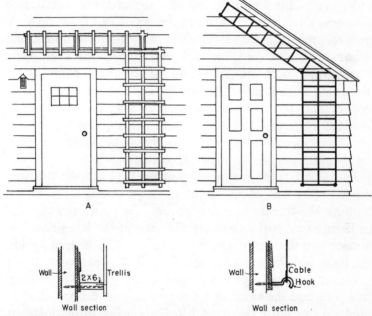

FIGURE 63. Vine supports.

A. A wood trellis is held away from the wall of the house by 2-by-6-inch pieces of wood or some other device.

B. Cables supported by hooks can be placed in any desired pattern. The vine will follow its support to give a planned foliage tracery.

COMBINING SECTIONAL PLANS

When you have decided on appropriate plantings for all sections of your house, as illustrated in Figures 56 through 62, arrange them on a plan in their proper positions. The assembled units will give a result equivalent to those in Figures 64 through 66 but will differ from them if the outline of your house is not the same. When the units are put together, duplicated or crowded plantings may need to be adjusted. Such an adjustment is illustrated at the right upper corner of Figure 64A where one plant overlaps another. One shrub from size group 3 serves both the entrance and the corner planting. A sketch or model made to scale will help you visualize the effect that your plans will produce.

Figure 64B is a photograph of a model planted accurately according to the arrangement designed in Figure 64A. As you see, this is a one-story house with the front door somewhat off center. As indicated on the plan and seen in the photograph, both the front- and side-entrance plantings are the same as that illustrated in Figure 56A, and each front-corner and the rear-left-corner plantings are the same as those in Figure 60A. If the owner of this house felt that the shrubs at these corners were too heavy, he could thin them by pruning out some of the crowded branches.

One shrub from group 3 is planted between the two windows to the left of the front door as in Figure 62C, but without the tree and ground covers; the planting suggested in Figure 62E is the chimney planting at the left side of the house; and the one suggested in Figure 62F is used against the back wall, where a basement-window areaway is shown.

Figure 64C pictures a two-story house with a low foundation wall and the same first floor window and door arrangement as in Figure 64, A and B. Only a few adjustments in the plantings have been made. At the right front and the rear left corners shrubs from group 6 replace those from group 5. A low-growing shrub and small tree at the left front corner replace the group designed for the one-story house. The shrub planted near the chimney at the left side of the house would be chosen from group 4 instead of group 3.

If either the one-story or the two-story house had a high foundation wall showing above the soil line, all the shrubs numbered 3 in plan 64A would be changed to number 4

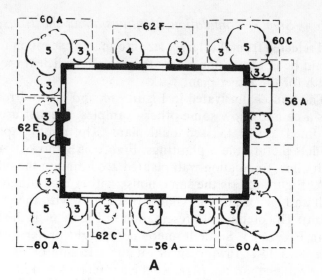

A

B

C

FIGURE 64A. Foundation planting plan for a one-story house with low foundation walls.

B. Effect produced by following plan 64A.

C. Effect produced by adapting plan 64A to a two-story house of the same general design.

and selected from this larger size group. An exception to this would be in a situation where there is not sufficient room in width for the larger plant.

The houses illustrated in Figures 65 and 66 are irregular in shape and show some other examples of exact use and modified use of the sectional plans. The photographs of models picture these plantings. Figure 65B shows a house with a low foundation wall planted according to the plan in 65A. Figure 65C is the same house with a high foundation wall and larger-growing plants in keeping with the greater height. The method of presentation in Figure 66 is the same as in Figure 65. Some homeowners might prefer to use a vine or a low-growing shrub at the left side of the front door rather than the pyramidal evergreen shown in Figure 66, B and C.

Follow these steps when planning each area.

1. Decide where each plant is to be placed.

2. Decide how large a plant will be suitable for each area.

3. Consider the spacing between plants, the spacing from the foundation, and the spacing from the walk or drive.

4. Select the plant of your choice from the proper size group for each place.

GENERAL RULES FOR FOUNDATION PLANTINGS

Do plant:

1. Only low-growing plants underneath windows. Flowers or ground covers may be used to advantage, or these places may be left unplanted except for extending the lawn to the foundation wall. If shrubs are used, they should be such varieties as will mature at least 1 to 2 feet below the window sill.

FIGURE 65A. Foundation planting plan for a one-story house, irregular in shape and with low foundation walls.

B. Effect produced by following plan 65A.

C. Effect produced by adapting plan 65A to the same house with a high foundation wall exposed above the soil line.

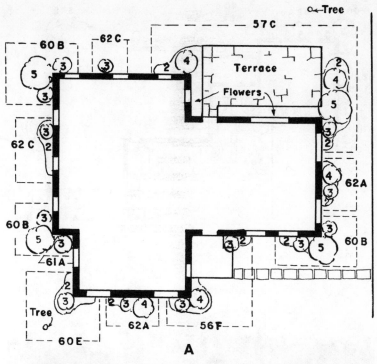

A

B

C

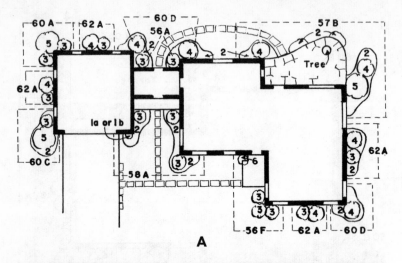

A

B

C

FIGURE 66A. Foundation planting plan for a one-story house, irregular in shape, with breezeway and garage attached, and with low foundation walls.

B. Effect produced by following plan 66A.

C. Effect produced by adapting plan 66A to the same house with a high foundation wall exposed above the soil line. The breezeway and garage have been left on the same level as in 66A and B.

2. Low-growing plants around porches. A vine or tree-form shrub can be used to provide partial shade or privacy.

3. Dwarf- to medium-sized plants at the sides of entrances and steps. A vine supported at the side of the doorway may supplement such a planting and may be preferable to an upright evergreen at either side of the door.

4. Medium- to tall-growing shrubs at the corner of the house except where a driveway or walk is too close. Here a vine may be used instead of a tall shrub. If there are windows at the corners, a tree-form shrub may be used to shade them, or low-growing shrubs may be used as suggested in number (1) above.

5. Medium-sized shrubs or vines in spaces along the foundation where the windows are far apart.

6. Ground covers, vines, or low-growing shrubs to cover most of exposed high foundation walls.

7. Vines on a chimney unless it is small. A small shrub may be used instead.

8. With some, but not too much, duplication of material.

By following the suggestions given in this STEP, *you can achieve as satisfying or better results from the revision of old, overgrown plantings as from new ones.*

Do not plant:

1. Tall-growing trees in the foundation planting.

2. A straight row of one variety of plant around the house except where a clipped hedge or formal planting is appropriate.

3. Tall-growing, dense shrubs in front of windows, as they darken the room and block the view toward the outside. An open, lacy-foliage effect is used sometimes to shade a large window or give some privacy from the outside.

4. Too great a variety of plants. Such plantings may look like a botanical collection, and each individual competes with the others for attention. Plants with brightly colored foliage or flowers should be used with caution.

Border Plantings and Outdoor Living Rooms

This STEP presents ways in which the home grounds, old or new, urban or rural, farm or nonfarm, may be integrated with the house to provide maximum use, pleasure, and beauty. The problem of steep banks is given special consideration.

Just as the house itself is planned for the use and enjoyment of the members of the family and friends, so the development of the yard should provide equal opportunities for satisfaction. At this stage, emphasis should be placed on the uses the property will serve.

Each room in the house is designed and equipped for certain functions necessary to daily living. Some of these rooms are separated, one from the other, by walls, with doorways to provide access from one "use area" to another. Sometimes these doorways are wide—in some cases so wide that only a suggestion of a wall separates the rooms.

The walls that enclose the house and those within the house have an outdoor counterpart in the border plantings which enclose the property and those which separate, more or less, the outside use areas. Openings in the plantings provide access from one "room" to another. The scale, however, is different in that most of these rooms are much larger.

From the standpoint of use, there are several similarities

between the inside and outside rooms. As the weather is seasonable, the family interests and living are transferred to outdoor settings. Instead of guests' being invited to the living room, they are taken to the terrace or a shaded lawn equipped with lawn furniture. The members of the family enjoy being outdoors while doing the mending, while reading, sunning, or indulging in some form of relaxation. Young children move from the nursery to the sandbox, swing, and teeter. The older children and adults go from the recreation room to the lawn equipped for badminton, croquet, or some other game.

Instead of eating every meal in the dining room, the family and friends adjourn to the picnic area where the meal is prepared and served. The hobbyist may want to transfer his indoor interests to some form of hobby gardening. Many whose livelihood is made from indoor work find rest and relaxation in working with ornamental plants, fruits, or vegetables.

Every member of the family should contribute ideas as to what activities are keyed to his interests and needs. Only in this way will the yard provide adequate areas for each desired use to the extent that space is available for it. This will make each property completely individualistic.

Usually, border plantings extend along a property line, but on medium to large places they may extend into the lawn to divide the home grounds into sections for different uses. Sometimes they are placed where they screen or block the view from the front to a side or rear lawn. A planted border may separate the vegetable garden or other service area from the lawn or provide seclusion for a picnic site or outdoor terrace. The type of border planting used on your home grounds depends upon its location with respect to adjacent properties, its size, and the function the planting is to fulfill. Homes in relatively closely built-up sections, cities, and villages probably need some privacy in certain parts of the lawn, usually at the side of the house or to the rear. To obtain the desired privacy, make a border planting in the line of view from the outside and tall enough to give seclusion (Figure 67, A, B, and C). Tall plantings are also located where they will block an uninteresting or displeasing view.

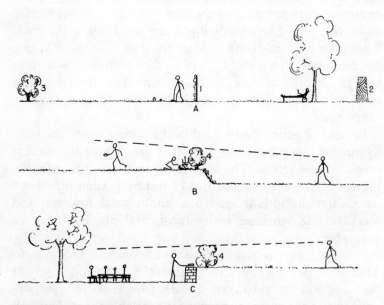

FIGURE 67. Border planting for privacy.

A. On level ground, the border planting should be 5½ or more feet in height to give privacy. This border might be a vine-covered fence (1), a clipped hedge (2), a single row of shrubs (3), or an informal border composed of shrubs and flowers.

B and C. On sloping ground, either up or down, the border need be only 3 or 4 feet high to give privacy.

You probably need a border planting parallel to your property line. This is sometimes made jointly by adjacent owners. Usually the shrubs are placed alternately on the two properties, each owner planting those on his side (Figure 68B). If one homeowner does the work without the aid of his neighbor, the planting should be made entirely on the land owned by the one doing the work (Figure 68, A, C, D, and E).

Planting a border or building a fence directly on a prop-

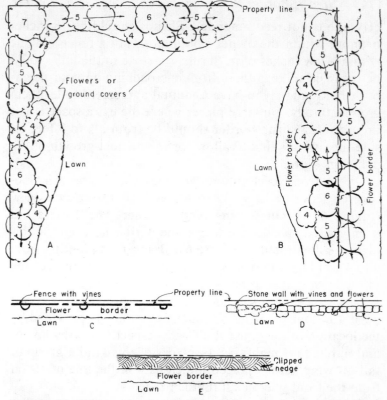

FIGURE 68. Types of border plantings.

A. Informal border plantings of shrubs and flowers require a width of from 8 to 12 feet or more. Therefore, these are most suitably used on a large property. The numbers in the plans refer to the size groups in the plant lists from which each plant is chosen.

B. A border is sometimes planted jointly by adjacent property owners. One side is shown here in an informal manner, the other side with a single row of shrubs. The shrubs on either side of the property line are placed alternately.

C. A vine-covered fence forms a good enclosure for small properties. The fence should be at least 5½ feet high to obtain privacy. On rural properties, farm or nonfarm, the fence should be only 3 or 4 feet high and should not be completely covered with vines. If desired, a few shrubs and a flower border may be used in front of it.

D. A low stone wall suitably defines the edge of the maintained lawn on rural home properties. Here and there a vine may grow over it, and some flowers may be placed informally in front of it.

E. A clipped hedge requires a width of from 3 to 5 feet. A flower border may or need not be used in front of it.

erty line is not recommended. Shrubs should be 18 inches or more within the owner's boundary, but a fence may be within a few inches of it. Shrubs set close to the line should be trimmed to keep them from encroaching on your neighbor's land unless you have a mutual agreement to let them grow naturally. On large places where the extra space is not important, a shrub border should be from 2½ to 3 feet inside the owner's line to allow for the normal growth of the plants in width.

On relatively level ground, you may use shrubs or a vine-covered fence at least 5½ to 6 feet high to screen a view (Figure 67A). On sloping land or where the ground has been graded on different levels, the border need not be this high. As illustrated in Figure 67, B and C, a planting from 3 to 4 feet high interrupts the line of vision from the outside to the lawn that is to be used for outdoor living.

Farm, rural nonfarm, and other large properties may not need a border planting. Frequently privacy is provided by the location of the house itself with respect to nearby homes and public thoroughfares. In places of this kind a group of tall-growing shrubs placed judiciously in the line of vision from the front may be all that is needed.

Seldom are the position of the house, garage, and other buildings, the position of the existing shade trees, and the slope of the ground the same on any two properties. Therefore, it is not likely that any one of the plans shown can be used in its entirety. You will have to make adjustments to conform to the variations on your land. You may, however, take some ideas from one plan and some from another. In this way your own plan will take shape according to your needs and to the opportunities afforded. The natural features of your yard, for example, may give you a clue as to what can be done. A group of trees may be used as a picnic site, a shady place for a wild-flower and fern garden, and a low, wet place for a swamp garden with plants that naturally do well in such places. Many plants are described in the plant lists as being adapted to such locations.

The plans shown in this STEP are drawn to scale, but no dimensions are given. Neither foundation plantings for the house nor shade trees are shown on these plans unless they directly supplement the borders. These are discussed in the STEPS pertaining to those phases of the work.

If the arrangement of your property is similar to any of the plans illustrated here but is reversed—that is, with the driveway on the other side of the house—turn the book so that the top of the page is toward you and hold a mirror at the bottom of the page. The image in the mirror will be a plan like yours.

Next draw to scale a tentative plan on cross-section paper. Include all buildings, sidewalks, driveways, shade trees, and any important existing features. Then roughly sketch in all of the use areas your family has decided will make your home grounds a more pleasant place. Stake out these use areas in the yard. It will help you to visualize more accurately the actual application of the plan. You may find that a few adjustments need to be made. Allow plenty of room for the growth of the plants. Include everything that does not now exist—walks and driveways, the border plantings, fences, trees, flower beds, outdoor terrace, fireplace, lawn for games, vegetable garden, clothes-drying yard, and other features. In the final plan you may add other things if there is room for them, or you may have to do without some of the things you wanted if there is insufficient room. This procedure will save you money as well as time, and you will have a more satisfying result for your whole family.

The details of each area are now drawn on the plan. For those who are garden-minded, the planning of a home property presents a challenge. It is an opportunity to do something individual and different. Clever planning and taking advantage of the existing characteristics of the home grounds will produce satisfying living for the garden hobbyist and for those who take pride in their home. Except for a few carefully placed shade trees, keep the lawn areas open, not broken up with specimen shrubs and flower beds. If your lawn now has specimen shrubs, transplant them to locations where they will conform to a better layout—one that will be easier to maintain.

Draw a circle for each plant in a similar way to that done

on the plans in this STEP. Place a number in each circle that corresponds to the suitable size group. Space the plants properly even though the planting will appear rather sparse for a few years. If you wish to obtain a more nearly immediate effect, you may add some temporary shrubs or other plants between the permanent ones, with the idea that as soon as the filler plants begin to crowd the permanent ones, the fillers will be removed.

After you have selected from this STEP the portions that are appropriate for you and have drawn your planting plan, you can then make out your order for plants. Order only the number and kinds you need. While you are waiting for the shrubs to be delivered, the soil in the areas to be planted can be prepared, and small stakes stuck in the ground where each shrub or tree is to be planted. When the nursery order arrives, the plants can then be set without delay.

If for financial or any other reason, it is unwise to complete the landscape job the first year, it may be done over a period of three or four years. Even though it is done gradually, the final result will be entirely satisfying if a suitable plan is adopted and followed.

GENERAL LOCATION FOR VARIOUS USE AREAS

1. The public area usually is located between the house and the street.

2. The outdoor living area is best on a terrace easily accessible from one of the living rooms of the house, or on a tree-shaded lawn. Either should be at the side or rear where it will be somewhat concealed from the street and where it will make an outdoor extension of the living rooms of the house.

3. The flower border, flower garden, rose garden, or other colorful feature should be in a position seen to advantage from the living room, dining room, or kitchen windows, and/or a frequented part of the lawn. It may be in a side or rear lawn.

4. The recreation area for lawn games should be relatively level and may be somewhat remote from the house.

5. Special hobby gardens, such as a wild-flower or fern garden, swamp garden, rock garden, or pool with aquatic plants, are located in proper natural settings or where suitable conditions can be provided.

6. The vegetable garden should be on the service side of the property, where the kitchen and garage are located, or across the back of the lot. This ideal arrangement may have to be changed because of unfavorable conditions, such as the slope of the ground, poor soil, or shade. On large rural properties the vegetable garden may be located outside the maintained home grounds.

7. The refuse cans should be located as conveniently near the kitchen entrance as is reasonable. In many situations a vine-covered trellis will effectively conceal them.

8. The outdoor incinerator sometimes is included in the construction of an outdoor fireplace. If located separately, it should be in an inconspicuous place and where the winds will carry the smoke away from the house.

SMALL CITY AND VILLAGE PROPERTIES

The Front Lawn

In urban places the homes along the street are relatively close together with few, if any, vacant lots, and the existing homes are 25 feet, more or less, back from the street.

A front lawn is considered a public or semipublic area. From the standpoint of the appearance of the entire street, it is usually better to have no border plantings separating the front lawn from the street (Figures 69 through 73). Side-border plantings should not completely separate the adjacent lawns, because a street appears more spacious with unbroken lawns extending throughout its length, except, of course, for a few properly placed shade trees and the necessary driveways and sidewalks.

Individual wishes or requirements may make this ideal lawn arrangement for the street difficult to achieve, because some properties may need a barrier to prevent a path or other encroachment on the lawn and some homeowners may wish to have a side or front border purely for ornament. The type of enclosure for either use is governed largely

by the purpose the planting is to serve and by the amount
of space available in width for it. The nearness of a driveway or sidewalk frequently limits the planting. If a sturdy
barrier is needed in a limited space, a vine-covered fence, a
clipped hedge, or an unclipped border of dense, low-growing shrubs may be used. A vine-covered fence requires a
space at least 1 foot wide. If more room is available, a flower
border 2 feet or more in width and placed adjacent to the
fence helps to make the planting more attractive (Figure
68C). A low-clipped hedge requires a width of 2 feet or a
little more (Figure 68E), while a single row of untrimmed
low-growing shrubs requires a space 3 feet or a little more
in width. A clipped hedge needs a considerable amount of
maintenance. If you choose a fence or shrub border, either
should be relatively low, no more than 3 feet high. A high
planting conceals the view and is a traffic hazard.

Even though you make a planting or place a fence at each
side, it is not necessary to do the same across the front. If
you want a complete enclosure, not all of it needs to be
alike. A fence at each side and a planting across the front,
or a fence across the front and plantings at the side, would
be good. If there are large shade trees along the street and a
front enclosure is desired, use a fence because the shade and
root competition given by the trees retards the growth of
nearby shrubs.

Remember that the front property line is usually about 1
foot inside the sidewalk. If there is no sidewalk, measure

FIGURE 69. A small enclosed lawn. In this plan a vine-covered fence,
a few shrubs, and flower borders enclose the small rear lawn. The
fence extending forward from the garage can be lower than the rest
of the fence. Steppingstones lead from the back door of the house to
the garage and through the gate at the rear right corner of the
house. Croquet, badminton, and tetherball could be played on this
small lawn. The removable clothesline is near the back door. The plan
could be altered to have a clothes-drying yard or small vegetable
garden behind the garage, and if a fireplace is desired, it could be
placed against the back fence facing the house.

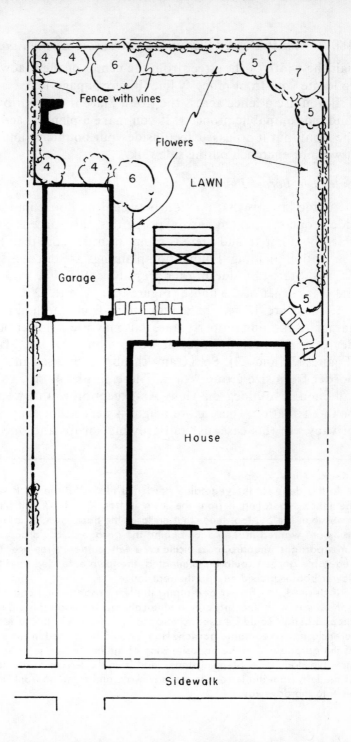

4 4 6 5 7

Fence with vines

5

Flowers

4 4 6

LAWN

Garage

5

House

Sidewalk

half the width of the street from the center of the roadway to locate your front property line (Figure 3, page 16).

If you use a fence across the front, place it on your own land, not on public property. If you make a planting across the front, put it at least 2 feet inside your boundary line so it will not encroach on the sidewalk.

Side-lawn Border Plantings

A side lawn is that portion between the house and the side property line. On narrow properties, this space is considerably limited, and there is room for little more than the foundation planting. Foundation plantings are discussed in STEP 8. Start this side-border planting somewhat back of the rear corner of the house (Figures 69, 70, and 72).

If there are 12 feet or a little more from the house or garage to the side property line, you may use a flower border or vine-covered fence, or both, along the boundary (Figures 71 and 73). Select any shrubs to be used in this border from size group 4 or 5. These shrubs do not grow tall enough to block the view. An exception to this would be in a situation where more height is needed for shade or privacy. In this case, use tall-growing shrubs and one or

---

FIGURE 70. A deep lot.

In this deep lot the vegetable garden is placed at the back, and the fence separating it from the lawn is from 2½ to 3 feet high, lower than the 5½-foot fence that encloses the back lawn. If no bush fruits are wanted in the space behind the garage, it could be used for asparagus, rhubarb, or a picnic area with outdoor fireplace. The vegetable garden could be eliminated, the lawn extended, and the flower border placed next to the rear fence.

If desired, the flower bed along the left property line could be done away with, leaving only a vine-covered fence on this side. A clipped hedge could be used to enclose the rear lawn, and a fence to enclose the vegetable garden. Hooks could be placed in the side of the garage and in the opposite wing of the house to support a removable clothesline. Steppingstones lead from the terrace to the gate at the left, from the terrace to the driveway, and from the front sidewalk to the driveway.

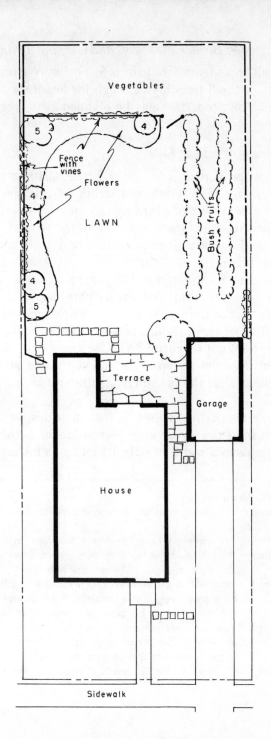

Vegetables

5 3

4

Fence
with
vines

Flowers

4

LAWN

Bush fruits

4

5

7

Terrace

Garage

House

Sidewalk

two small trees from size group 6. You may trim the side branches of small trees high enough for headroom.

Wide urban properties may be planned as is suggested for rural properties.

Development of a Rear Lawn

On most properties, a rear lawn is the part best suited for outdoor living. The width and depth of this space determines the best type of plantings in locations where other established residences surround the home grounds. The descriptions and illustrations presented here show a few ways to obtain privacy.

The house and sometimes the garage blocks a portion of the view from the front, and border plantings or a vine-covered fence make the rest of the enclosure. On level ground the planting or fence should be above the eye level, 5½ feet or more in height (Figure 67A). Use vines from size group 1a or shrubs from groups 5 or 6. On sloping ground you may wish to alter the plantings, as illustrated in Figure 67, B and C.

Narrow properties, about 50 feet in width, are best enclosed at the sides by a vine-covered fence, as this type of border requires a width of only 1 foot to 18 inches (Figures

---

FIGURE 71. A corner lot.

This corner lot is somewhat wider than those shown in Figures 69 and 70.

A 5½-foot vine-covered fence encloses the rear lawn, but the fence opposite the house at the left may be stepped down to about 3 feet high. A grass path extends between the two flower borders at the side of the house. The picnic area suggested behind the garage might instead be a small vegetable garden. If additional space for flowers is wanted, a bed could be prepared next to the fence along the left side. If less space is needed for flowers, the bed beside the fence at the right side of the property could be omitted. Stepping-stones lead from the terrace to the garage and through the entrance gate to the front sidewalk. The flagstone terrace is at the back of the house.

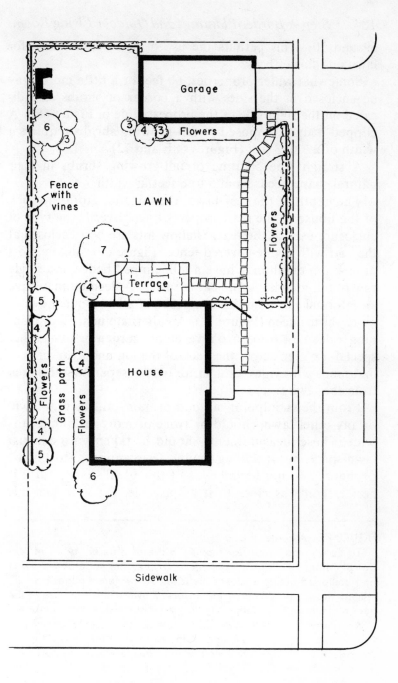

Garage

3 4 3 Flowers

6 3

Fence with vines

LAWN

7

Flowers

4

Terrace

5

4

4 House

Flowers

Grass path

Flowers

4

5

6

Sidewalk

69 and 70). This permits the use of a maximum area for lawn and flower beds.

Somewhat wider properties, 60 feet or a little more, may be enclosed at the sides with a border of shrubs as indicated on the right side of the property line in Figure 68B. A clipped hedge composed of tall-growing shrubs requires a width of 2½ to 3 feet (Figures 68E and 72).

A straight-line planting of tall-growing shrubs in their natural shape needs from 5 to 6 feet in width.

The depth of the rear lawn, the distance from the back of the house to the rear property line, governs the type of enclosure used at the rear. Shallow lots are best enclosed at the rear with a vine-covered fence (Figure 69). Building lots of medium depth may have a tall, clipped hedge or a single row of tall-growing shrubs at the back. A deep lot may have an informal shrub border composed of a bed planted two or more shrubs deep (Figure 73). An alternate method of planning a deep lot is to have a vegetable garden or some other special-use area across the back of the lot, and a flower border, fence with vines, or a shrub border separating this area from the lawn (Figure 70).

From the standpoint of good proportion, the rear lawn, or any other lawn, should be twice or more as long as it is wide. These measurements should be taken on the actual lawn space, not including the border plantings. Most home properties do not have lawns of this ideal shape, but it is best to come as close to it as possible. On wide lots this

---

FIGURE 72. A corner lot.

This plan of a corner lot shows the use of different types of border plantings. A vine-covered fence screens the vegetable garden and a clipped hedge encloses the lawn. A low fence edges a small, intimate flower garden near the terrace. Flowers also are used at the back of the lawn. The clothes-drying yard is at the side of the garage.

An alternate suggestion would be to erect a horizontal bar or trellis and locate it at the left end of the terrace. Hooks placed in the crosspiece and in the back wall of the garage would support a removable clothesline.

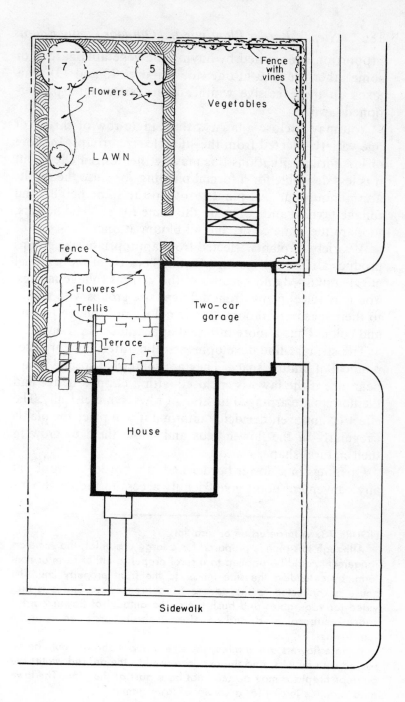

proportion is obtained by having the vegetable garden or some other use area at one side (Figures 72 and 73). This takes up the excessive width and leaves a better-proportioned lawn.

You may enclose a lawn with a single row of shrubs of one variety selected from the suitable size groups. In more or less formal situations this may be the desired effect, but it is less desirable for informal plantings because the results are monotonous. All plants grow to the same height, and foliage texture and color are the same for all. The flowers, too, are the same color, and all bloom at once.

A variety of plants selected from appropriate size groups produce a more interesting planting because of the seasonal effects obtained and because of the various foliage masses. You may select plants from different size groups with regard to their season of bloom, flower color, and foliage texture and color. Thus a more informal appearance is produced.

The straight-line developments illustrated here are economical of limited space. They are somewhat formal in appearance if the lawn is enclosed with a clipped hedge and the flowers are arranged in straight rows, symmetrically. The effect is, however, decidedly informal if you place the plants irregularly in the flower beds and allow them to grow in their natural shape.

Openings in a flower border and in a border of shrubs at any convenient point give friendly access to the neighbor's

FIGURE 73. A large urban or rural lot.

Although this plan is prepared for a large urban lot, the same arrangement could be applied to a rural property, either farm or non-farm, by extending the side fences to the front property line. The house is connected to the garage by a breezeway. Space is provided for vegetables and bush fruits. The amount of flower garden space is subordinated, and an informal shrub border encloses the rear lawn.

If more flowers are wanted, the size group 4 shrubs could be replaced with flowers, and the bed increased to the desired width. The outdoor fireplace may or need not be a part of the plan. The lawn area is ample in size for a variety of lawn games.

property (Figures 69 through 73). A gate in this opening
may be necessary to confine children or pets.

The lawn could be used for croquet or any other lawn
games that may be played in a small area.

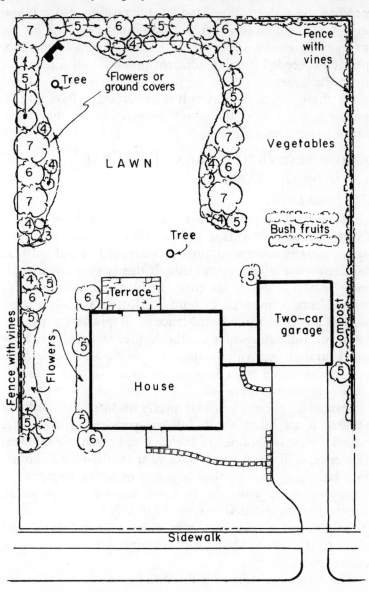

Small Corner Lots

Corner lots are developed in much the same way as other lots. A vine-covered fence or border of shrubs is used, depending upon the width of the lot, the position of the buildings, and the desired effect. Two different positions for the garage are shown in Figures 71 and 72. On inside lots, privacy is needed from an adjacent property; on corner lots, from the street.

On these corner properties it is important to have no tall-growing plants near the street intersection, as they are a serious traffic hazard.

LARGE PROPERTIES, URBAN OR RURAL, FARM OR NONFARM

The Front Lawn

Most rural properties, farm and nonfarm, have a wider front lawn than do village and city places. Also, rural properties usually have a pasture, a cultivated or unkept field bordering the lawn on each side. If this is your situation, it may be best to define the entire maintained home grounds with a fence, stone wall, or border planting. Usually a stone wall or a two- or three-board fence of simple design, painted white or the same color as the house, is appropriate for most rural places. An unpainted rail or hurdle fence is more in keeping with a home in a naturalistic setting or with rustic architecture (Figure 74).

Instead of a fence you may prefer an informal border of shrubs; if so, select shrubs of low-growing varieties over which a view is obtained of the road approach. Be sure that the fence, wall, or planting is on your own land, and not on that belonging to the public highway or to the neighbor.

Vines may be grown on the fence, and irregularly spaced shrubs may be planted in front of it. If you wish, you may plant a flower border 2½ feet or more wide in front of and close to the fence. The flower border need not extend the entire length.

The space between the driveway and the edge of the

maintained lawn or property line may be only a few feet
wide. If any planting is desired in this area, consider (1) the
direction of the prevailing winds and (2) the width of the
area. If the winds are from this edge of the lawn toward
the driveway, a hardy shrub planting or a fence of fairly
close construction would cause snowdrifts to form in the
drive. Here you might use a fence of open construction such
as a three-rail fence. You could use vines such as clematis

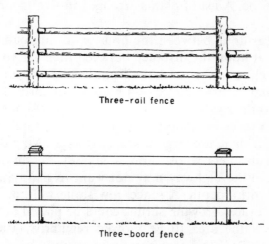

Three-rail fence

Three-board fence

FIGURE 74. Two types of fences.

or China fleece-vine (silver-lace vine) on the fence as either
may be cut to the ground in the fall, so that snow will not
drift in the driveway. Either vine makes a full growth and
flowers in one season. Annual vines, such as morning glory
or sweetpeas, also are suitable. An annual or perennial
flower border may be planted between the fence and the
drive (Figure 76).

If you want a border planting and no fence, shrubs such
as snowhill hydrangea or Anthony Waterer spirea may be
used in a space from 5 to 6 feet wide. Peonies also would be
suitable. They all may be cut to the ground each fall.

If the prevailing winds are in a direction from the house

toward the driveway, use a three-board fence, a picket fence, or a woody shrub planting at the edge of the lawn. Use only low-growing shrubs at the front near the road, as they will not obstruct the view. You may plant medium-sized shrubs that grow from 4 to 6 feet high opposite the house and plant taller-growing ones toward the back.

A fence treatment is best for a space as narrow as 2 feet, but may still be used if the lawn is wider. An informal shrub border should not be planted in a space less than from 8 to 10 feet wide. A list of plants arranged in size groups begins on page 253.

What is done between the house and the road depends somewhat upon the distance between them. If your house is fairly close to the road, the front lawn need not be separated from it with a fence or a planting of shrubs, but may extend to the roadside. If, however, some division seems desirable, a fence of suitable design is usually preferred, particularly if there are large roadside trees growing there.

Rural dwellers whose homes are several hundred feet back from the highway may not want to maintain a lawn for this entire depth. A fence, low stone wall, or a border planting of low-growing shrubs could be placed at the front portion of the area to be mowed regularly with a lawn mower. Outside this area a grain crop could be planted, or it could be allowed to develop naturally with field grasses.

FIGURE 75. A plan for many uses.

This rural property provides for most uses any family would want, including a flower garden enclosed for privacy, a vegetable garden, and a large lawn for outdoor recreation. The boundary fence extends to the front line and need be only 3 to 4 feet high and of rather open design. The fence at the right of the vegetable garden should be of the same design but could be lower. A low stone wall extends across the front of the lot.

An alternate suggestion would be to have the fence enclose the rear lawn and a low stone wall extend from the end of this fence to and across the front of the property. The border plantings at the edges of the rear lawn are purposely kept simple, with vines and dwarf shrubs used in places where there are desirable distant views.

Mowing once in June with a sickle-bar mower will keep such areas reasonably tidy. This space might also be used as a pasture for grazing horses, calves, or sheep. This area may

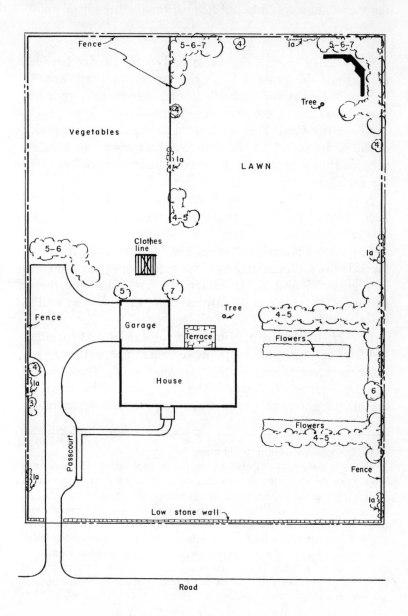

be sown with a mixture of 5 pounds of broadleaf birdsfoot trefoil mixed with 10 pounds of Kentucky bluegrass for each acre. The narrowleaf birdsfoot trefoil is a lower-growing variety and could be substituted for the broadleaf trefoil.

Side Lawns

On wide properties there is usually ample space between the side of the house or garage and the property line. If, however, this space is small on one side or the other, the same ideas that have been suggested for small properties can be carried out. This is a logical arrangement for the side of the house on which the garage and driveway are located, provided these service areas are on the less spacious side of the grounds.

A space of 20 feet or more at the side of the house most accessible to the living areas provides enough room for a flower garden or play area. The addition of a few shrubs, appropriately placed, will break the view from the road into the side lawn. Suggestions for such developments are given in Figures 75 and 77. In either of these plans, the flower garden is where it can be enjoyed from the house as well as from outside.

Larger side lawns may be used for games and for other outdoor recreation. The plans for rural properties do not show so much detail in the plantings as do the plans of small properties, because of the small scale. The detail for the plantings on rural homes can be patterned after similar

---

FIGURE 76. A plan for a rural home.

This is a simple but effective plan for a rural home. The plantings have been carefully located to give privacy to the rear lawn and to screen the clothes-drying yard. Adjustments will have to be made to conform with the position of the service buildings and the desired amount of lawn space. If more flowers are wanted, they could be planted in a prepared bed near the fence at the left side of the lawn.

A property with no barn would be planned with a fence located at the edge of the back lawn, a planting at the rear right corner, and only enough driveway to provide room to turn around. These changes are indicated by dotted lines.

ones on the small property plans and those in Figure 68, A and B.

Development of a Rear Lawn

The opportunities to develop the rear or side lawn on rural properties are much greater than on small places. On

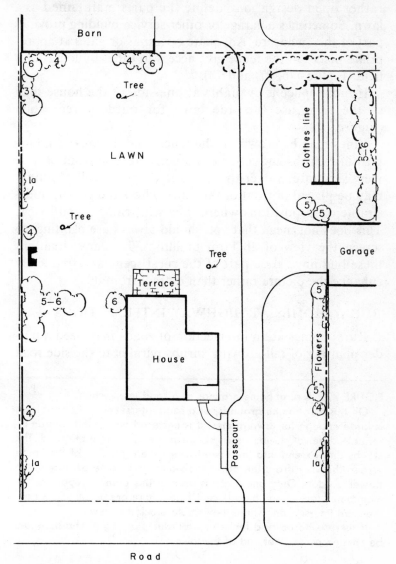

farm and nonfarm rural home grounds, the position of the rear lawn gives considerable privacy because there are no nearby neighbors at the side and to the rear. Plan this area to give a feeling of openness. The horizon may be the margin of enclosure. Large lawns developed in a simple way sometimes provide the most satisfying effects. A fence of rather open design may define the parts maintained as a lawn. Sometimes a garage or other service building provides part of the enclosure. Adequate openings or gates at appropriate places in the fence give access to other buildings or a field (Figures 76, 77, and 78).

If more space is available at one side of the house than at the rear, use the side lawn for outdoor recreation (Figure 78).

Vines may be grown on the fence, and, if you wish, low-growing shrubs and a flower border placed in front of it. A view is obtained over these to the horizon. Tall plantings may be placed in front of the fence where the view is undesirable or in positions where they will frame a good view. This does not mean that you should always use plantings to screen the view of all farm buildings. In many situations these buildings are a part of the rural scene and frequently enhance the picture rather than detract from it.

RURAL HOMES AT HIGHWAY INTERSECTIONS

Rural homes at an intersection of roads may need a border planting of tall-growing shrubs parallel to the side road

---

FIGURE 77. A rural home grounds at a road intersection.

On this rural home grounds, at a road intersection, the rear lawn is large enough for lawn games. It is enclosed on the left with an informal border of shrubs which obstructs the view from the road. The shrubs that extend into the lawn toward the right side of the house screen the view from the other road and give some privacy in the flower garden. Only one fence is used in this plan. It separates the maintained lawn from the adjacent field. There are no plantings near the road intersection, where they would block the view.

If there is no barn, a fence or a border planting of shrubs would be located across that end of the lawn.

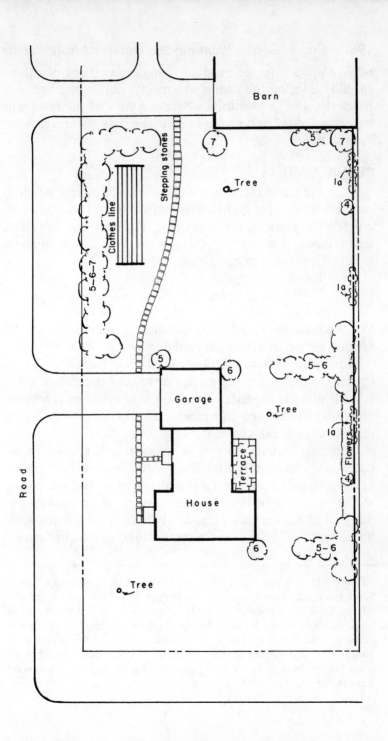

Barn

7   5 7

Tree   1a

4

1a

Stepping stones

Clothes line

5-6-7

5-6

5   6

Garage

Tree

House

1a

4

Flowers

Terrace

6   5-6

Tree

Road

to give privacy in the outdoor living areas. Such plantings should be set on the owner's property, not on the highway property, and in positions where the view of the lawn will be screened effectively. Never make tall plantings near intersections.

SERVICE AREAS

In any of the plans shown here, whether for large or small properties, a socket and clothes reel could be located in any convenient place in the rear lawn. The reel can be folded and removed for storage. The socket is set low enough so that the lawn mower can be run over it.

An alternate arrangement for drying clothes is given in Figure 72. Hooks are placed in the side of the garage and on a crossbar opposite. Place the hooks from 6 to 6½ feet high and remove the clothesline when not in use so that the terrace will be available for outdoor living.

Put the compost pile in any out-of-sight location, such as the corner of a vegetable garden or behind the garage. Only a small space is needed, for garbage and refuse cans reasonably near the kitchen entrance. A small vine-covered trellis effectively conceals the cans.

If an outdoor incinerator is necessary, it should be located at a safe distance from the house or garage. Consideration should be given to the direction of the prevailing winds. A corner of the vegetable garden or an inconspicuous part of the rear lawn frequently is used for this purpose. Some types of incinerators are safer than others. Either one

---

FIGURE 78. A rural home lawn with semicircular driveway. Sometimes the rural home ground is wider than it is deep, and a semicircular driveway breaks up the only large lawn area. If this space is large enough, it may be used for lawn games. A flagstone terrace is more private if it is placed on the opposite side of the house even though this space is comparatively small. A flower garden and picnic area feature this outdoor living space. The clothesline is screened from the road.

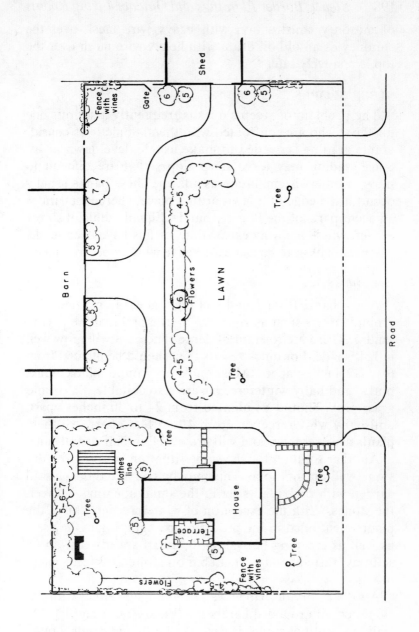

of masonry construction with heavy wire mesh over the chimney or an old oil drum with heavy wire mesh over the top is relatively safe.

STEEP SLOPES

The problem of steep slopes is frequently a serious one for those who are confronted with them. Sometimes considerable grading is needed to make usable, level lawn areas. Such grading may leave steep slopes that are difficult to mow or otherwise maintain as a lawn. These banks usually occur at the edge of a lawn or in a place where it separates adjacent parts of the home grounds. Equally difficult slopes are left where highway excavations or fills have been made. All these banks can be made attractive with proper treatment.

Low Banks

A low bank, from 2 to 4 feet high, is easily planted with ground covers such as common myrtle or Japanese pachysandra. These are tolerant of dense shade but will grow well in half shade. For quick results they should be planted from 6 to 12 inches apart. Moss pink or ground phlox, grass pinks, and baby wintercreeper are also suitable. Phlox and grass pinks should be planted from 24 to 30 inches apart, and baby wintercreeper, from 4 to 5 feet apart. All these plants are evergreen and will grow well in half or full sun.

Another solution for the same situation is to build a dry stone wall on the slope. This may be converted into a wall garden with rock plants set in the small openings between the stones. With the exception of wintercreeper, any of the plants mentioned in the preceding paragraph may be used, as well as creeping babysbreath, dwarf speedwells, dwarf sedums, tufted sandwort, Lebanon stonecress, and many others.

A satisfactory dry stone wall can be made either with flat stones or with rounded hardheads (Figure 79, A and B). The wall made of flat stones is easier to build and needs a pitch of only 1 to 2 inches for each foot in height. A round-stone wall should have a pitch of at least 3 to 5 inches for each foot in height. In either wall, the stones should fit snugly together and slope slightly into the bank. Good soil should be wet and tamped firmly in place behind the wall as each tier of stones is laid. Unless this is done, the wall may collapse during or soon after a hard rain.

Masonry walls may be used instead of dry stone walls. In locations where the winters are severe, masonry walls should be provided with a footing extending below frost line, and openings placed through the wall for drainage.

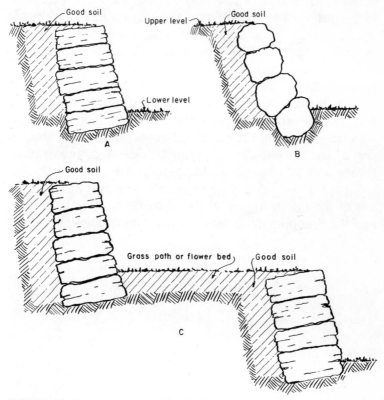

FIGURE 79. Dry stone retaining walls.

A. Flat-stone wall.

B. Round-stone wall. Both A and B are for low banks, 2 to 3 feet high.

C. Double stone wall—for high banks.

High Banks

A high bank, 5 feet or more in height, may be developed with two or more dry stone walls separated by a level portion 3 or more feet wide. This level portion may be used as a path or a flower bed (Figure 79C).

A satisfactory and easy treatment for a high bank is to plant it with vines, dwarf shrubs, and shrubs with a drooping habit of growth. Vines suitable for this purpose include sharpleaf wintercreeper, English ivy, Hall's honeysuckle, and memorial rose. These may be planted on the bank and in staggered rows about 6 feet apart. With new plantings it is advisable to place a mulch of peat, sawdust, clean straw, or lawn clippings on the ground underneath the plants. This mulch checks weed growth, checks erosion, and retains moisture in the soil.

Low-growing shrubs for bank plantings include coralberry, snowberry, Japanese barberry, and Scotch rose. These may be planted on the bank and in staggered rows about 6 feet apart. If a very dense planting is desired, any of these shrubs may be underplanted with myrtle or pachysandra.

Weeping forsythia may be set about 6 feet apart at the top of a bank or high wall. It grows from 4 to 6 feet high, and the drooping branches often trail down about 8 feet.

Recreation at Home

The suggestions given here are intended for use on home properties by the family and friends but may be used equally well by public-spirited individuals to provide needed recreation for community use.

The activities described here provide recreation which may be enjoyed fully by persons of various ages. Some promote team play, but most of them are played by only a few contestants. Many of them require only a fairly level lawn, which may be used for several different games. Some of the equipment need not be duplicated, as one net can be used for volleyball and tennis. A small net can be used for badminton, deck tennis, and paddle tennis. The same paddles can be used for tetherball and paddle tennis. One of the poles supporting the net should extend 10 feet above the lawn; the other 8 feet. The higher pole is used for tetherball, and both poles will be long enough to permit the net to be raised and lowered for various games.

Sometimes the only lawn available for games is somewhat smaller than is required for a court of standard dimensions. In such situations smaller courts may be made if those who are to use them are willing to adapt their game to the smaller scale. One can decrease the size of the total area by shortening the end and side zones and, if necessary, by proportionately decreasing the dimensions of the playing space.

The grass on small areas that are used intensively becomes worn and thin. As the interest of the players changes from one game to another, the grass recovers where it has become worn. If the interest in the game does not change, the intensively used portion may be shifted. If this is not possible, the family can take the attitude that the worn places are providing healthful fun which, for the time being, is more valuable than the better appearance of a beautiful turf.

GAMES THAT REQUIRE SMALL AREAS

Toddler's Play Yard

Compared with the recreation area of older children and adults, the play space and the equipment for toddlers is of temporary interest. If possible, locate it where the sandbox, teeter, swing, and other equipment is shaded by a tree, building, or awning, and where it is seen easily from the house. Sometimes it is necessary to enclose this play space with a temporary fence. When this stage is outgrown, it may be used for other activities.

Box Hockey

Box hockey is a good game for two or four persons. A tournament may begin in May and last all summer. Make the box of 1-inch lumber or of plywood 5 or 6 inches wide. A larger box may be made with two or three equally spaced center partitions instead of one as shown in the diagram. A wooden disk 2 inches in diameter and from ¾ to 1 inch thick is used for the puck, and each contestant uses a broom handle about 30 inches long or a small hockey stick.

Play is started with the puck in the notch at the top edge of the middle board. The players stand on opposite sides of the box, and each strikes the floor and his opponent's stick alternately three times before trying to knock the puck into his opponent's court and from there out of the box through the opening at the bottom of the board to his left. The person or side accomplishing this wins the game. If the puck hops out of the box, play is resumed in the same side that it left. When four play, partners stand on the same side, the two opponents opposite.

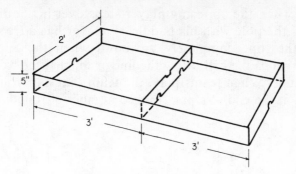

FIGURE 80. Box hockey.

Tetherball

Tetherball is a game enjoyed by teen-agers and young adults who like a sport requiring quick physical reactions and a considerable amount of stamina. The equipment can be made of inexpensive materials. A space 20 feet in diameter is large enough for outdoor play. A sturdy pole about 2½ inches in diameter is placed in the ground so that 10 feet extend above the soil level. A hole drilled in the concrete driveway or a pipe set vertically in the ground makes the socket for the pole. A line is painted or taped around the pole at from 5 to 6 feet above the ground. A rope 7 to 8 feet long is attached at the top of the pole. To the other end of the rope is tied or sewed a fine-mesh net or leather bag containing an old tennis ball or any rubber ball about that same size and weight. Two wooden paddles with handles about 6 inches long and blades about 6 by 9 inches are used—one for each player. These may be constructed of 3-plywood. A volleyball may be used instead of a tennis ball. In this case the ball is hit with the hands.

Only two players play at a time, although teams may be formed. The players knock the ball in opposite directions trying to wind the rope its full length around the pole and *above* the 5-to-6-foot mark. A player scores a game (1) when he winds the rope completely above the mark on the pole, or (2) when the opposing player steps over his bounds or strikes the pole with his paddle. A player has a free serve with the rope completely unwound when the opposing player winds the ball below the line or touches the ball with his hands. When teams play, the team that has won more games at the end of a prearranged number of rounds wins.

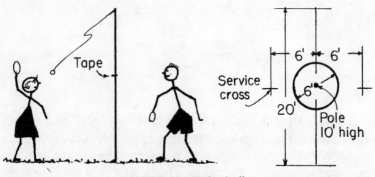

FIGURE 81. Tetherball.

Table Tennis

Table tennis is most popular as a winter, indoor game, but some like to take the equipment to the lawn for summer play. A large outdoor terrace is ideal. Some of the equipment required is easy to construct.

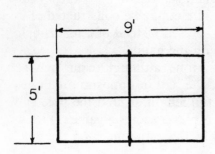

FIGURE 82. Table tennis.

GAMES THAT REQUIRE MEDIUM-SIZED AREAS

Deck Tennis

Deck tennis is a good game for a lawn about 25 by 50 feet in size where a net can be suspended across the center of the court at a height of 4 feet 6 inches. The game is played by throwing across the net a rubber ring or one made of ¾-inch rope 6 inches in diameter. The rings may be obtained at any sporting-goods store under the name of "teniquoit." Two or four persons play. All throws, including the service, are from any place behind the end boundary line; first from the right-hand, then from the left-hand court, as in tennis. A net serve that drops into foul territory, between the foul line and the net, gives the server another try. A net service into fair territory may be played or not, as the receiver wishes. Only the serving side may score one point at a time as a result of the opponent's "fault." A fault consists of catching the ring with both hands, catching the ring against the body, batting the ring, failure to catch the ring, failure to return it over the net, overhand throw, or the touching of the ring by more than one player of a side on a single play. The game is for 15 points.

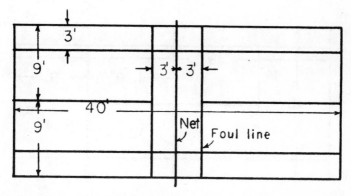

FIGURE 83. Deck tennis court. Net 4 feet 6 inches high at center.

Paddle Tennis

Four wooden paddles, similar to tetherball paddles, a sponge rubber ball, and a net hung 26 inches high complete the equipment needed for paddle tennis. Two or four persons may play at a time. The game is played and scored as in tennis except that the ball is bounced before serving from behind the end boundary line.

One can score the game in a simple way. The serving side can score one point at a time as a result of an opponent's "fault." If the serving side faults, the serve goes to the opponent and no point is scored. A fault consists of failing to return the ball to within the boundaries of the opposite court, allowing the ball to bounce more than once before it is returned (the ball may be returned before it touches the ground), batting the ball with either hand or with some other part of the body, or more than one player of a side batting the ball on a single play. With these rules the game may be played for 6 points or any number agreed upon before the game starts. This game gives much of the fun of tennis but can be played on a small lawn and with homemade paddles.

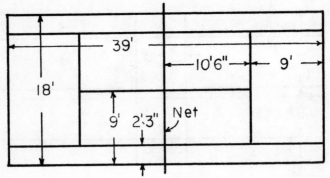

FIGURE 84. Paddle tennis court. Net 26 inches high at center.

Clock Golf

Clock golf can be set up in various ways, with the putting cups placed in a spiral, as in the diagram, or in a circle or arc. The distance between cups may vary between 4 and 15 feet, as indicated. The equipment needed is golf balls and putters. Tin cans with both ends cut out and sunk in the ground can serve as the cups for either this or pitch and putt golf. Any number of persons can play. The object is to see who can sink all the putts in the least number of shots. Each of the twelve cups should be numbered clearly. Each shot is made from the center mark. When the grass becomes worn, the position of the cups and the starting point should be changed. Covers should be provided for the cans when they are not in use.

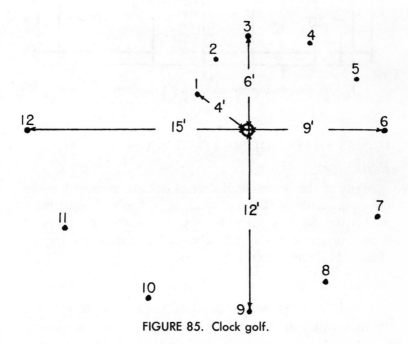

FIGURE 85. Clock golf.

Badminton

Badminton, an ancient game, has gained popularity in this country. A lawn 54 by 24 feet is a good size for the game.

The rackets, shuttlecocks, and net are not expensive. It is a good fast game for proficient players, but even children may enjoy it because the rackets are light and easily handled. Two or four persons may play at one time. The rules are included with the set.

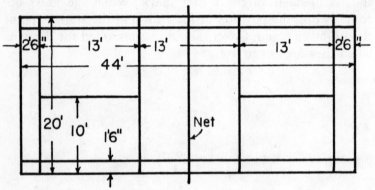

FIGURE 86. Badminton court. Net 5 feet high at center.

GAMES THAT REQUIRE LONG, NARROW SPACES

Darts

Many of the commercial dart games are suitable for outdoor play and are enjoyed by all ages. Probably dart baseball is the most popular. Both targets and some types of darts may be constructed at home. These games require close supervision when being used.

Horseshoe Pitching

Forty feet is the proper distance for horseshoe pitching. Women pitch at 30 feet; children may want the stakes closer.

Iron stakes that extend 8 inches above the soil level are placed in the center of a 6-foot-square pitcher's box. The box may be made by setting two-by-fours in the ground with about an inch left above the surface. Leaners and the closest shoe or shoes of one player count 1 point each. A ringer counts 3. If one player's ringer tops the opponent's ringer, both are canceled and the next-nearest shoe counts 1. According to the rules, a shoe farther than 6 inches from the peg does not count, but a greater distance than this may be agreed upon. The game is 21 points. Complete official rules may be obtained from the National Horseshoe Association, London, Ohio.

Shuffleboard

The equipment for this game can be made at home, but the playing space must be carefully prepared with a level, reinforced concrete slab 6 by 45 feet in size. The surface should be made smooth with a steel trowel and painted. Eight wooden disks (four red and four black) are used; each is 6 inches in diameter and 1 inch thick. The shovel can be made with a dowel or bamboo pole from 5 to 6 feet long and hinged onto a flat piece of wood that is cut to fit the disk. Two or four persons play, as in horseshoe pitching; one side has the red disks, and the other the black.

First the red disk is pushed from the 10-off space to the opposite triangle; then a black disk is pushed; and so on until all the disks are played. The object is to knock the opponent's disk out of the counting triangles and leave the player's in. To count, a disk must be entirely within the numbered area, not touching a line. A disk left in the 10-off area takes 10 from the score. The game is for 50 or 100 points. Complete official rules may be obtained from a sporting-goods store, or from references on page 218.

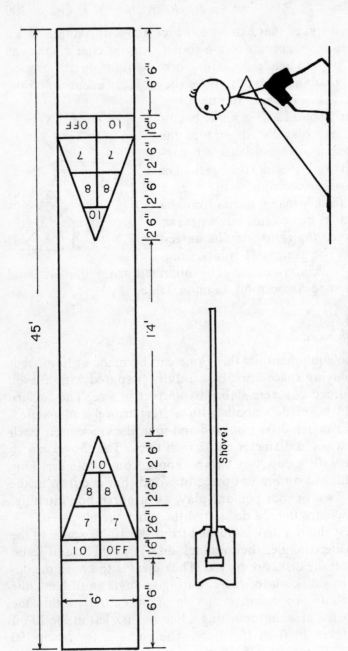

FIGURE 87. Shuffleboard.

Archery

Archery is an ancient and honorable game that takes considerable practice. Young people want a range of about 25 yards, which may be increased to 35 yards or more for adults. The target can be made of canvas, with straw padding from 4 to 5 inches thick. It is 48 inches in diameter, with painted bands outlining the circular areas. The center bull's-eye is gold (9½ inches in diameter); around it are red, blue, black, and white bands, each 4¾ inches wide.  The points are scored from the bull's-eye outward—9, 7, 5, 3, and 1. Some players may wish to make their own archery tackle. A helpful booklet is *How to Make Bows and Arrows* from the Boy Scouts of America, New Brunswick, New Jersey. Complete instructions on scoring, skills, and tournaments may be obtained from a sporting-goods dealer.

Bowling on the Green

Two or four persons may bowl on the green at a time, and the scoring is the same as in horseshoe pitching. A fairly level, smooth lawn varying from 50 feet long and 10 feet wide to 100 by 20 feet may be used. This can be marked out  with a light rope. Each player is supplied with two balls (croquet balls will do). One smaller white ball, the "jack" (another croquet ball), is rolled from one end of the green at least three-fourths the length of the field by the lead player of one of the teams. If it goes out-of-bounds laterally, it is returned to the center of the court straight in from where it lies; if it goes over the far end of the court, it is brought in 2 yards. The same person then bowls his first ball as near the jack as possible. The alternate players on each side bowl their balls. The team with one or more balls nearer the jack than any opponent's ball scores 1 for each such ball. The game is for 21 points. Both the jack and the opponents' balls may be hit. It is the final position of the jack that is used in scoring.

GAMES THAT REQUIRE LARGER AREAS

Croquet

The regulation playing space for croquet is 30 by 60 feet, but the size and shape may be varied to fit the available space. If necessary, one may play around trees or on slightly sloping ground; a few hazards add to the fun. There are different arrangements for the wickets. The rules usually are included with the equipment.

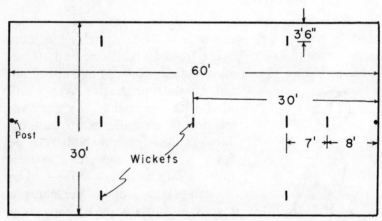

FIGURE 88. Croquet court.

Pitch and Putt Golf

A lawn 30 by 50 feet is large enough for nine holes. With the plan indicated in the diagram, a putter is the only club that will be needed. If a large lawn is available, increase the distance for each hole so that it will include a No. 7 or No. 8 iron shot. Make each distance different; mix the short and long holes. Start with the cross (tee) and sink a cup for each of the nine holes. The diagram shows a possible arrangement. Number the holes and the tees *(1)*and*(1)*, *(2)*and*(2)*, and so on to prevent confusion. See who can make the nine holes in the least number of shots.

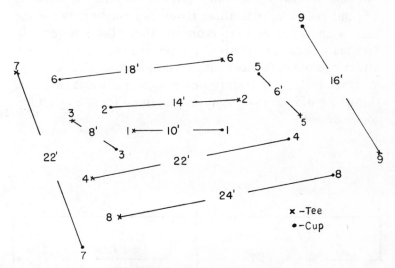

FIGURE 89. Pitch and putt golf.

Volleyball

Volleyball is one of the best sports for informal playing. As many as twelve or more persons can play at a time. It requires a space about 40 by 70 feet.

Each side serves from behind the right-end boundary line. The ball must not be helped over the net on a serve. Serving, and all hitting of the ball, must be with the open hands. A net ball (one touching the net) is not allowed on a serve but is good on following plays. Only the serving side can score one point at a time as a result of the opponent's "fault." If the serving side faults, the serve goes to the opponents, and no point is scored. A fault consists of a failure to return the ball to within the boundaries of the opposite court before the ball touches the ground. A team loses the ball also if the ball hits the body of a player, if a player catches or kicks the ball, or if a player touches the net. The ball can be batted from one player to another on the same side but not more than three times. No player may bat the ball twice in succession before another player touches it. The team receiving the ball for service shall immediately rotate one position clockwise so that each player serves in his turn. Fifteen or twenty-one points constitutes a game. Complete official rules may be obtained from a sporting-goods dealer.

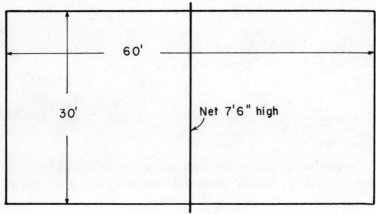

FIGURE 90. Volleyball.

Tennis

The standard space required for tennis is 60 by 120 feet, including the end and side zones. It may be played on a smooth and level dense-grass turf, a clay court, or one constructed of asphalt or concrete. Two or four persons play at a time.

Most tennis courts are made with a surface composed of a mixture of sand and clay. The proportions used vary with the character of these materials available in your community. Experiment with small quantities and different mixtures to obtain a material that will not crack excessively when dry. Four or five inches of this mixture is spread on the surface of the court, including the end and side zones. This is raked and rolled until a smooth surface and slight crown in the center is obtained. Clay courts are sometimes maintained by broadcasting brick dust on the surface and brushing it in with a stiff broom. The rules for this game are found in an official guide published annually by the United States Lawn Tennis Association, 120 Broadway, New York City.

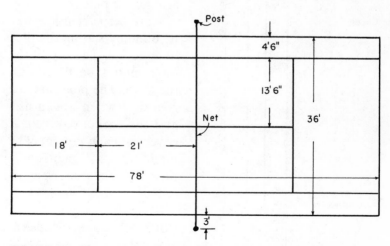

FIGURE 91. Tennis court. The net is hung 36 inches high at the center, 42 inches high at the sides. The wire backstops are 10 feet high and located at each end 21 feet behind the end boundary line.

EQUIPMENT EASY TO MAKE

Poles and Sockets

One set of poles will serve for tetherball, deck tennis, paddle tennis, volleyball, and badminton if the same lawn is to be used for all these games. The poles may be cut from a wood lot; straight seedlings about 2½ inches in diameter at the base are best. One should be 12½ feet long and the other 10 feet. The long pole is used for tetherball. Both are used to support a net for the games named above; the net is adjusted at the proper level for each game. The large end of the pole must be fitted to the inside of the socket.

Sockets for these poles should be set 30 feet apart across the center of the court. If there is room to play the game north and south, the poles are set on an east-and-west line. Small holes are dug 3 feet deep for the sockets. Then 6 inches of gravel are put in the bottom of the hole, a 2½-inch pipe, 2½ feet long, is put in, and the soil packed firmly around the pipe (Figure 92). A more permanent job may be done by setting the pipe in concrete. The top of the pipe should be flush with the lawn. The poles may be removed when not in use, and the socket covered. A cover for each pipe may be made from a 3-inch-square piece of sheet copper or

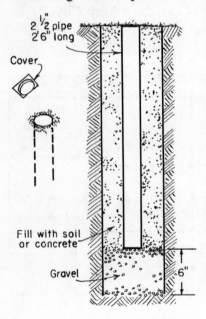

2½" pipe
2'6" long

Cover

Fill with soil
or concrete

Gravel

6"

FIGURE 92. Construction details of socket.

galvanized iron screwed to a block of wood that fits into the top of the pipe.

Paddles

Four paddles made according to the diagram (Figure 93) are needed for both tetherball and paddle tennis.

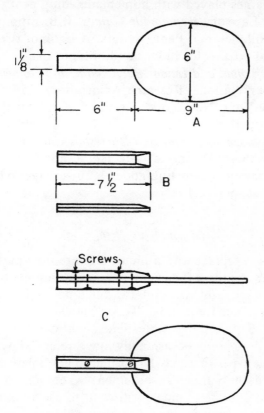

FIGURE 93. Construction details of paddle.

A. Size and shape of paddle. Made of ¼-inch 3-ply wood.

B. Handle made of soft wood 7½ inches long, 1⅛ inches wide, and 7/16 inch thick. Outer edges are beveled.

C. Paddle assembled. Screws must be tightened securely to support handle.

REFERENCES

E. O. Harbin, *The Fun Encyclopedia,* Abington Press, Nashville, Tennessee. Includes hundreds of games for home play with a section on "Fun with Sports."

Lynn Rohrbough, *Handy I* and *Handy II,* Cooperative Recreation Service, Delaware, Ohio. These books include sections on games played with homemade equipment.

Arthur H. Lawson, *Homemade Games,* J. B. Lippincott Company, Philadelphia, Pennsylvania. A book of twenty-six games and puzzles for indoor and outdoor play.

Home Playground and Indoor Play Room, and Homemade Play Apparatus, National Research Association, 315 Fourth Avenue, New York, New York. A small pamphlet with designs and instructions.

How to Organize and Promote a Horseshoe Club, and *How to Play Horseshoes,* Diamond Calk Horseshoe Company, Duluth, Minnesota. Sporting-goods stores have official guides for most sports.

Outdoor Fireplaces

An outdoor fireplace and a picnic site are now parts of many home grounds as they provide entertainment and recreation for the family, friends, and neighbors. For families who use them frequently, the permanent types illustrated in this STEP are desirable. Those who wish to cook meals out of doors only occasionally may prefer to buy one of the portable types that may be pushed to any shady place and stored in the garage or basement when not in use. Those who do not like to picnic will want to use all of their space for other purposes.

In planning a picnic area, the location of the fireplace, with its furnishings, and the design and construction of them are important. Some fireplaces are elaborate and, therefore, costly; but these are not necessarily the best unless the surroundings demand one of intricate design. A simple fireplace that fits into a carefully planned scheme is inexpensive to construct and is in keeping with most situations.

FIRE HAZARD

The fire hazard from any of the designs shown is not great, particularly if nearby buildings are built with fireproof materials or if the fireplace is about 50 feet from the nearest building. It is best if prevailing winds carry the smoke away from nearby buildings. One seldom builds a roaring fire, for a fire burned down to coals provides the best cooking heat. Wood that crackles and snaps should not be used. A charcoal fire is excellent. Someone usually is nearby all the time the fire is burning, and quick action can be taken in any emergency. The fire usually burns out of its own accord before the meal is over or soon after, but, before leaving, one should be sure that it is completely out. Any local fire regulations must be observed.

LOCATION OF FIREPLACE

Some individuals may prefer the fireplace near the house, where it will be convenient to carry food and utensils to it. The plans suggest only a few of the usual arrangements. Figure 94A illustrates a fireplace built into a house chimney. If this is done, a separate flue should be made for it. This flue should have a damper or be plugged in winter to prevent any interference with the draft in the flue of the home heating plant.

Another outdoor fireplace located conveniently near the house is illustrated in Figure 94B. This one is also planned as a part of a terrace development but is not a part of the house construction and need not be built with a chimney. It may be of the type illustrated in Figures 96 or 98 or one with only a low flue opening at the back of the fire pit. The plans in Figure 94, A and B, are suitable for either large or small properties.

Two outdoor fireplace developments closely associated with the garage are shown in Figure 94, C and D. The one illustrated in Figure 94C involves the construction of a chimney extending above the roof of the garage. A wire screen placed over the top of the flue gives added safety. The terrace may be shaded with a vine-covered pergola, at the choice of the owner.

Figure 94D illustrates a similar plan sometimes used effectively on a narrow lot. The terrace here is rather large, possibly large enough for table tennis. This table might also be used for picnics. The terrace is enclosed along the property line with a high, vine-covered fence.

On large properties it is possible to locate a fireplace

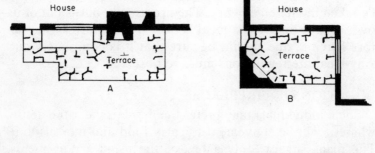

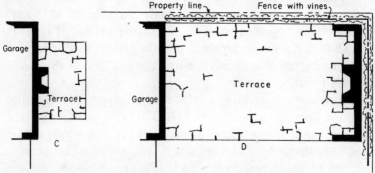

FIGURE 94. Outdoor fireplaces near the house or garage.

A. The flue of this outdoor fireplace is built into the house chimney. The unpaved area under the window is planted.

B. This outdoor fireplace is constructed as a part of the terrace.

C. This outdoor fireplace is constructed at the side of the garage.

D. This outdoor fireplace is constructed at the end of a large terrace.

farther from the house. Some families value the greater seclusion thus obtained more than they do the convenience of having it near the house. Such developments are more informal in character and are provided with a shrub background. Some home properties have a small grove of trees which may be made suitable for a picnic ground with naturalistic surroundings.

Figure 95, A, B, and C, shows plans that may be adapted to either level or slightly sloping ground. The arrangement in Figure 95A suggests a border planting at a rear corner where the lawn is reasonably level. A fireplace without a chimney should face the prevailing winds so that the smoke will be blown away from the cook and the table. A tree at the west or southwest of the picnic area provides shade for the table and chairs.

If the slope of the ground in front of the fireplace is such that furniture cannot be used comfortably, some grading and construction should be done as shown in Figure 95, B and C. Either of these designs provides a level place for the furniture, and the enclosing walls can be made high enough (about 20 inches above the floor of the terrace) to be used for seats at the table.

CONSTRUCTION PLANS

None of the plans shown need be followed exactly. The drawings merely illustrate three types most often used, any of which may be adapted as desired. The one shown in Figure 96 need not be made of stone, and the one in Figure 98 need not be made of brick. Materials used are those most conveniently available, but they should be in harmony with the surroundings.

It is more difficult to obtain good results with round field stones than with flat stones, such as limestone. The firebox should be made of firebrick or of highly glazed brick, because most types of stone crack or "explode" if submitted to intense heat. The foundation is made of concrete: one part cement, two parts of sand, and three parts of gravel. A small fireplace with or without a chimney needs only a concrete

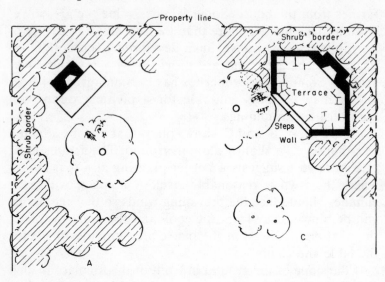

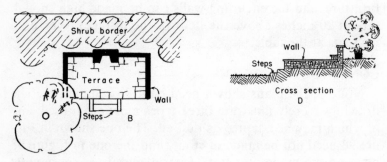

FIGURE 95. Outdoor fireplaces located at some distance from any buildings.

A. This outdoor fireplace is located at a rear corner of a level lawn. The shrub border provides some privacy from adjacent properties and partially separates the picnic area from the rest of the lawn.

B and C. These outdoor fireplaces are designed for sloping lawns but may be on a level lawn where no steps would be necessary. The plantings give some privacy, and the tree provides shade. The clump of three small-growing trees in C supplements the shrub border in giving privacy.

D. Cross section of a terrace and fireplace built on sloping ground.

slab from 4 to 6 inches thick and reinforced with old wire or metal rods. A larger fireplace, especially one with a chimney attached to a building, should have a foundation that extends below the frost line. One sack of cement, 2 cubic feet of sand, and 3 cubic feet of gravel, will make about 3 to 3½ cubic feet of concrete. Three parts of sand and one part of cement are mixed into a mortar and used for the walls and the firebox.

Special metal grates are sometimes used, but makeshift parts may be made from old pipes or metal sheets. The top section of an old wood or coal-burning kitchen range could be used. This assembly sometimes includes a reservoir for heating water.

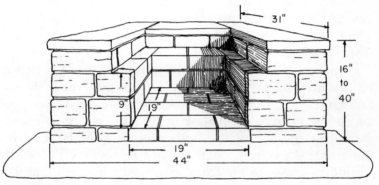

FIGURE 96. Construction details of a wood-burning fireplace. A wood-burning fireplace usually is better in appearance if it is low but is more comfortable to use if it is higher.

The wood-burning fireplace shown in Figure 96 has a firebox about 19 inches square and 9 inches high. The height and depth of any wood-burning fireplace should not vary much from these dimensions. The length of the firebox and the outside dimensions may vary with the size of the available grates and according to the desire of the owner. The shelves on each side of the grate should be large enough to set dishes and food near the cooking surface. The firebox is built first, and then the shelf space.

Charcoal makes the best fire for cooking. A charcoal shelf or grate that may be bent to fit a wood-burning fireplace is shown in Figure 97. This may be made from a sheet of

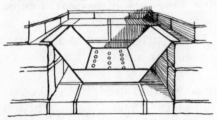

metal, 28 inches by 18 inches for a 19-inch square firebox. Lightweight metal can be supported from underneath with bricks to prevent warping or bending. The depth of this adapter, or grate, should be about 5

FIGURE 97.   A wood-burning fireplace, with this metal adapter, can be used with charcoal for fuel.

inches, and the sides should slope as shown. The bottom level is 8 inches wide. This, with the sloping sides and shallow depth, conserves fuel and gives a good cooking heat. The front edge should have a low siding to keep the coals from falling on the hearth.

When charcoal only is used for fuel, one might better build a fireplace for this purpose. One of this type is shown in Figure 98. The distance from the fine-mesh grate on which the charcoal is placed to the cooking grate above should be about 5 inches. Both grates may be larger than indicated if a larger cooking space is desired. The grate should be closer to the front than to the back so that the cooking surface will be easier to reach.

An elaborate fireplace is shown in Figure 99. There are many variations of this type, which include not only a wood-storage box but warming ovens, grills, places to store outdoor furniture, and many other knickknacks that add to its usefulness. Shelves as shown on the chimney are convenient for salt and pepper shakers, cooking spoons, forks, and small pans.

Unless large fires are built, the chimney need not be lined with flue tile. Such lining, however, is desirable, because of the cracking of most stones and soft brick when subjected to sudden intense heat.

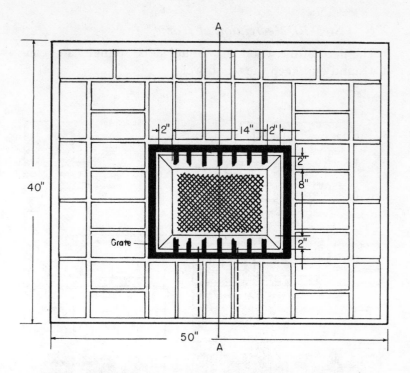

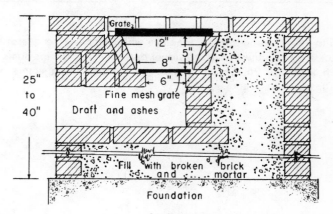

Section AA

FIGURE 98. Construction details of a charcoal-burning fireplace.
   A. Top view.
   B. Section AA. This shows the arrangement of the fire pit, grates, and draft. Firebrick should be used in the fire pit. This fireplace may be made of stone or brick.

The floor of the wood box should slope so that water cannot stand and keep the wood wet.

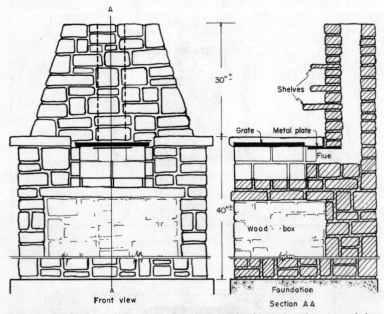

FIGURE 99. A wood-burning fireplace with chimney. The size of the firebox may be adjusted to individual desire or may be the same as shown in Figure 96. Section AA shows the flue arrangement and storage place for wood.

Hobby Gardens

The purpose of this STEP is to suggest phases of gardening which may be developed into hobbies according to family interests, abilities, and resources.

Gardening, as a hobby, has become increasingly popular with both men and women as a change from indoor work and for the healthful exercise it provides. Many of those who start as amateurs become so proficient in a specialized gardening hobby that they acquire almost professional skill and knowledge. The pride of achievement is all that is necessary to launch the enthusiast on a study of the vast variety of literature available and the sharing of information with others through garden clubs and other contacts.

Many books, magazine articles, catalogues, and other publications give detailed information on a wealth of subjects. Different varieties of plants are produced constantly, and new research provides us with greater knowledge of plant functions and better management.

FLOWER GARDENS

In most situations, flower borders such as those illustrated in the STEP on border plantings give adequate color and as much occupation as many homeowners care to devote to the project. This arrangement of having flower borders at the edge of a lawn conserves both space and time and produces attractive results. A large selection of annuals and perennials may be grown in a location where sun is available for all or perhaps three-quarters of the day. Shady spots are better for other varieties, including ferns. Soil con-

227

ditions can be improved, if necessary, by adding organic materials and fertilizers as described in STEP 6, page 85.

Most gardeners find satisfaction in planting flower beds informally, arranging irregular and overlapping clumps of the various kinds, occasionally repeating certain favored ones. The large-growing plants and those with the largest and most showy flowers sometimes are used singly, as one plant produces a sufficient mass of color. Smaller plants and those less prominent in color may be used in groups of three or more. Thus "drifts" of different, harmonizing colors are blended together (Figure 100).

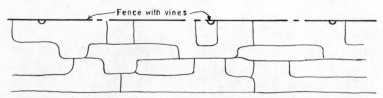

FIGURE 100. A plan for an informal flower bed. Clumps of flowers arranged in "drifts" produce the informal border. Each area outlined is planted with a different kind of plant from those in the adjacent areas.

The choice of plants and flower color rests with the individual. The desired combinations may not be obtained at the first planting, but as years pass and as planned transplanting is done, the garden becomes more and more to the liking of its owner.

These same ideas may be used in all flower beds whether they occupy a place along a border or in a small area especially devoted to growing flowers. Special flower gardens are most appropriately located near the house, where they can be enjoyed from the living rooms (Figure 101, A, B, C, and D, and the plans in STEP 9), particularly if there is easy access to them from the house. Such flower gardens usually are enclosed with a vine-covered trellis, a shrub border, or a clipped hedge. The enclosure serves both to give privacy and to provide a background for the flowers. The shrubs or vines used in such a border should be those that grow about 5 feet high and are not so aggressive in growth that they crowd out everything else.

The flower beds may form three sides of this garden except where breaks in the planting provide "doorways." The fourth side may be a wall of the house. If the beds along the outer borders of this garden do not provide as much space for growing flowers as is desired, part of the enclosed grass area may be sacrificed for flower beds, as is suggested in Figure 101, B and D. Any one of many different patterns may be used, but it is best to avoid acute-angle corners. The design must be modified and adapted to the size and shape of the space available and must be in character with the entire development.

The width of such garden beds should not be greater than can be reached easily from the edges, perhaps 3 to 5 feet. Wider spaces than this are hard to work in wet weather and are more difficult to maintain.

The amount of lawn within this garden usually should exceed that devoted to flower growing. Grass paths should be at least 3 feet wide, and if there is room for wider grass panels, so much the better. There may be room for a garden bench or other lawn furniture so that this colorful place may be enjoyed in comfort and at leisure.

Herbaceous Perennial Flowers

Many people have a special interest in herbaceous perennials. Most of these are produced easily from seed and live more than two years. Some continue to live at least as long as those who planted them. As a rule, when produced from seed, perennials do not flower the first year but do each year of their life thereafter, usually reaching their peak of perfection about the third year. The majority of them die to the ground in the fall, but the root lives through the winter and produces new growth in the spring.

While most perennials bloom during the period from early spring until midsummer, before annuals are in season,

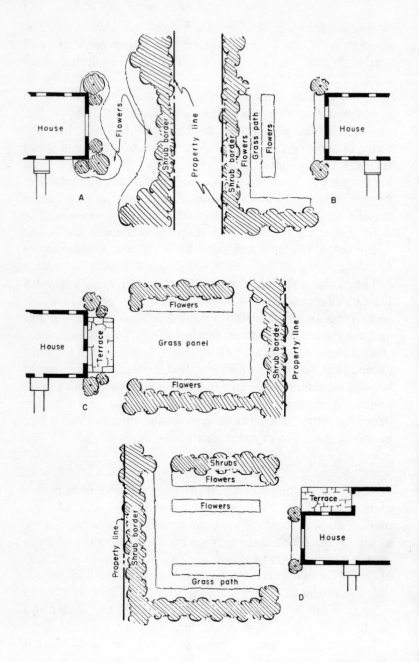

House

Flowers

Shrub border

Property line

Shrub border

Flowers

Grass path

Flowers

House

A

B

House

Terrace

Flowers

Grass panel

Flowers

Shrub border

Property line

C

Property line

Shrub border

Shrubs

Flowers

Flowers

Grass path

Terrace

House

D

careful selection enables the gardener to have their color through the summer until after light frosts have killed many of them to the ground. Chrysanthemums and anemones give color late in the season; the Christmas rose produces waxy, white flowers during the winter; and winter aconite opens its yellow cups in February or March.

As the flowers fade, it is best to cut them off and burn them or add them to the compost pile. Certain plants, such as phlox, produce seed prolifically. This seed germinates readily and produces so many plants the next season that they tend to crowd out the parent stock. The original plant retains its individual identity, but the seed produced from cross-pollination may result in a considerably different flower color from that of the parent plant.

Some perennials produce flowers over a period of several weeks, but most of them are colorful for only a week or two before they fade. If the first flowers are cut off and the ground fertilized, a second flowering from many of these plants will be induced, thereby extending the pleasure they afford. A few of them die to the ground soon after they are through flowering, leaving bare places in the border; but most of them remain in leaf for the season.

Within this class of plants are many different varieties of certain groups such as peonies, delphiniums, columbines, poppies, and phlox. Any one or more of these presents the possible hobby of growing and knowing many different varieties. As interest in these plants increases, the gardener

FIGURE 101. Small flower gardens. All these gardens are shown enclosed with an informal shrub border. Individual preference or more limited space may dictate an enclosure composed of a clipped hedge, a vine-covered fence, or trellis.

A. The curved lines add to the informality of this small flower garden, designed for a narrow side lawn.

B. The extra bed here provides additional flower-growing space.

C. The terrace and grass panel enclosed by flower beds and shrubs make this a pleasant outdoor living area.

D. The inside flower beds improve the proportion of the central grass panel.

may want to grow some from seed, propagate them from stem cuttings or by root division, or even try something more technical such as cross-pollination to obtain a new strain.

Many perennials are used effectively for cut flowers.

Biennials

There are relatively few different biennials commonly used in home flower gardens. Bellflower, or Canterbury bell, is one of the fine old-fashioned flowers in this class. Most biennials are easily produced from seed. They make good growth the first year but do not produce flowers until the second season. This means that new plants should be started from seed every year. An alternate plan is to buy year-old plants. Self-sown plants are apt to produce disappointing results.

Annuals

Annual flowers are popular in the garden because they produce continuous bloom from early summer until late fall. Some of them withstand light frost, retaining their color until a heavy freeze kills them. Many of them are produced easily from seed, and all of them complete a life cycle in one year. They grow to maturity, produce flowers and seeds, and die in the fall.

Sometimes gardeners start the seeds of these plants outdoors, in the beds where they are to remain for the summer. Flowering is then somewhat delayed. The avid gardener is not satisfied with this shorter season of effectiveness and purchases plants of flowering size from a florist or, during the late winter, starts these seeds indoors and transplants them to the flower beds as soon as danger of frost is past. If suitable indoor facilities are available at home and careful planning is done to start the seed in time, flowering plants may be obtained early in the season.

Although annual flowers, except for those that are self-sown, must be replaced each year, the total amount of work involved is not great, and there are certain advantages. The beds may be fertilized, spaded, and cleaned free of weeds just previous to the time planting is done. After the annuals have been set, all of the bed may be mulched with a 1-inch layer of peat or other suitable material. This will help to retain moisture in the ground and, to a large degree, decrease the growth of weeds. Thus the chief maintenance necessary is the cutting of flowers that have faded.

Many annuals produce flowers that are effectively used for house decoration. They may be used alone effectively, or in combination with other materials to provide a variety of color and texture. Some who enjoy making flower arrangements grow a row or two of annuals in the edge of the vegetable garden especially for cutting.

In a flower garden separate beds may be planted to annuals exclusively, or a single bed may be used for annuals, perennials, and bulbs. There is an advantage when all are used in one bed, as perennials and bulbs produce color from early spring until early summer, when the annuals take over and give lasting color for the rest of the season.

Bulbs

Bulb gardening is an interesting hobby, especially for families who are at home through the spring and then move to another location for the summer. Some, even though they stay at home all summer, may wish to have a special hobby for the early season. Most bulbs are spring-flowering plants and are tolerant of shady locations.

The long list of different tulips and daffodils is being lengthened continually as hybridizers work to obtain better and somewhat different flowers. Daffodil is the common name used for both the large trumpet types and those with small cups. The small-cup types frequently are called narcissus.

Many varieties of narcissus, tulip, and crocus produce an annual supply of bulblets, thus perpetuating these plants for several years. The first year these bulblets mature into plump bulbs and produce just one leaf and no flower. During the second season, they produce two leaves and one or more flower stalks.

Many varieties of bulbs grown in the garden are excellent to use in the house.

WILD-FLOWER GARDENS

Gardeners who like to roam through the fields and woods may have a particular flair for growing wild flowers and ferns. Some of those that grow in great abundance in your vicinity may be transplanted to the home garden, provided they are not protected by state law and a near duplication of their natural habitat can be provided. However, the best way to get them is to order the seeds or plants from a nursery specializing in them.

Beds in which these plants are to be grown should be prepared with great quantities of woods dirt or with high proportions of organic matter such as leaf mold or peat. Any of these materials may be mixed with the existing soil by spading them together.

Most wild flowers and ferns grow well in a shady location. This may be a small grove of trees, a border planting of large shrubs and small trees, or a prepared bed along the north side of a building.

Many wild flowers and their ancestors have in their background interesting stories and legends, some based purely on superstition and others on fact. The subject offers interesting reading and research for winter evenings.

ROCK GARDENS

Once upon a time rock gardens were popular, so popular that most home grounds had them on display regardless of their suitability for the location and the available materials. A wheelbarrow load or two of soil deposited in the center of the lawn and a few stones sprinkled on top were characteristic. A display of rocks collected from widely separated sources may have considerable sentimental value but is not appropriate for a good rock garden. Fads of this kind come and go, but a naturalistic rock garden becomes a permanent part of the well-planned landscape.

Occasionally native rock outcroppings occur on a home property. These can be planted with rock-garden plants to obtain a truly naturalistic effect. If such a setting is not available and there is an urge to have a rock garden, it may be designed in a manner in keeping with the existing conditions. Although level land is not well adapted to such a development, it can be utilized by clever and careful planning. If the ground is sloping, either up or down, the opportunities are better.

The maker of a realistic rock garden must have a rather clear understanding of natural rock formations and the mechanical ability to reproduce them if he is to construct one that approaches in appearance an outcropping left by glacial action or exposed by erosion. Stones should not be dropped on the surface and left. They will appear more stable, more as if they belonged with the surroundings, if they are "planted" in the ground so that only a small portion of the stone shows. Large stones are better than small ones. Use the kind of stones native to the area, and arrange them as nearly as possible in a natural manner.

Another type of rock garden sometimes is called a wall garden. This is constructed by grading the lawn and building a dry stone wall as suggested in STEP 3, profiles B, E, and F, and Figure 13, A and B, and planting rock-garden plants in the crevices between the stones. This type of rock garden is not difficult to construct, and the results are satisfying.

Anyone contemplating starting a rock garden should keep in mind that a large amount of detailed hand weeding must be done. Some of the plants are tiny; others spread aggressively, and the spaces are so small that patient fingers are a necessity. Those who enjoy this kind of work will derive great satisfaction from being able to grow some plants not suited to other types of gardens.

ROSE GARDENS

A good soil for garden roses is clay loam into which has been mixed large amounts of organic matter. Good drainage is essential. Garden roses may be planted either in the fall or in the spring, spring planting being preferred in the northern part of this country. The main stem of budded plants has a swelling near the ground level. When planted, this point of budding should be set 1 to 2 inches below the surface of the soil.

Thrifty growth can be stimulated by applying fertilizers to the soil each year and placing a 1- or 2-inch mulch over the bed. The mulch will help to retain moisture in the soil and discourage the growth of weeds.

Roses are subject to certain insect and disease pests and should be sprayed or dusted frequently during the growing season. Preventing the attack of these pests is far better than checking them after infestation has occurred. Combination dusts and sprays are available. They avoid the use of two or three separate materials.

In cold climates, tender rose plants should be protected during the winter. The best method known at present is to mound the soil about a foot high around the base of each plant after the surface of the ground is frozen. The soil used for this purpose can be taken from the rose bed if care is used not to damage the roots seriously. If the bed is not large enough to provide sufficient soil for this purpose, it may be obtained from the vegetable garden or from a shrub border. In the spring, after the last frosts are past, the mounds are removed.

Although garden roses require a considerable amount of attention, their beauty and usefulness compare favorably with those of our best ornamental plants.

Hobby gardening with roses is an interesting challenge to anyone who wishes to work with a genus having many different varieties. A wide range of flower color is available, and some kinds produce blooms from early summer to late autumn. They are excellent for flower arrangements.

If the gardener wishes to have only a few rose plants, it probably is best to set them in a flower border rather than to prepare a small, separate bed for them. However, if roses are to be the subject of a hobby, a separate garden is preferred, the design of which may be similar to one of the plans shown for flower gardens. It should be in a sunny location with no large trees nearby. It may be enclosed with a trellis if this is in keeping with the rest of the garden. This would provide facilities to grow two more rose types: the climber and pillar roses. The beds would be planted with the bush-type roses: hybrid teas, hybrid perpetuals, and polyanthas, sometimes called floribundas.

Many of those that are winter-hardy in the area where they are sold are grown on their own roots. Those that are likely to be killed by low temperatures are grown on the hardy root of a common rose, usually *Rosa multiflora.* They are propagated by a process called budding, whereby a bud of the desired variety is inserted low on the stem produced by the common rootstalk. When this bud has grown into a stem of sufficient length, all the stems produced by the rootstalk are cut off, leaving only the top growth of the desired variety. Thus each rose plant so produced will have the root of a common rose and the top of another. All stems arising from below the point of budding are from the original stock and must be cut off at the ground level or below. These are strong-growing stems, and if they are not removed, they will crowd out all the stems of the variety purchased.

FLOWER ARRANGEMENT

All kinds of enticing suggestions and illustrations of flower arrangements confront us at every turn. A wide variety of colors and textures of material present a challenge to anyone interested in this prevailing hobby. Not only the selection of the right container becomes important, but the choice of colors which will fit into a garden scheme. The form, line, and texture of the plants, the character of the arrangement in its relation to the place where it is to be used, and the desire for interesting materials affect the selection of plants for the home grounds.

Early-flowering shrubs and small trees, such as flowering quince, forsythia, flowering crab, flowering dogwood, and redbud provide stems for forcing flowers indoors in the late winter and early spring. Material with which to make your Christmas decorations can be grown at home. Some of those most often used include winterberry, bayberry, and both broad- and narrow-leaved evergreens such as laurel, rhododendron, mountain andromeda, leucothoe, Japanese yew, balsam, and pines in variety.

Thus the contribution of the out-of-doors becomes not only seasonal, but a year-round pleasure in the hands of the flower-arranging hobbyist.

GARDENING FOR BIRDS

Those fond of birds may wish to grow some of the plants attractive to them. A tree or two, large shrubs, and some vines provide nesting places. Birdhouses also give shelter, but any unnatural form of "housing," as well as birdbaths and feeding stations, should be used sparingly and be located in inconspicuous places.

Many ornamental woody plants produce fruit that birds feed upon in the late summer, autumn, and winter. The fruit of two evergreens, yew and red cedar, are eaten by a number of birds. Only the pistillate-flowering form of yew should be used because this is the kind that will bear fruit. Several kinds of low-growing trees are fine "feeding stations." They include shadblow, flowering dogwood, cornelian cherry, hawthorn, flowering crab, and mountain ash. In the border plantings, viburnums and shrubby dogwoods are among the best of our woody flowering plants as their season of interest covers much of the summer, and the fruit they produce is freely used by birds. Among the many species of viburnum are blackhaw, nannyberry, wayfaringtree, arrowwood, highbush cranberry, witherod, mapleleaf viburnum, and many others. The shrubby dogwoods include red-osier dogwood, silky dogwood, gray dogwood, and roundleaf dogwood. Honeysuckle (in variety), privet (in variety), elderberry, summersweet, spicebush, and many others could be added to the list of plants successfully used to attract birds.

Gardening for birds is a hobby speciality that is enjoyed by many. Although some progress can be made in this direction on small city lots, the opportunities probably are greater in larger rural or suburban properties.

SWAMP GARDENS

Large home properties occasionally have low swampy places which may be rather extensive yet are not suitable for the development of a pond. If it is desirable to make this space available for a lawn, for recreation or for some other use, it is possible to eliminate the excess water. Filling the depression may be sufficient, or regrading the area to provide surface drainage will distribute the water elsewhere. If necessary, tile may be laid to drain it.

If this low land is not more valuable for some other purpose and if it offers a challenge as a swamp garden, it can be made accessible by providing steppingstone paths. The planting and culture of trees, shrubs, and wild flowers which thrive under such growing conditions is an interesting study in itself.

In fairly large swamps, American arborvitae can be used for year-round greenness, and tamarack, tupelo, red maple, and quaking aspen for spring and autumn color. To these could be added the shrubs and wild flowers that would be used exclusively in smaller swamps. They include winterberry, for its brilliant red fruit so valuable in the winter landscape and in Christmas wreaths and other arrangements; American and scarlet elderberry, for their interesting combination of flower and fruit; many of the viburnums and shrubby dogwoods, for their flower, fruit, and autumn color; swamp azalea, for its early pale pink flowers; summersweet, for its spikes of white, sweet-scented flowers in midsummer; and red and black chokeberry for midsummer fruit color and red autumn foliage. These shrubs and trees give attractive results as seen either nearby or at a distance. Many different wild flowers, including marsh marigold, small white ladyslipper, pitcherplant, wintergreen, cinnamon and royal ferns give added interest for close inspection.

Thus an area that would otherwise be a difficult situation can be made into an attractive place. Troublesome insects that multiply in such locations can be controlled with insecticides.

POOLS

Many persons who live on small home grounds and on rural properties are interested in building a pool to add to the beauty of their property and provide an opportunity for a hobby of growing aquatic plants. A little hard work, backed by some mechanical ability, will enable anyone to have a water garden. The cost varies with the size of the pool because a larger pool requires more materials. A large pool, such as one that might be built on a rural property, may afford some fire protection.

Once it is decided to have a pool, several questions arise: Where is the water supply? What disposal can be made of the overflow? Shall the pool be formal, informal, or naturalistic? Where is it to be and of what material shall it be made? What size and shape shall it be? What plants shall be used in and near it? Unless these important questions are answered correctly, the pool may be a failure in operation or appearance.

A pool, like all other landscape features, must be in keeping with the surroundings. Sloping land with no level space presents the most difficult situation unless much grading is done. However, many properties have a natural setting for a pool.

In a sandy or gravelly soil, the pool must be cemented. In heavy clay soil, cement need not be used if the bottom of the basin is puddled so that it is almost watertight, or tight enough to maintain a constant level when there is a continuous supply of water. For a small pool the soil, while moist, may be pounded with a heavy tamper. Rocks may be wedged in around the edge, and the joints plastered with damp clay. Puddling is advised only for a natural pool. A small stone or cement dam constructed at the point of overflow maintains a constant water level. The construction of this dam may be partly concealed by a planting of shrubs and evergreens. The water from this pool may be deflected back into the course of the stream or into a nearby ditch.

Water Supply

A pool must have a supply of fresh water. This may come from a stream, a spring, clean drainage water, a city or private reservoir, or from a well. Sometimes a continuous drip of water from the main source keeps the pool clean, or, with an electric pump and storage tank, the same water may be used over and over. A pool must not be too large for the supply. Unless there is a steady inflow, a small pool need not have an outflow. Because of natural evaporation, water must be added at intervals. If the water becomes stagnant, it should be baled out or siphoned off and replaced with clean water.

The growth of algae, or green slime, can be prevented by adding 1 ounce of copper sulphate (blue vitriol) for each 8,000 gallons of water. This may be reduced or increased in proportion to the size of the pool—⅛ ounce for each 1,000 gallons, or 2 ounces for each 16,000 gallons. Most fish are susceptible to the poisonous effects of copper sulphate. If goldfish are kept in the pool and are not removed while treatment is being made, only ⅛ ounce of copper sulphate should be used for each 2,500 gallons of water. The stronger treatment may be used if the fish are removed and are not replaced until the pool has been drained, flushed out, and refilled with clean water.

Place and Type of Pool

The most desirable place for the pool should be selected even if a little extra trouble is involved in supplying it with water. Since one of the principal values of a pool is its reflecting surface, it should be placed in front of a plant or group of plants, a pergola, or some other architectural feature. If a reflection is to be seen on the pool, the surface of the water must be near the ground line, and the pool so placed that the reflection will show from one of the porches of the house, from a terrace, a pergola, or some frequented place in the garden.

A pool affords an opportunity for the culture of water plants. If waterlilies, which need at least full morning sun to produce good blooms, are to be grown, the pool must be in a sunny spot. The pool might be in the center of a grass panel where it forms a central feature of a garden, or it might be near the house or at the far end of a grass panel and immediately in front of the object to be reflected.

The pool will harmonize with formal surroundings if it has formal outlines and is square, oblong, round, oval, or some slight variation of one of these shapes.

Usually a pool in a formal or semiformal setting should have a neat coping of cement, brick, slate, or tile. The top surface of this coping usually should be nearly flush with the ground. Just as a landscape developed along straight lines need not be planted in a strictly formal way, so a formal-shaped pool may be somewhat informal in appearance if the planting is grouped irregularly.

If the garden plan is along curved lines, or if it is naturalistic in design, the pool should have a curved margin, and

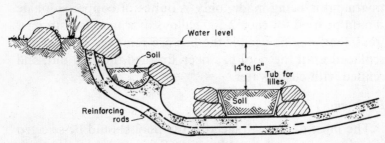

FIGURE 102. Round-stone edging. These construction details of an informal pool show the position of stones to conceal the cement, pocket for shallow-water plants, and the lily tub.

might be placed at one side of the property or near the rear. A definitely outlined coping around a pool of this kind is not needed. The pool will have a more natural appearance if grass is grown down to meet the water in some places and stones form the edges at other places. All the cement should be screened from view; a few rocks and low-growing plants, well placed, will soften the edge and hide unsightly construction (Figures 102 and 103). If the pool is shallow and made of concrete, the white bottom will be glaring, and the pool will not act as a reflecting medium unless the bottom is painted with asphalt or some dark-colored, waterproof paint. This also helps to protect the concrete. A dense border of shrubs and evergreens behind the pool forms a suitable background.

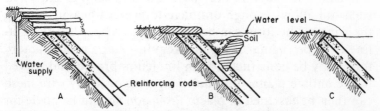

FIGURE 103. Construction details of different edgings.
   A. Naturalistic waterfall with supply pipe concealed under the stone edging.
   B. Flat-stone coping and pocket for shallow-water plants.
   C. Grass edging. The concrete is beveled to give some soil depth for grass to grow near the water's edge.

Construction

The size of the pool must be in accord with the size of the grounds or the part of the grounds in which it is placed. A suitable size may be determined either by drawing a plan to scale or by laying a rope or garden hose on the ground to mark the outline, and changing it until the desired size and shape are obtained. The smallest surface in which waterlilies can be grown successfully is about 15 square feet.

If waterlilies are to be grown, the depth will be determined by the height of the waterlily tubs. The minimum size for a tub is 15 inches square and not less than 8 inches deep. These are usually made of cypress or pine. The surface of the water should be from 14 to 18 inches above the tops of the tubs.

The sides should be sloping and rounded or angular at the bottom. The surface width should be greater than that at the bottom so that there will be less danger of the concrete's cracking if the water freezes. Cracks that appear in later years can be mended with a rich mixture of cement or with heavy asphalt paint.

In a clay soil the excavation can be dug to the size and shape of the pool, allowing an extra foot of depth—6 inches for cinders, as a foundation, and 6 inches more for concrete. The cinder foundation may be omitted in sand or gravel, as such soil allows enough drainage to prevent heaving during the winter. The form can be built with old boards if the outline is to be regular. For an irregular shape a satisfactory form may be constructed with linoleum, braced and curved to the outline planned. Reinforcing rods or heavy wire mesh can then be fastened in place. Provision should be made for a supply pipe or water inlet and for an overflow pipe or outlet (Figure 104). The plumbing may be simple. Brass piping, although more expensive at the start, will not rust and may be bent to do away with couplings and joints. As a protection to small children or to small animals that might fall into the pool, a coarse wire netting might be stretched over a pipe framework, some 2 or 3 inches under the proposed water level.

Informal or naturalistic pools should have no coping of stone, cement, or brick; and no concrete or cement shows in a cleverly constructed pool of this kind. Many pools are spoiled by stones of various sizes and shapes set at angles around the edge. Flat or round stones, placed informally before the concrete has hardened, may be used for the edging, or grass may be allowed to grow to the water's margin.

If the sides have a slight slope, it may not be necessary to use any forms, and stiff concrete may be troweled in the excavation.

If lilies are to be planted in sunken tubs, holes may be dug to an extra depth of 8 inches in the desired positions. The tubs are then set in place, and concrete is poured around them. The tub must be tapped, both inside and outside, to fill the voids and make it watertight. A 1-2-3 mixture of concrete is used, or one part of good cement, two parts of clean, sharp sand, and three parts of crushed rock.

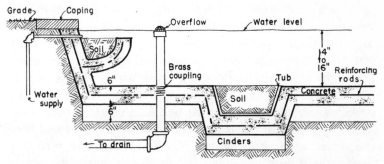

FIGURE 104. Construction details of a formal pool showing a dressed-stone coping, plumbing details, pocket for shallow-water plants, and lily tub.

All the concrete is poured at one time to make it more watertight. Cups for shallow-water plants may be made at irregular intervals in the side of the pool. The top of these should be from 3 to 4 inches under the water level, and they should be large enough to hold at least ¾ cubic foot of soil. The inside of the pool is brushed with a rich mixture of cement—one part of cement and one part of sand, before the concrete has set. The cement is then covered with straw so that it will dry slowly and become thoroughly cured before any water is put into the pool. At least two weeks are allowed for curing. The first filling of water should be allowed to stand for another two weeks to absorb the alkali from the new concrete. The pool should then be drained and filled with clean water before stocking it with plants or fish.

Planting

Plantings for a pool need little attention. Water gardens are likely to be overplanted. The surface should not be covered with foliage, because much of the beauty lies in a reflecting surface. For waterlilies, a pool surface of about 40 square feet should not have more than two lily tubs with one plant in each tub. A better effect is obtained if only one water lily is used with other aquatic plants.

A catalogue from a reliable nursery is a good guide for selecting plants. The two types of waterlilies are the tender, or tropical, and the hardy lilies. Tropical lilies are divided into two classes according to habit—the day-blooming and the night-blooming—and come in a wide range of color. The tender tropicals usually are treated as annuals, and are replaced each year. Care must be taken not to set them out in the spring until frosts are past and the weather will keep the water in the pool warm. Cold water seriously retards their growth both in foliage and in bloom, but with a warm start in spring they will bloom all summer and on into the fall, until frost kills them.

Hardy lilies have a wide range of color, including yellow. They can be kept from year to year with a small amount of winter care. Some persons prefer to remove the tubs, put them in the basement, and keep them moist all winter. Others drain the pool, put all the tubs in one corner, and cover them with a heavy mulch of straw and leaves. Still others prefer not to disturb the lilies but leave the water in the pool, cover the entire surface with boards, and put straw and leaves on top. Any one of these practices is satisfactory.

Since waterlilies are gross feeders, they are planted in two parts of good soil and one part of well-rotted cow manure. If cow manure is not available, at least 1 quart of blood meal is mixed in a bushel of soil. The tubs are filled to within an inch of the top, and the root is planted so that the crown is at the surface. A top layer of sand or fine-screened gravel keeps the soil from washing into the pool, which is then filled with water to the top of the tubs and allowed to warm in the sun for a few days. As the pool is filled gradually, the shock of cold water will not retard the growth of the plants. The second year the soil should again be fertilized by working in a little well-rotted cow manure or blood meal. The third year new soil should be put into the tubs, and the root divided by taking off the new side shoots and planting the old root.

Descriptions of many other plants to make the pool more attractive and interesting are given in the catalogues of reliable nurseries which specialize in aquatic plants. Submerged plants which give off oxygen will keep the water in good condition for goldfish. Fanwort and loosestrife serve this purpose and do not require planting in the soil, but they may be held in place if they are anchored in the side pockets or in the lily tubs. Other plants are water hyacinth and water snowflake, which float on the surface. Low-growing, shallow-water plants for the side pockets of the pool are watercress, floatingheart, and waterpoppy. Medium-height plants are arrowhead, sweetflag, waterplantain, and wild calla. For a tall plant, use cattail.

For small pools the border plants should be selected from a group of low-growing perennials, shrubs, and evergreens. Large plants may be used near large pools and in the background planting for both large and small pools.

Small fish of various kinds may add to the interest of the pool and help to keep the water clean and free of mosquito larvae. Other aquatic animals also may be used if desired. Snails are good scavengers, as they clean the pool of decayed vegetable matter; frogs and turtles live on insects. All these plants and animals help to form a complete balance.

Once the work is done, a pool is an unending source of pleasure. The better it fits its surroundings, the greater will be the feeling of permanency, and the water garden will not fall into that class of fads which come and go from year to year.

Rural Ponds

Many large properties, particularly those in rural areas, have a place where a sizable pond could be made. A soil-conservation specialist or an engineer with experience in this work should first check the supply of available water and the water-holding capacity of the existing subsoil. If conditions are such that success is assured, a bulldozer is used to grade the basin. Pipe or tile is laid, and a valve installed, so that the pond may be drained when necessary.

A pond of this kind is more than an attractive feature. It will satisfy children's boating ambitions and provide a place to swim or skate. Many times such ponds are stocked with fish which, when mature, offer recreation for the fishing enthusiast and a delicacy for the dinner table. Also, in rural areas where a public water supply is not available, a pond furnishes water for fire-fighting equipment in case of emergency.

Plant Lists

SELECTION OF PLANTS

The selection of plants for your use depends upon your familiarity with them and upon personal choice. Since most homeowners know few different kinds, this phase of landscaping is the most difficult one to direct.

When your general landscape plan is outlined and specific plants are chosen, you are ready to make out your order. Purchase only the number and kinds you need. Select the plants you know and like, or refer to a reliable book or nursery catalogue for descriptions and illustrations of less familiar plants. A still better procedure is to go to a nearby nursery, ask to see the plants you are interested in, and learn about their characteristics. Obtain complete information about them, including their mature size, the color of the flower and fruit, and the time of year each is effective.

SIZES TO BUY

It is customary for nurseries to have available several sizes of each variety they grow. In general, a shrub 3 to 4 feet high costs more than a 1½- to 2-foot shrub of the same variety because of the longer time and more labor required to produce it. Because the larger plant gives a more nearly immediate effect, some homeowners are willing to pay more for it. However, in a few years the smaller size will produce the same effect as the large one. Probably most homeowners buy medium-sized plants, as they produce a reasonably good appearance when they are planted, have a good root system, stand transplanting well, and are moderate in cost.

When very small sizes are used, the new planting appears sparse and inadequate, but if the plants purchased are proportional in size to their mature character, the general effect of the new planting will be suggestive of their appearance after several years' growth.

If only a limited number of mature or semimature shrubs is to be used, preference should be given to those planned for use near the base of the house. The appearance of the house will then be greatly improved immediately after the planting is done. Except where it is desirable to screen an objectionable view or give immediate privacy, it does not make so much difference if the border plantings require a few additional years to produce the desired effect, and smaller-sized plants may be used.

Evergreens, both narrow-leaved and broad-leaved types, and some deciduous plants that are difficult to transplant successfully with bare roots are sold with a ball of earth on the roots and wrapped in burlap. They are listed in nursery catalogues as "B and B."

If for financial, or any other reason, it is unwise to do the complete landscape planting at one time, it may be done over a period of three or four years. Although some time is lost in getting the plants started as soon as possible, the final results will be entirely satisfying if a suitable plan has been adopted and followed.

TIME OF BLOOM

Information as to the time of flowering is taken from records made in Ithaca, New York. Even in one locality the date of bloom of an individual plant varies from year to year. Likewise the date of bloom varies in different localities. Flowering will be later in areas having long winters and earlier in places having short winters. However, the sequence of bloom will be the same.

GUARANTY

Some nurserymen guarantee their plants to survive because their customers wish to have this assurance. Obviously, the nurserymen who guarantee their plants to live must either have their own men plant them and charge a higher price for their product or run the risk of losing considerable sums of money replacing plants that have died for reasons over which they have no control. If their own men plant and maintain them for the first growing season, the nurserymen have assurance the work has been done properly and they can reasonably accept the responsibility for them. If the purchaser plants the stock and maintains it without regard to proper procedure, the grower should not be held responsible. However, if the plants have been set and taken care of according to approved practices, he probably will lose less than 10 per cent of his order.

In any event, the nurserymen can, and probably should, guarantee their plants to be of a specified size and age, true to name, and in good condition when they are delivered.

ORDERING PLANTS EARLY

If possible, place your order for plants two or three months before the planting season, as this gives the nurseryman time to plan his work efficiently and enables him to make deliveries on time. The nursery business is a seasonal one, and a tremendous amount of work must be done during the short planting periods. In addition to filling your orders, he must restock his nursery.

The days between the time when the order is sent and that when the plants are delivered can be gainfully used preparing the soil in areas to be planted. Small stakes stuck into the ground where each plant is to be set facilitate quick planting when the order is delivered.

Plant Lists

The plants listed here are suitable for use in most of the northeastern quarter of the United States, south through Tennessee, and west to the foothills of the Rocky Mountains. Those classified as "tender" may not survive the winters of the coldest parts of this area. In the warmer portions more plants could be added.

Although this list is basic, no one can state the precise territorial or climatic limits of all these plants. There are pockets within this range where some of them may not grow successfully, and many of them are used satisfactorily hundreds of miles beyond. Some of them may survive in certain locations but will be of no special landscape value because they fail to produce flowers or fruit.

Probably much of the inconsistency in plant behavior can be traced to several factors, important among which is that of providing suitable soil. Other factors include fertility of the soil, moisture, temperature, and sunlight. A malnourished plant or one weakened by insect or disease attack will be less resistant to winter injury than one of the same variety that is growing thriftily. We are continually learning about successful attempts with well-known plants in new locations where they were heretofore believed to be unreliably hardy. Adventuresome home gardeners can lead the way to the successful use of an ever-greater variety of plants in an ever-expanding area.

Homeowners living beyond the reaches of this plant list should consult reliable sources such as their state colleges of agriculture, local nurserymen growing plants in the area, and experienced home gardeners to learn the names of plants that grow successfully in their locality.

These lists are arranged in size groups, but it should be kept in mind that soil and moisture will influence somewhat the mature size of a plant. Good soil with ample moisture produces a larger plant than does poor, dry soil. Also, the same variety will grow larger in a mild climate than in a colder one. Light annual pruning, if necessary, keeps them within the size group listed. The following plants are classified according to the heights they attain under New York State conditions.

The scientific names follow L. H. Bailey's *Manual of Cultivated Plants,* published in 1949. The name in parentheses is the old one.

Group 1. Vines

The vines named in groups 1a and 1b usually are listed in nursery catalogues according to their age. A two- or three-year-old plant is a good size to order. Those used near a wall should be planted as close as possible.

GROUP 1a. TWINING VINES FOR FENCES AND TRELLISES

Small-growing vines used on a fence enclosing a private lawn should be planted about 10 feet apart; large-growing vines, 15 feet or more apart. Fences not intended to give privacy to a lawn should be only partly covered. Usually one vine is enough for a small trellis. Seldom, if ever, should a wall be completely covered with vines.

Deciduous

BOWER ACTINIDIA: *Actinidia arguta* [ak-tee-nid′-ee-uh are-goo′-tah]
Leaves: Yellow in autumn.
Flowers: White in May, hidden somewhat by the leaves.
Remarks: Large-growing, clean foliage plant, tolerant of shade or sun.

FIVE-LEAF AKEBIA: *Akebia quinata* [ah-kee′-bee-ah kwin-a′-tuh]
Leaves: Five leaflets peculiarly notched at the tip, remain green late into autumn.
Flowers: Beautiful, dark red with showy yellow stamens in May, fragrant, hidden somewhat by leaves.
Remarks: Small-growing, dense; use in sun or shade; free of insect and disease attack.

DUTCHMAN'S PIPE: *Aristolochia durior* [a-ris-toe-low′-key-ah du′-ree-or]
Leaves: Large, coarse texture.
Fruit: Interesting, pipe-shaped.
Remarks: Provides dense screen; use in sun or shade.

AMERICAN BITTER-SWEET: *Celastrus scandens* [see-las′-trus skan′-dens]
Leaves: Yellow in autumn.

Fruit: Orange clusters in late summer and through the winter, useful for house decoration.

Remarks: Large-growing; use in sun or shade; pistillate-flowering plants produce fruit.

ORIENTAL BITTER-SWEET: *Celastrus orbiculatus* [see-las'-trus or-bic-u-lay'-tus]

Remarks: Similar to native variety.

CLEMATIS: Only three of the more commonly used varieties are described here, but there are available many large-flowering species that have a wide color range—white, pink, red, scarlet, blue, and yellow. They vary in size, and the flowering season extends from early summer to autumn. Some of the large-flowering kinds are difficult to grow successfully and are not recommended for the beginning gardener. All varieties of clematis are relatively small-growing vines and will grow well in sun or light shade.

SWEET AUTUMN CLEMATIS: *Clematis dioscoreifolia robusta (paniculata)* klem'-uh-tis die-os-ko-ree-eye-foe'-lee-uh roe-bus'-tah]

Flowers: Billowy mass of small white flowers in September, fragrant.

JACKMAN CLEMATIS: *Clematis jackmanii* [klem'-uh-tis jack'-man-ee-eye]

Flowers: Large, purple in July.

VIRGIN'S BOWER: *Clematis virginiana* [klem'-uh-tis vir-gin-ee-a'-nah]

Flowers: White in July.

Fruit: Showy, fluffy heads, autumn to late winter.

HALL'S HONEYSUCKLE: *Lonicera japonica halliana* [low-niss'-er-uh ja-pon'-ih-cah hal-lee-ain'-uh]

Leaves: Semievergreen.

Flowers: White in mid-June, fade yellow, fragrant.

Remarks: Strong-growing; will smother nearby plants if not restricted by pruning; tender.

TRUMPET HONEYSUCKLE: *Lonicera sempervirens* [low-niss'-er-uh sem-per'-vee-rens]

Flowers: Orange, yellow, and scarlet trumpets in June.

Fruit: Red in late summer.

Remarks: Relatively small-growing, use in sun or partial shade.

CHINA FLEECE-VINE: *Polygonum aubertii* [po-lig′-on-um
au′-ber-tee-eye]

Flowers: Showy, white in September.

Remarks: Large, rapid-growing, tender, roots survive, send up
new shoots in spring.

CLIMBING AND RAMBLER ROSES: Usually classified as twining
vines, but the stems need to be tied to or curved through the
fence or trellis support. They are very popular, and many
varieties are available, with a choice of flower color from
white to yellow, to several shades of pink and red.

JAPANESE WISTERIA: *Wisteria floribunda* [wiss-tee′-ree-ah
flo-ree-bun′-duh]

Flowers: Blue-violet in late May, white-flowering variety about
a week later.

Remarks: Large-growing, tender, needs protected location.

CHINESE WISTERIA: *Wisteria sinensis* [wiss-tee′-ree-ah si-nen′-sis]

Flowers: Same but darker than Japanese wisteria.

Remarks: Somewhat more tender than Japanese wisteria. Both
should be grafted plants with scions taken from a freely
blooming vine.

GROUP 1b. CLINGING VINES FOR MASONRY WALLS

Plant these wines where there is a large wall that would
be more attractive if it is partly covered with foliage. One
vine is adequate for a small wall. If a wide, unattractive wall
needs to be concealed, space the vines 15 or 20 feet apart.
Some may be used on a fence to enclose a lawn.

Deciduous

TRUMPET-CREEPER: *Campsis (Bignonia) radicans* [camp′-sis
ray-die′-cans]

Flowers: Large, orange trumpets in mid-July through August.

Remarks: Large-growing vine, rootlike holdfasts not strong enough to hold to wall without aid of straps or other support; successful on trellis or fence enclosing lawn or garden; shoots often sprout from roots; tender.

CLIMBING HYDRANGEA: *Hydrangea petiolaris* [high-dran'-gee-ah pet-ee-oh-lair'-is]
Flowers: Showy, white in early June.
Remarks: Excellent vine, should be used more often, probably tender.

VIRGINIA CREEPER: *Parthenocissus (Ampelopsis) quinquefolia* [par-then-oh-sis'-us kwin-kwi-foe'-lee-uh]
Leaves: Brilliant red in autumn.
Remarks: Large-growing, densely covers large wall or fence.

BOSTON IVY: *Parthenocissus (Ampelopsis) tricuspidata* [par-then-oh-sis'-us tri-cus-pih-day'-tuh]
Leaves: Dark red in autumn.
Remarks: Large-growing, densely covers large wall.

JAPANESE HYDRANGEA-VINE: *Schizophragma hydrangeoides* [shy-zoh-frag'-mah high-dran-gee-oh-eye'-des]
Remarks: Similar to climbing hydrangea, flowers about a month later.

Evergreen

BIG-LEAF WINTERCREEPER: *Euonymus fortunei (radicans) vegetus* [yew-on'-ih-mus for'-too-nee-eye veg'-ee-tus]
Leaves: Broad-leaf.
Fruit: Pink and orange clusters; remain on vine most of winter.
Remarks: Large-growing; rootlike holdfasts do not hold it without other support; used successfully on fence or trellis to enclose lawn or garden; tender; sometimes erroneously called "evergreen bittersweet." There are several varieties of wintercreeper, one of which has small leaves and is less rank in growth. It is BABY WINTERCREEPER: *Euonymus fortunei minimus* [min'-ee-mus].

ENGLISH IVY: *Hedera helix* [hed'-er-uh he'-lix]
Leaves: Broad-leaf.
Remarks: Large-growing; best in shady location such as north side of building; covers large wall spaces, but restricted by

pruning, it is successfully used to cover a foundation wall. Several varieties are available, of which *baltica* [ball'-tih-kuh] probably is the most hardy.

Group 2. Ground Covers

Ground covers are sold as clumps, as is true with common periwinkle, sometimes called myrtle; by age, as with vines; and by diameter spread of the branches, as with prostrate forms of juniper. The best spacing of ground covers varies considerably among the individuals listed here. Each plant is marked with numbers, such as 18"–3'–2'. The first figure (18") represents the distance to plant them from a wall; the second figure (3') represents the distance apart to plant them; and the third figure (2') the distance to plant them from a walk, drive, or lawn edge.

Deciduous

MEMORIAL ROSE: *Rosa wichuraiana* [roe'-zuh wich-ur-ih-ain'-uh] 18"–3'–2'
Leaves: Small, glossy, remain green until well into winter.
Flowers: White in mid-July, fragrant.
Remarks: Long, trailing stems densely cover ground; best in sun.

Evergreen

GOLDEN-TUFT: *Alyssum saxatile* [ah-liss'-um sax-at'-ill-ee] 18"–3'–2'
Leaves: Gray-green.
Flowers: Yellow in mid-May.
Remarks: Dense, best in sun.

ROSE DAPHNE: *Daphne cneorum* [daff'-nee nee-oh'-rum] 1'–2'–18"
Leaves: Light green.
Flowers: Pink in mid-May, fragrant.
Remarks: Protect in winter with evergreen boughs; hardy in most areas; does best in well-drained soil, sunny location.

COTTAGE PINK: *Dianthus plumarius* [die-an'-thus plu-may'-ree-us] 18"–3'–2'

Leaves: Gray-green.
Flowers: Fringed, white, or pink in mid-June, fragrant.
Remarks: Dense, best in full sun.

SHARPLEAF WINTERCREEPER: *Euonymus fortunei (radicans acutus)*
  2′–4′–3′ [yew-on′-ih-mus for′-too-nee-eye]
Leaves: Purplish underneath in winter.
Remarks: Dense, trailing, use in sun or shade.

BABY WINTERCREEPER: *Euonymus fortunei minimus*
  [yew-on′-ih-mus for′-too-nee-eye min′-ih-mus] 18″–3′–2′
Leaves: Small, dark, glossy green.
Remarks: Dense, will cling to wall; use in sun or shade.

ENGLISH IVY: *Hedera helix* [hed′-er-uh he′-lix] 18″–3′–2′
Leaves: Dark, glossy green.
Remarks: Dense, best in shady locations, will cling to wall,
  tender.

EDGING CANDYTUFT: *Iberis sempervirens* [eye-ber′-iss
  sem-per′-vee-rens] 8″–18″–12″
Flowers: Showy, white in May.
Remarks: Dense, sometimes used as edging for flower beds.

SARGENT JUNIPER: *Juniperus chinensis sargentii* [joo-nip′-er-us
  chi-nen′-sis sar′-gen-tee-eye] 2′–4′–3′
Leaves: Light, blue-green.
Remarks: Does best in full sun, tolerant of dry soil.

CREEPING JUNIPER: *Juniperus horizontalis* [joo-nip′-er-us
  hoh-rih-zon-tay′-liss] 2′–4′–3′
Leaves: Darker green than Sargent juniper.
Remarks: Does best in full sun, tolerant of dry soil.

WAUKEGAN JUNIPER: *Juniperus horizontalis douglasii*
  [joo-nip′-er-us hoh-rih-zon-tay′-liss doug′-las-ee-eye] 2′–4′–3′
Leaves: Blue-green.
Remarks: Does best in full sun, tolerant of dry soil.

TRUE LAVENDER: *Lavandula officinalis* [la-van′-due-lah
  oh-fiss-ih-nay′-lis] 8″–18″–12″
Leaves: Gray-green, fragrant.
Flowers: Lavender in late June, fragrant.
Remarks: Does best in full sun, tender.

HALL'S HONEYSUCKLE: *Lonicera japonica halliana* [low-niss'-er-uh ja-pon'-ih-cah hal-lee-ain'-uh] 3'–6'–5'
Leaves: Semievergreen.
Flowers: White in mid-June, fade yellow, fragrant.
Remarks: Best used on large banks; rank in growth and may be a nuisance if not controlled; use in sun or shade.

JAPANESE PACHYSANDRA: *Pachysandra terminalis* [pak-ih-san'-dra ter-mih-nay'-liss] 6–"12"–9"
Leaves: Light, yellow-green.
Flowers: White in early May.
Remarks: Grows best in shady places and high-organic soil.

MOSS-PINK: *Phlox subulata* [flox sub-u-lay'-tuh] 1'–2'–18"
Leaves: Small, yellow-green.
Flowers: White, pink, or purple in early May.
Remarks: Compact, grows well in sun or light shade.

COMMON PERIWINKLE, MYRTLE: *Vinca Minor* [vin'-ka my'-nor] 6"–12"–9"
Leaves: Dark green, glossy.
Flowers: Light blue in late April, some bloom throughout summer.
Remarks: Best in shade but tolerant of full sun; white- and purple-flowering varieties available.

Group 3. Low-growing Shrubs from 1½ to 3 Feet High

The low-growing plants listed here usually are classified in nursery catalogues by the height of the plant when purchased, but some of them may be classified by the spread of the branches. Most people buy plants about half their mature size. These shrubs may be used in appropriate places in foundation and border plantings.

The spacing for this group is indicated as for ground covers. The first figure represents the planting distance from a wall, the second figure the distance apart to plant them, and the third, the distance to plant them from a walk, drive, or lawn edge.

Deciduous

BOX BARBERRY: *Berberis thunbergii minor* [ber'-ber-is
thun'-ber-gee-eye my'-nor] 18"–3'–2'
Leaves: Small, bright red in autumn.
Fruit: Bright red in fall and winter.
Remarks: Like Japanese barberry but smaller-growing, tolerant
of shade.

NEW-JERSEY-TEA: *Ceanothus americanus* [see-ah-noh'-thus
ah-mair-ih-cay'-nus] 18"–3'–2'
Flowers: White in early July.
Remarks: Difficult to transplant successfully, usually sends up
new shoots from the roots in midsummer, definitely worth
having as it adds to our limited variety of low-growing shrubs.

DWARF JAPANESE QUINCE: *Chaenomeles japonica* [ky-nom-ell'-ees
ja-pon'-ih-cah] 18"–3'–2'
Leaves: Yellowish in autumn.
Flowers: Orange to red in early May.
Fruit: Yellow when ripe; used sparingly gives tart flavor to
apple jelly.
Remarks: Flower buds above snow line sometimes killed by late
frosts in Northern areas.

ROCK COTONEASTER: *Cotoneaster horizontalis* [coh-tone-ee-ass'-ter
hoh-rih-zon-tay'-liss] 18"–3'–2'
Leaves: Small, glossy, red in autumn.
Fruit: Abundant, red in late summer, effective well into winter.
Remarks: Tender, dense, horizontal branching.

BIG-FLOWER BROOM: *Cytisus supinus* [site'-ih-sus soo-pie'-nus]
18"–3'–2'
Flowers: Showy, yellow in mid-June.
Remarks: Green stems, tender.

SLENDER DEUTZIA: *Deutzia gracilis* [doot'-zee-uh grass'-ill-iss]
18"–3'–2'
Flowers: Showy, white in late May.
Remarks: Tender.

GOLDEN ST. JOHNSWORT: *Hypericum frondosum* [hy-pair'-ih-cum
fron-doe'-sum] 18"–3'–2'

Flowers: Showy, yellow in early July.
Remarks: Tender.

THIBETAN HONEYSUCKLE: *Lonicera thibetica* [low-niss'-er-uh
  ty-bet'-ih-kuh] 2'–4'–3'
Leaves: Small, whitish underneath.
Flowers: Small, lilac in mid-May.
Remarks: Low-rounded shape, tender.

SHRUBBY CINQUEFOIL: *Potentilla fruticosa* [poe-ten-till'-uh
  froo-tih-koh'-suh] 2'–4'–3'
Flowers: Showy, yellow, late May to mid-June.
Remarks: Does well in full sun, tolerant of shade, probably
  hardy. The variety *veitchii* [veetch'-ee-eye] similar, but has
  showy white flowers in June.

FLOWERING ALMOND: *Prunus glandulosa sinensis* [proo'-nus
  glan-du-low'-sah sy-nen'-sis] 18"–3'–2'
Flowers: Double, pink in mid-May.
Remarks: Good, old-fashioned plant, tender.

SCOTCH ROSE: *Rosa spinosissima* [roe'-suh spy-noh-siss'-sih-mah]
  2'–4'–3'
Flowers: Showy, white in late May.
Remarks: Available in pink- and yellow-flowering varieties.

ANTHONY WATERER SPIREA: *Spiraea bumalda anthony waterer*
  [spy-ree'-ah boo-mal'-duh an'-tho-nee wat'-ter-er] 18"–3'–2'
Leaves: Reddish in autumn.
Flowers: Pink-purplish in late June.
Remarks: Use in sun or light shade, white- and red-flowering
  varieties available.

CORAL-BERRY: *Symphoricarpos orbiculatus (vulgaris)*
  [sim-foe-rih-car'-pos or-bik-yew-lay'-tus] 18"–3'–2'
Fruit: Dark red in autumn and through the winter.
Remarks: Does well in full sun, tolerant of dense shade.

DWARF CRANBERRY-BUSH: *Viburnum opulus nanum* [vie-bur'-num
  oh'-pu-lus nay'-num] 18"–3'–2'
Leaves: Red in autumn.
Remarks: Dense, compact, globe-shaped.

Evergreen

JUNIPER: There are several varieties of low-growing junipers, two of which are listed here. They will do best in sunny locations and are tolerant of dry soil conditions.

PROSTRATE JUNIPER: *Juniperus communis saxatilis* [joo-nip'-er-us koh-mew'-niss sax-ah'-tee-liss] 2'–4'–3'
Leaves: Narrow, light blue-green.
Remarks: Wide, prostrate branching habit.

ANDORRA JUNIPER: *Juniperus horizontalis plumosa* [joo-nip'-er-us hoh-rih-zon-tay'-liss ploo-moe'-suh] 2'–4'–3'
Leaves: Narrow, blue-green in summer, beautiful dark purple in winter when exposed to full sun.

DROOPING LEUCOTHOE: *Leucothoe catesbaei* [loo-koh'-thoh-ee kates'-bee-eye] 2'–4'–3'
Leaves: Broad, bronze in winter when in full sun.
Flowers: Drooping, lily-of-valley-like white flowers in late May.
Remarks: Tender, best in high-organic, acid soil.

MOUNTAIN ANDROMEDA: *Pieris floribunda* [pie'-ee-ris floh-rih-bun'-duh] 2'–4'–3'
Leaves: Similar to mountain laurel but smaller.
Flowers: Upright, lily-of-valley-like, white in late April.
Remarks: Protect from sun and drying winds; best in high-organic, acid soil.

RHODODENDRON: The two rhododendrons listed here should be provided with the same growing conditions described for mountain andromeda.

DAPHNE RHODODENDRON: *Rhododendron arbutifolium* [roe-doe-den'-dron ar-bu-tih-foe'-lee-um] 2'–4'–3'
Flowers: Showy, rose in early June.

MYRTLE RHODODENDRON: *Rhododendron myrtifolium* [roe-doe-den'-dron mir-tih-foe'-lee-um] 2'–4'–3'
Flowers: Showy, light pink in early June.

GROUND-HEMLOCK, CANADA YEW: *Taxus canadensis* [tax'-us can-ah-den'-sis] 30''–5'–3'
Leaves: Narrow, dark green throughout the year.
Fruit: Red, use pistillate-flowering plants.

Remarks: Grows several feet in diameter, can be restricted by cutting side branches.

DWARF JAPANESE YEW: *Taxus cuspidata nana* [tax'-us cus-pih-day'-tuh nay'-nah] 2'–4'–3'
Leaves: Narrow, dark green throughout the year.
Fruit: Red, use pistillate-flowering plants.
Remarks: Dense, compact. The variety *densa* may be used instead. The spreading English yew is good but tender.

LITTLE GEM ARBORVITAE: *Thuja occidentalis pumila* [thoo'-yuh awk-sih-den-tay'-lis pum'-ih-lah] 18"–3'–2'
Leaves: Narrow, yellow-green, browns somewhat in winter.
Remarks: Dense, compact, globe-shaped, can be used as clipped specimen or hedge.

Group 4. Shrubs That Mature 4 to 5 Feet High

Shrubs in this size group usually are purchased about one-half their mature size, 2- to 2½-foot plants. Except where otherwise noted, all of them should be planted 2 feet from a wall, 4 feet apart, and 3 feet from a walk, drive, or lawn edge. The order of these numbers is the same as for ground covers.

Deciduous

BLACK CHOKEBERRY: *Aronia melanocarpa* [ah-roe'-nee-ah mel-an-oh-car'-pah]
Leaves: Glossy, dark red in autumn.
Fruit: Black in early fall, attractive to birds.
Remarks: Grows in moist woodlands, will do in well-prepared garden soil.

JAPANESE BARBERRY: *Berberis thunbergii* [ber'-ber-iss thun'-ber-gee-eye]
Leaves: Small, bright red in autumn.
Fruit: Bright red in fall and winter.
Remarks: Use in full sun or full shade.

BUTTERFLY-BUSH: *Buddleja davidii* [bud-lee'-ah day'-vid-ee-eye]
Flowers: Long, cylindrical, lilac in late July, fragrant.

Remarks: Open habit of growth, tender. Other varieties have purple, red, pink, or white flowers.

BEAUTY-BERRY: *Callicarpa dichotoma (purpurea)* [cal-lih-car′-pah dic-hoe′-toe-mah]
Flowers: Small, pink in August.
Fruit: Violet.
Remarks: Tender; stems die to ground in winter; new stems grow from root in spring.

HYBRID JAPANESE QUINCE: *Chaenomeles (Cydonia) superba* [ky-nom-ell′-ees soo-per′-bah]
Flowers: Showy, red in early May.
Fruit: Large, fleshy, yellow when ripe; small amount gives tart flavor to apple jelly.
Remarks: Flower buds above snow line sometimes killed by late frosts in Northern areas.

SPREADING COTONEASTER: *Cotoneaster divaricata* [coe-tone-ee-ass′-ter die-vare-ih-cay′-tah]
Leaves: Small, dark green, glossy, dark red in autumn.
Flowers: Small, pink.
Fruit: Abundant, red, late summer into winter, attractive to birds.
Remarks: Wide, rounded shape, tender.

FEBRUARY DAPHNE: *Daphne mezereum* [daff′-nee me-zee′-ree-um]
Leaves: Dark red in autumn.
Flowers: Purple, early April before the leaves.
Fruit: Red in midsummer, attractive to birds.
Remarks: Grows in moist woodlands, will do in well-prepared garden soil.

LEMOINE DEUTZIA: *Deutzia lemoinei* [doot′-zee-uh lee-moin′-ee-eye]
Flowers: Showy, white clusters in late May.
Remarks: Upright in growth, tender.

DROOPING GOLDEN-BELL: *Forsythia suspensa* [for-sith′-ee-ah sus-pen′-sah] 3′–5′–4′
Leaves: Yellow in autumn.
Flowers: Yellow in mid-April before the leaves.
Remarks: Best used on large, steep bank or at top of wall; flower buds above snow line sometimes killed by late frosts in Northern areas.

HILLS-OF-SNOW HYDRANGEA: *Hydrangea arborescens grandiflora*
[hy-dran'-gee-ah   are-bow-res'-cens   gran-dee-flo'-rah]
Leaves: Large, heart-shaped.
Flowers: Showy, snowball type in early July.
Remarks: Coarse texture; stems may die to the ground in
winter.

SHRUBBY ST. JOHNSWORT: *Hypericum prolificum*
[high-pare'-ih-cum   pro-liff'-ih-cum]
Leaves: Yellowish in autumn.
Flowers: Showy, yellow in early July.
Remarks: Tolerant of dry soil.

KERRIA: *Kerria japonica* [kair'-ee-ah   ja-pon'-ih-cah]
Leaves: Yellow in autumn.
Flowers: Showy, yellow in mid-May.
Remarks: Tender; slender twigs green throughout the year;
twigs often tip-killed in winter.

REGEL PRIVET: *Ligustrum obtusifolium (ibota) regelianum*
[lie-gus'-trum   ob-too-sih-foe'-lee-um   ree-gal-ee-ay'-num]
Leaves: Purplish in autumn.
Flowers: White clusters in mid-June, similar to lilac but smaller.
Fruit: Black clusters in fall throughout winter, attractive to
birds.
Remarks: Horizontal branching habit. Get plants propagated
vegetatively (from cuttings) from true Regel privet.

WOLF HONEYSUCKLE: *Lonicera syringantha wolfii* [low-niss'-er-ah
suh-ring-gan'-tha   wolf'-ee-eye]
Leaves: Small, dark green above, light gray beneath.
Flowers: Small, pink in mid-May, fragrant.
Fruit: Red in midsummer, attractive to birds.
Remarks: Rounded mass of arching branches, suitably planted
at top of low wall.

LEMOINE MOCK-ORANGE: *Philadelphus lemoinei* [phil-ah-del'-fus
lee-moin'-ee-eye]
Leaves: Yellowish in autumn.
Flowers: Showy, white in mid-June.
Remarks: Upright form; several Lemoine hybrids are available.

BEACH PLUM: *Prunus maritima* [proo'-nus   mair-ih'-tee-mah]
Flowers: White in early May.

Fruit: Purple in midsummer, useful for jam or jelly.
Remarks: Tolerant of dry soil.

AZALEAS: Only two of the most hardy azaleas are listed here. They grow best in a high-organic, acid soil and are tolerant of light shade. There are many hybrids available some of which are tender. They are a good subject for the plant hobbyist.

JAPANESE AZALEA: *Rhododendron (Azalea) japonicum* [row-doe-den'-dron ja-pon'-ih-cum]
Leaves: Reddish in autumn.
Flowers: Showy, salmon in late May.

PINXTER-FLOWER: *Rhododendron (Azalea) nudiflorum* [row-doe-den'-dron new-dih-floh'-rum]
Leaves: Yellowish in autumn.
Flowers: Pink to white in early May.

FRAGRANT SUMAC: *Rhus aromatica* [russ air-oh-mah'-tih-cah]
Leaves: Compound, three leaflets, dark red in autumn.
Flowers: Small, yellow in early May before the leaves.
Fruit: Clusters, red in midsummer, attractive to birds.
Remarks: Sprawling, tolerant of shade.

RUGOSA ROSE: *Rosa rugosa* [row'-sah roo-goh'-suh]
Leaves: Yellow in autumn.
Flowers: Showy, lavender-pink in mid-June.
Fruit: Large for rose hips, red in late autumn.
Remarks: Stems densely thorny.

WHITE RUGOSA ROSE: *Rosa rugosa alba* [row'-sah roo-goh'-suh al'-bah]
Remarks: Same as above but with white flowers.

VIRGINIA ROSE: *Rosa virginiana* [row'-sah vir-gin-ee-an'-uh]
Leaves: Red in autumn.
Flowers: Pink in early June.
Fruit: Red in late summer, attractive to birds.
Remarks: Red stems throughout the year, sparsely thorny.

URAL FALSE-SPIREA: *Sorbaria sorbifolia* [sore-bay'-ree-uh sore-bih-foe'-lee-ah]
Leaves: Long, compound.
Flowers: Large clusters, white in early July.
Remarks: Coarse texture, dense in summer, open branching in winter.

BILLIARD SPIREA: *Spiraea billiardii* [spi-ree'-ah bill-ih-ar'-dee-eye]
Leaves: Small, dark red in autumn.
Flowers: Pink in early July.
Remarks: Compact, upright branching.

THUNBERG SPIREA: *Spiraea thunbergii* [spi-ree'-ah
  thun'-ber-gee-eye]
Leaves: Small, reddish in autumn.
Flowers: Small but showy, white in early May.
Remarks: Fine texture, good background for flower border, ten-
  der; stem tips killed during winter in Northern areas.

CUT-LEAF STEPHANANDRA: *Stephanandra incisa* [steff-an-and'-rah
  in-size'-ah]
Leaves: Small, deeply lobed, yellowish in autumn.
Flowers: White in June.
Remarks: Graceful, arching branching habit, tender.

SNOWBERRY: *Symphoricarpos albus laevigatus (racemosus)*
  [sim-for-ih-car'-pos al'-bus lay-vih-gay'-tus]
Fruit: Showy, white in late summer.
Remarks: Dense, tolerant of shade.

DOCKMACKIE, MAPLE-LEAF VIBURNUM: *Viburnum acerifolium*
  [vie-bur'-num ay-cer-ih-foe'-lee-um]
Leaves: Purplish-red in autumn.
Flowers: Flat, creamy-white clusters in mid-May.
Fruit: Clusters, black in late summer, attractive to birds.
Remarks: Open habit of growth.

BURKWOOD VIBURNUM: *Viburnum burkwoodii* [vie-bur'-num
  burk'-wood-ee-eye]
Leaves: Dark red in autumn.
Flowers: Pink in bud, white when expanded in mid-May,
  fragrant.
Remarks: Tender.

FRAGRANT VIBURNUM: *Viburnum carlesii* [vie-bur'-num
  kar'-leez-ee-eye]
Leaves: Dark red in autumn.
Flowers: Pink in bud, white when expanded, very fragrant.
Remarks: Hardy, own-root plants are best. Grafted plants
  usually produce sucker shoots which, if not cut off, will crowd
  out the more desirable shrub.

EVA RATHKE WEIGELA: *Weigela eva rathke* [wye-gee'-lah eve'-ah rath'-kuh]
Leaves: Dark red in autumn.
Flowers: Red in late June.
Remarks: Probably tender; several different varieties are available.

Evergreen

PFITZER JUNIPER: *Juniperus chinensis pfitzeriana* [joo-nip'-er-us chi-nen'-sis fit-zer-ih-an'-ah] 3'–6'–4'
Leaves: Narrow, gray-green throughout the year.
Remarks: Horizontal branching when young, wide pyramid when old.

SAVIN JUNIPER: *Juniperus sabina* [joo-nip'-er-us sah-bye'-nah]
Leaves: Narrow, blue-green, sharp-pointed.
Remarks: Upright, vase-shape.

MOUNTAIN-LAUREL: *Kalmia latifolia* [kal'-mee-ah lat-ih-foe'-lee-ah]
Leaves: Broad, dark green.
Flowers: Pink bud, white flower clusters in mid-June.
Remarks: Best in high-organic, acid soil, and in shade.

HOLLY MAHONIA: *Mahonia aquifolium* [mah-hoe'-nee-ah ak-wih-foe'-lee-um]
Leaves: Broad, compound, bronze in winter.
Flowers: Yellow clusters in early May.
Fruit: Blue clusters in midsummer.
Remarks: Tender, give protected location.

MUGO PINE: *Pinus mugo mughus (montana mughus)* [pie'-nus mu'-go mu'-gus]
Leaves: Narrow, two in bundle, stiff, twisted.
Remarks: Get plants propagated vegetatively from a true specimen.

CAROLINA RHODODENDRON: *Rhododendron carolinianum* [roe-doe-den'-dron care-oh-lie-nee-an'-num]
Leaves: Broad, dark green.
Flowers: Showy, pink in mid-May.
Remarks: Best in high-organic, acid soil and protected location; several different varieties are available; tender.

SHRUB JAPANESE YEW: *Taxus cuspidata* [tax'-us cus-pih-day'-tah]
 3'–6'–4'
Leaves: Narrow, dark green throughout the year.
Fruit: Red in autumn, attractive to birds.
Remarks: Tolerant of shade; get plants propagated vegetatively
 from fruiting stock.

WARE ARBORVITAE: *Thuja occidentalis robusta (wareana)*
 [thoo'-yah ox-ih-den-tay'-liss roe-bus'-tah]
Leaves: Narrow, scalelike.
Remarks: Several similar varieties are available.

Group 5. Shrubs That Mature 6 to 8 Feet High

Shrubs in this size group usually are purchased as 2½- to
3-foot plants. All those listed here should be spaced 3 feet
from a wall, 5 feet apart, and 4 feet from a walk, drive, or
lawn edge, unless otherwise noted by three numbers following the name of the plant. These numbers are in the order
given above.

JAPANESE MAPLE: *Acer palmatum* [a'-sir pal-may'-tum]
Leaves: Deeply lobed, green in summer, red in autumn.
Remarks: Several varieties are available, some with deeply cut
 leaves; some remain red all summer.

RED CHOKEBERRY: *Aronia arbutifolia* [ah-roe'-nee-ah
 are-bu-tee-foe'-lee-ah]
Leaves: Small, glossy, red in autumn.
Flowers: Small, white in mid-May.
Fruit: Red in late summer, attractive to birds.
Remarks: Tolerant of wet locations.

COMMON BARBERRY: *Berberis vulgaris* [ber'-ber-iss vul-gare'-iss]
Leaves: Dark red in autumn.
Flowers: Yellow clusters in late May.
Fruit: Red clusters in late summer, attractive to birds.
Remarks: Stems have thorns. This, as well as the purple-leaved
 form, are alternate hosts to wheat rust and should not be
 planted in wheat-growing regions.

CAROLINA ALLSPICE, SWEET-SHRUB: *Calycanthus floridus*
[cal-ih-can′-thus flor′-ih-dus]
Leaves: Yellowish in autumn, sweet-scented when crushed.
Flowers: Interesting, reddish-brown, May to July, fragrant.
Remarks: Good old-fashioned shrub, tender, sometimes called
  "pineapple shrub."

JAPANESE QUINCE: *Chaenomeles lagenaria (Cydonia japonica)*
[ky-nom-ell′-ees lah-gen-a′-ree-ah]
Flowers: Red in early May.
Fruit: Green with some red; used in small quantities to give tart
  flavor to apple jelly.
Remarks: Flower buds above snow line sometimes killed by
  late frosts in Northern areas; several different varieties
  available.

SUMMER SWEET, SWEET PEPPERBUSH: *Clethra alnifolia* [klee′-thra
al-nih-foe′-lee-ah]
Leaves: Brown in autumn.
Flowers: White, upright clusters in late July, spice-scented.
Fruit: Brown, upright clusters all winter, seeds attractive to
  birds.
Remarks: Tolerant of moist soil.

SHRUB DOGWOODS: The shrub dogwoods are among the best of
  our woody flowering plants, as they have long seasons of interest: in flower, in fruit, in autumn color, and some with bright
  stem color. Those listed here all have dark red autumn color
  and are tolerant of wet soil. The fruit of these shrubs is attractive to birds.

TATARIAN DOGWOOD: *Cornus alba* [kor′-nus al′-bah]
Flowers: White flat clusters in early June.
Fruit: White clusters in late summer.
Stems: Bright red throughout the year.
Remarks: Other varieties available.

SILKY DOGWOOD: *Cornus amomum* [kor′-nus am-moe′-mum]
Flowers: White flat clusters in late June.
Fruit: Light-blue flat clusters in late summer.
Stems: Dark red throughout the year.

GRAY DOGWOOD: *Cornus racemosa (paniculata)* [kor′-nus
ray-see-moe′-sah]

Flowers: White clusters in mid-June.

Fruit: White clusters on bright red fruit stalks, showy well into winter.

RED-OSIER DOGWOOD: *Cornus stolonifera* [kor'-nus stow-lon-if'-er-ah]

Flowers: White flat clusters in late May.

Fruit: White clusters in late summer.

Stems: Red throughout the year.

Remarks: A yellow-stemmed variety, *flaviramea* [flah-vir-am'-ee-ah], is available.

WINGED EUONYMUS: *Euonymus alatus* [yew-on'-ih-mus ah-lay'-tus] 3½'–6'–4½'

Leaves: Brilliant red in autumn.

Fruit: Small, scarlet-orange, in clusters, stay on plant most of winter.

Stems: Interesting corky wings.

Remarks: Horizontal branching.

PEARL-BUSH: *Exochorda racemosa (grandiflora)* [ex-oh-cord'-ah ray-cee-moe'-suh]

Leaves: Brown in autumn.

Flowers: Showy, white clusters in mid-May.

Remarks: Grown in tree or shrub form.

SHOWY FORSYTHIA: *Forsythia intermedia spectabilis* [for-sith'-ee-ah in-ter-mee'-dih-ah spec-tab'-ih-liss]

Leaves: Reddish or yellowish in autumn.

Flowers: Showy, yellow in mid-April before the leaves.

Remarks: Upright habit of growth; flower buds killed by late frosts in the North; other varieties available.

SHRUB-ALTHEA: *Hibiscus syriacus* [hi-bis'-cus see-rye'-ah-cus] 2½'–4½'–3'

Leaves: Yellowish-green in autumn.

Flowers: Rose to purple in late July.

Remarks: Upright in growth habit; several varieties available with flowers; lavender, white, or blue, single or double.

WINTERBERRY, BLACK-ALDER: *Ilex verticillata* [eye'-lex ver-tiss-ih-lay'-tah]

Leaves: Yellow in autumn.

Fruit: Bright red, useful in Christmas decorations.

Remarks: Sexes separate; use four or five fruiting plants to one male plant; best in wet soil.

DOUBLE KERRIA: *Kerria japonica pleniflora* [kair'-ree-ah ja-pon'-ih-cah plee-nih-flo'-rah]
Leaves: Yellow in autumn.
Flowers: Showy, double in late May.
Stems: Bright green throughout the year.
Remarks: Stems may be tip-killed during the winter.

SPICE-BUSH: *Lindera benzoin (Benzoin aestivale)* [lin-dee'-rah ben'-zoe-in]
Leaves: Yellow in autumn.
Flowers: Yellow in mid-April before the leaves.
Fruit: Red in midsummer, attractive to birds.
Remarks: Sexes separate; use same as winterberry; best in wet soil.

HONEYSUCKLE: There are several honeysuckles that could be listed in this size group. They are good fillers in border plantings and are occasionally used in foundation plantings. The fruit, usually red but sometimes yellow or orange, ripens in late summer and is attractive to birds.

WINTER HONEYSUCKLE: *Lonicera fragrantissima* [low-niss'-er-ah fray-gran-tiss'-ih-mah]
Leaves: Green in autumn, semievergreen.
Flowers: Fragrant, white in early April, before the leaves.
Remarks: Tender.

MORROW HONEYSUCKLE: *Lonicera Morrowii* [low-niss'-er-ah more'-row-ee-eye] 4'–6'–5'
Leaves: Yellowish in autumn.
Flowers: White in late May, fade yellow.
Remarks: Wider than high.

BAYBERRY: *Myrica pensylvanica* [mee-rye'-cah pen-sill-van'-ih-cah]
Leaves: Glossy, brown in autumn.
Fruit: Gray, remain on plant all winter, used in Christmas and other house decorations.
Remarks: Sexes separate; use fruiting plants; grows well either in light or heavy soils.

JETBEAD: *Rhodotypos tetrapetala* [row-doe'-tie-pos tet-rah-pet'-ah-lah]
Leaves: Greenish in autumn.
Flowers: Showy, white in mid-May.
Fruit: Shiny, black in tight clusters; stays on all winter.
Remarks: Dense, broad, rounded form.

MISSOURI CURRANT: *Ribes odoratum* [rye'-bees oh-doe-ray'-tum]
Leaves: Greenish in autumn.
Flowers: Yellow in early May, spicy fragrance.
Remarks: Good old-fashioned shrub, tolerant of shade, alternate host to white-pine blister rust.

ROSE ACACIA: *Robinia hispida* [roe-bin'-ee-ah his'-pih-dah]
Leaves: Greenish in autumn.
Flowers: Showy, rose in late May.
Remarks: Sprawling, open growth; may sucker badly from roots.

HARISONS YELLOW ROSE: *Rosa harisonii* [roe'-sah ha'-rih-so-nee-eye]
Leaves: Greenish in autumn.
Flowers: Showy, double yellow in early June.
Remarks: Good old-fashioned shrub; may sucker from roots.

HUGO ROSE: *Rosa hugonis* [roe'-sah hue-go'-niss]
Leaves: Greenish in autumn.
Flowers: Showy, single yellow in late May.
Remarks: Similar to Harison's yellow rose; stems very thorny.

JAPANESE ROSE: *Rosa multiflora* [roe'-sah mul-tih-floe'-rah]
Leaves: Greenish in autumn.
Flowers: Showy, white in early June.
Remarks: Recommended by some conservation specialists for "living fences." Does well in good soil, not well in poor soil.

AMERICAN ELDER, ELDERBERRY: *Sambucus canadensis* [sam-bue'-cus can-ah-den'-sis]
Leaves: Yellow in autumn.
Flowers: Large, flat, white clusters in late June.
Fruit: Large, flat, black clusters in late summer, attractive to birds, used in various ways for human consumption.
Remarks: Does well in wet soil.

AMERICAN RED ELDER: *Sambucus pubens* [sam-bue'-cus
pew'-bens]
Leaves: Yellowish in autumn.
Flowers: Showy, creamy-white in mid-May.
Fruit: Red in late June with flower of American elder.
Remarks: Does well in wet soil.

BRIDAL WREATH: *Spiraea prunifolia plena* [spy-ree'-ah
proo-nih-foe'-lee-ah plee'-nah]
Leaves: Dark red in autumn.
Flowers: Showy, double white in early May.
Remarks: Fine old-fashioned shrub.

VANHOUTTE SPIREA: *Spiraea vanhouttei* [spy-ree'-ah
van-hou'-tee-eye]
Leaves: Dark red in autumn.
Flowers: Showy, white clusters in late May.
Remarks: Fine plant but much overused.

CHINESE LILAC: *Syringa chinensis* [see-ring'-ga chi-nen'-sis]
4'–6'–5'
Leaves: Greenish in autumn.
Flowers: Showy, rose-lavender in late May.
Remarks: Dense, shrub-form. White-flowering variety is available.

VIBURNUM: These are among the best of our woody, flowering
shrubs as they have a long season of interest, in flower, fruit,
and rich, red autumn color. The fruit is attractive to birds.

WITHE-ROD: *Viburnum cassinoides* [vie-bur'-num
cas-in-oh-eye'-des]
Flowers: Showy, flat clusters, white in mid-June.
Fruit: Flat clusters, green, changing to red and black.
Remarks: Tolerant of moist soil.

ARROW-WOOD: *Viburnum dentatum* [vie-bur'-num den-tay'-tum]
Flowers: Showy, flat clusters, white in early June.
Fruit: Flat clusters, black in late summer.
Remarks: Tolerant of moist soil, upright in growth.

LINDEN VIBURNUM: *Viburnum dilatatum* [vie-bur'-num
dil-ah-tay'-tum]
Flowers: Flat clusters, showy, white in early June.

Fruit: Flat clusters, red in late summer.
Remarks: Tender.

EUROPEAN CRANBERRY-BUSH: *Viburnum opulus* [vie-bur'-num
  oh'-poo-lus]
Flowers: Interesting, showy, flat clusters, white in early June.
Fruit: Drooping red clusters in autumn through the winter.

SNOWBALL: *Viburnum opulus roseum (sterile)* [vie-bur'-num
  oh'-poo-lus roe'-zee-um]
Flowers: Showy, snowball type, white in late May.
Remarks: Badly attacked by aphids.

JAPANESE SNOWBALL: *Viburnum plicatum (tomentosum sterile)*
  [vie'-bur-num ply-cay'-tum] 4'–6'–5'
Flowers: Showy, snowball type, white in late May.
Remarks: Not attacked by aphids.

DOUBLEFILE VIBURNUM: *Viburnum plicatum tomentosum*
  [vie-bur'-num ply-cay'-tum toe-men-toe'-sum] 4'–6'–5'
Flowers: Interesting, showy, flat clusters, white in late May.
Remarks: Horizontal branching habit, may be tender.

AMERICAN CRANBERRY-BUSH: *Viburnum trilobum (americanum)*
  [vie-bur'-num tril'-oh-bum]
Flowers: Showy, flat, white clusters in early June.
Fruit: Flat clusters, red; stay on shrub most of winter.
Remarks: Like European cranberry-bush.

Evergreens

RHODODENDRON [roe-doe-den'-dron]. The broad-leaved evergreen rhododendrons have been hybridized extensively, and
  many kinds are available, with flower colors ranging from
  white to pink, magenta, and red. Many of them should be
  listed in this size group, 6 to 8 feet high. A few are larger and
  a few smaller. They will all do best in a high organic, acid
  soil and, in the North, where they are protected from the winter sun.

HATFIELD YEW: *Taxus media hatfieldii* [tax'-us mee'-dee-ah
  hat'-field-ee-eye]
Leaves: Narrow, dark green throughout the year.

Fruit: Red, get plants propagated vegetatively from heavily fruiting stock.
Remarks: Upright in growth.

Group 6. Large Shrubs and Small Trees That Mature 8 to 15 Feet High

The plants in this size group usually are purchased as 3- to 4-foot plants, although they may be obtained either larger or smaller. Most of them may be kept in tree form by cutting off, at the base, all except two to perhaps five of the main branches. All those listed here should be spaced 4 feet from a wall, 6 feet apart, and 5 feet from a walk, drive, or lawn edge, unless otherwise noted by three numbers following the name of the plant. These numbers are in the order given above.

Deciduous

SMOKE-TREE: *Cotinus coggygria (Rhus cotinus)* [coe′-tin-us cog-gig′-ree-ah]
Leaves: Usually red, sometimes yellow in autumn.
Flowers: Fluffy, creamy, white clusters in mid-July.
Fruit: Showy, fluffy, purple clusters in mid-August.
Remarks: Use pistillate-flowering (fruiting) plants.

WAHOO: *Euonymus atropurpureus* [yew-on′-ih-mus at-roe-pur-pur′-ee-us]
Leaves: Red in autumn.
Fruit: Scarlet, remains on shrub well into winter.
Remarks: Tolerant of moist soil and partial shade.

AMUR PRIVET: *Ligustrum amurense* [lie-gus′-trum am-moor-en′-see]
Leaves: Purplish in autumn.
Flowers: White clusters in late June.
Fruit: Black clusters in late summer, attractive to birds.
Remarks: Upright in growth, often used for clipped hedge.

HONEYSUCKLE: There are several honeysuckles that might be listed in this size group.

LATE HONEYSUCKLE: *Lonicera maackii podocarpa* [low-niss'-er-ah
mack'-ee-eye poe-doe-car'-pah] 5'–8'–6'
Leaves: Greenish in autumn.
Flowers: Pink in early June.
Fruit: Red in late summer, attractive to birds.
Remarks: Dense, wide branching habit.

TATARIAN HONEYSUCKLE: *Lonicera tatarica* [low-niss'-er-ah
ta-tar'-ih-cah] 5'–8'–6'
Leaves: Dark purplish in autumn.
Flowers: Pink in late May.
Fruit: Red in midsummer, attractive to birds.
Remarks: Dense, upright in growth.

MOCK-ORANGE: There are several other mock-oranges that might
be listed in this size group.

SWEET MOCK-ORANGE: *Philadelphus coronarius* [fill-ah-del'-fus
coe-roe-nay'-ree-us]
Leaves: Yellow in autumn.
Flowers: Showy, white in early June, sweet-scented.
Remarks: Upright in growth habit, the old-fashioned kind,
sometimes incorrectly called "syringa."

LARGE-FLOWERED MOCK-ORANGE: *Philadelphus grandiflorus*
[fill-ah-del'-fus gran-dee-floe'-rus]
Remarks: Similar to sweet mock-orange, but with larger flowers
about a week later, only slightly sweet-scented.

VIRGINAL MOCK-ORANGE: *Philadelphus virginalis* [fill-ah-del'-fus
vir-gin-nay'-liss]
Remarks: Similar to sweet mock-orange, but with double or
semidouble flowers only slightly sweet-scented.

FRENCH HYBRID LILACS: These hybrids are showy in flower with
singles and doubles and ranges of flower color from white to
blue, lavender, and shades of pink to deep purple. Hundreds
of named varieties have been produced, but two or three of
each color range will satisfy all except the lilac hobbyist.

LATE LILAC: *Syringa villosa* [suh-ring'-gah vil-low'-sah]
Leaves: Yellowish in autumn.

Flowers: Showy, lilac-lavender in early June, sweet-scented.
Remarks: Extends the lilac flowering season.

COMMON LILAC: *Syringa vulgaris* [suh-ring'-gah vul-gare'-iss]
Leaves: Yellowish in autumn.
Flowers: Showy, lavender in late May, sweet-scented.
Remarks: Fine old-fashioned shrub. A white-flowering variety is
   available.

WAYFARING-TREE: *Viburnum lantana* [vie-bur'-num lan-tan'-ah]
Leaves: Dark red in autumn.
Flowers: Showy, flat, white clusters in mid-May.
Remarks: Dense, long season of interest as with other viburnums.

Evergreen

THREAD RETINISPORA, CYPRESS: *Chamaecyparis pisifera filifera*
   [cam-eye-cip'-ah-riss pie-sif'-er-ah fie-lif'-er-ah]
Leaves: Narrow, overlapping scales like arborvitae.
Remarks: Grows with central leader in a wide-base pyramid,
   tender.

COLUMN CHINESE JUNIPER: *Juniperus chinensis columnaris*
   [joo-nip'-er-us chi-nen'-sis co-lum-nay'-riss]
Leaves: Narrow, light blue-green.
Remarks: Dense, narrow, upright form.

UPRIGHT JAPANESE YEW: *Taxus cuspidata capitata* [tax'-us
   cus-pih-day'-tah cap-ih-tay'-tah] 5'-8'-6'
Leaves: Narrow, dark blue-green throughout the year.
Fruit: Red in late summer.
Remarks: Dense, grows with central leader, wide-base pyramid
   form, sometimes used as clipped hedge, tolerant of shade.

HICKS YEW: *Taxus media hicksii* [tax'-us mee'-dee-ah
   hick'-see-eye] 2'-4'-3'
Remarks: Same as upright Japanese yew, except that it branches
   from the base and grows in a narrow, upright form.

PYRAMIDAL ARBORVITAE: *Thuja occidentalis douglasii pyramidalis*
   [thoo'-yuh awk-sih-den-tay'-liss dug'-lass-ee-eye
   pyr-ah-mid-day'-liss] 2'-4'-3'
Leaves: Narrow, scalelike, yellow-green.
Remarks: Dense, narrow, upright form; use in sun or shade.

Group 7. Small Trees That Mature from 15 to 30 Feet High

These small trees usually are purchased from 5 to 10 feet high. They should be used sparingly and carefully in any foundation planting near large buildings but occasionally may be used near small homes to shade a sunny window or entrance or to form a part of a corner planting. In border plantings, they are used to frame a good view, screen an objectionable view, or give an interesting variation in height.

The spacing of these plants varies considerably according to the desired effect. Usually they would be planted from 6 to 8 feet from a wall but may be a little nearer if necessary. Branches that begin to rub the side of the house may be pruned back. When set from 2 to 3 feet apart, they crowd each other, often producing a picturesque group with curving trunks and branches. Spacing them from 10 to 15 feet apart produces more normal-shaped plants. So, when using small trees in a foundation planting, set them according to the available space and according to the desired effect. They may be planted within 3 feet of a walk or driveway, provided the lower branches are cut off to allow head room or car room. A usual spacing from a walk or driveway is about 12 feet.

Frequently, single trees from this size group, or groups of them, are planted 15 or more feet from a corner of a house with good results. Because there is considerable variance in the distance that these trees may be spaced, your own preference will determine your choice.

Some of the plants listed here occasionally grow in shrub form. They may be kept in tree form by cutting off most of the main branches at the base.

Deciduous

AMUR MAPLE: *Acer ginnala* [a'-sir gin'-nay-lah]
Leaves: Small, bright red in early autumn.

Remarks: May be used as clipped hedge or a shade tree along narrow streets, tender.

STRIPED MAPLE: *Acer pensylvanicum* [a'-sir pen-sil-vah'-nee-cum]
Leaves: Large, bright yellow in autumn.
Remarks: Vertical, white stripes in green bark, good winter effect, does well in shade.

SHADBLOW: *Amelanchier laevis* [am-ee-lan'-chi-er lee'-vis]
Leaves: Red in autumn.
Flowers: Showy, white in early May before the leaves.
Fruit: Red in June, attractive to birds.
Remarks: Best used in front of dark background; other varieties and species are available.

PAPAW: *Asimina triloba* [ah-sim'-ih-nah trill'-oh-bah]
Leaves: Large, yellow in autumn.
Flowers: Large, purple, before the leaves.
Fruit: Large, fleshy, edible.
Remarks: Somewhat tropical in character, may be tender.

SIBERIAN PEA-TREE: *Caragana arborescens* [care-ah-gay'-nah are-boe-res'-ens]
Leaves: Small, lacy, yellow to brown in autumn.
Flowers: Pealike, yellow in mid-May.
Fruit: Brown capsule, interesting but not attractive.
Remarks: Tolerant of adverse growing conditions.

AMERICAN HORNBEAM: *Carpinus caroliniana* [car-pie'-nus care-oh-lie-nee-a'-nah]
Leaves: Reddish in autumn.
Remarks: Smooth, ridged bark, interesting, tolerant of shade.

KATSURA-TREE: *Cercidiphyllum japonicum* [sir-sid-ih-fil'-um ja-pon'-ih-cum]
Leaves: Small, heart-shaped, yellow in autumn.
Remarks: Dense, round form, tender.

REDBUD, JUDAS-TREE: *Cercis canadensis* [sur'-siss can-ah-den'-sis]
Leaves: Heart-shaped, yellow in autumn.
Flowers: Purple in mid-May, before the leaves.
Remarks: Flower buds sometimes killed by late frosts, tender. White-flowering form available.

FRINGE-TREE: *Chionanthus virginica* [kye-oh-nan'-thus vir-gin'-ih-cah]

Leaves: Yellow in autumn.
Flowers: Lacy, white in early June.
Remarks: Tender.

FLOWERING DOGWOOD: *Cornus florida* [kor'-nus floe'-ree-dah]
Leaves: Bright red in autumn.
Flowers: Showy, white in mid-May.
Fruit: Red in late summer, attractive to birds.
Remarks: Interesting, horizontal branching habit, tender. Variety *rubra* has pink flowers.

KOUSA DOGWOOD: *Cornus kousa* [kor'-nus koo'-sah]
Leaves: Red in autumn.
Flowers: White in early June.
Fruit: Not so showy as flowering dogwood.
Remarks: Similar to flowering dogwood but later-flowering, tender.

CORNELIAN CHERRY:*Cornus mas* [kor'-nus mass]
Leaves: Red in autumn.
Flowers: Small, but effective in front of dark background, yellow in early April before the leaves.
Fruit: Red, showy; have been used for making jam.
Remarks: Probably more hardy than flowering dogwood.

HAWTHORN, THORNAPPLE: Several species and varieties of hawthorns are available at many nurseries. They are frequently used in border plantings where dense foliage masses are desirable and are satisfactorily used as a clipped hedge. The red fruit produced is attractive to birds.

COCKSPUR THORN: *Crataegus crus galli* [crah-tee'-gus crus gall'-lee]
Leaves: Reddish in autumn.
Flowers: White in early June.

DOWNY HAWTHORN: *Crataegus mollis* [crah-tee'-gus mol'-liss]
Leaves: Reddish in autumn.
Flowers: White in early June.
Fruit: Red, larger than most other hawthorns.

ENGLISH HAWTHORN: *Crataegus oxyacantha* [crah-tee'-gus ox-ee-ah-can'-tha]
Leaves: Glossy, small, brownish in autumn.
Flowers: White in early June.

Remarks: Several varieties are available with white, pink, or scarlet flowers, some with double flowers. The double-flowering varieties are very showy but do not bear fruit.

WASHINGTON THORN: *Crataegus phaenopyrum* [crah-tee′-gus fee-no-pie′-rum]
Leaves: Red in autumn.
Flowers: White in early June.
Fruit: Red in late summer and stay on plant all winter.

GREAT SILVER-BELL: *Halesia carolina (tetraptera)* [ha-lee′-zee-ah ca-roe-line′-ah]
Leaves: Yellow in autumn.
Flowers: Unusual white bells in mid-May.
Remarks: Tender.

GOLDENRAIN-TREE: *Koelreuteria paniculata* [coal-roo-tee′-ree-ah pa-nic-u-lay′-tah]
Leaves: Yellowish in autumn.
Flowers: Large, upright clusters, yellow in mid-July.
Fruit: Large, upright clusters, yellow in late summer.
Remarks: Dense, tender.

SCOTCH LABURNUM: *Laburnum alpinum* [lah-bur′-num al-pie′-num]
Leaves: Small, lacy, greenish in autumn.
Flowers: Drooping, pealike, yellow in late May.
Remarks: Tender.

SAUCER MAGNOLIA: *Magnolia soulangeana* [mag-no′-lee-ah soo-lan-gee-a′-nah]
Leaves: Large, yellowish in autumn.
Flowers: Large, pink in bud, turning white when open in early May.
Remarks: Tender.

STARRY MAGNOLIA: *Magnolia stellata* [mag-no′-lee-ah stel-lay′-tah]
Leaves: Medium in size, yellowish in autumn.
Flowers: Medium in size, white in early May.
Remarks: Tender.

FLOWERING CRABS: *Malus* [may′-lus]. Many species and varieties of flowering crabs are available. Their main qualification for attention is their showy display of flowers, single and double, white, pink, and purplish. They bloom during the last half of May.

FLOWERING CHERRIES: *Prunus* [proo'-nus]. Many species and varieties of flowering cherries are available. They have about the same range of flower color as the flowering crabs but bloom a little earlier, from late April to the middle of May.

PUSSY WILLOW: *Salix discolor* [say'-lix dis'-color]
Leaves: Yellowish in autumn.
Flowers: Interesting, hairy catkins in early April.
Remarks: Grows best in moist soil, tolerant of drier soil.

SASSAFRAS: *Sassafras albidum* [sass'-ih-fras al'-bih-dum]
Leaves: Variously colored but usually yellow in autumn, shaped with different lobing.
Remarks: In some situations grows to be a large tree with picturesque branching habit.

MOUNTAIN-ASH: *Sorbus americana* [sore'-bus ah-mair-ih-can'-ah]
Leaves: Yellow in autumn.
Flowers: Large, white clusters in late May.
Fruit: Large, orange clusters in autumn and early winter, attractive to birds.
Remarks: If this tree does not succumb to borer attack, it may grow larger than should be listed in this size group. Other species are available.

JAPANESE TREE LILAC: *Syringa amurensis japonica* [suh-ring'-gah ah-moor-en'-sis ja-pon'-ih-cah]
Leaves: Yellowish in autumn.
Flowers: Showy, white clusters in mid-June, not fragrant.
Remarks: One of the largest-growing hardy lilacs.

NANNY-BERRY: *Viburnum lentago* [vie-bur'-num len-tay'-go]
Leaves: Dark red in autumn.
Flowers: Showy, flat, white clusters in late May.
Fruit: Drooping, black clusters in late summer, attractive to birds.
Remarks: Upright in growth, tolerant of shade.

BLACK-HAW: *Viburnum prunifolium* [vie-bur'-num proo-nih-foe'-lee-um]
Leaves: Bright red in autumn.
Flowers: Showy, flat clusters, white in late May.

Fruit: Flat clusters, black in late summer, attractive to birds.
Remarks: Horizontal branching habit, tolerant of shade.

Evergreens

CHINESE JUNIPER: *Juniperus chinensis* [joo-nip'-er-us chi-nen'-sis]
Leaves: Narrow, sharply pointed, blue-green.
Remarks: Tolerant of dry soil, several varieties available, some narrow and columnar in shape, others a wide-base pyramid shape.

RED-CEDAR: *Juniperus virginiana* [joo-nip'-er-us vir-gin-ih-an'-ah]
Leaves: Narrow, dark green.
Remarks: Same as Chinese juniper.

JACK PINE: *Pinus banksiana* [pie'-nus bank-see-an'-ah]
Leaves: Narrow, two in bundle, short, stiff, and twisted.
Remarks: Irregular, curving branching, picturesque.

SWISS STONE PINE: *Pinus cembra* [pie'-nus sem'-bra]
Leaves: Narrow, long, dark green, five in bundle.
Remarks: Dense, regular in branching habit, slow in growth; may eventually grow beyond this size group.

SWISS MOUNTAIN PINE: *Pinus mugo (montana)* [pie'-nus mu'-go]
Leaves: Narrow, short, sharp-pointed, two in bundle.
Remarks: Branches from base, forming rounded outline. See *Pinus mugo mughus* for dwarf form.

AMERICAN ARBORVITAE: *Thuja occidentalis* [thoo'-yuh awk-sih-den-tay'-liss]
Leaves: Narrow, scalelike, dark green to yellow-green, usually browns in winter sunlight.
Remarks: Grows best in moist soil and shaded location. Frequently used as a clipped hedge.

A Few of the Best Plants for Clipped Hedges

The smaller-growing plants may be set 18 inches apart and about 12 to 15 inches from the property line, the medium-sized ones about 2 feet apart and 2 feet from a property line, and the tall ones about 3 feet apart and about 2½ feet from the property line.

Low hedges from 1½ to 3 feet high

JAPANESE BARBERRY: *Berberis thunbergii*
BOX BARBERRY: *Berberis thunbergii minor*
REGEL PRIVET: *Ligustrum obtusifolium regelianum*
DWARF NINEBARK: *Physocarpus opulifolius nanus*
DWARF CRANBERRY-BUSH: *Viburnum opulus nanum*
JAPANESE YEW: *Taxus cuspidata* (evergreen)
DWARF JAPANESE YEW: *Taxus cuspidata densa* and *nana* (evergreens)

Medium hedges from 4 to 5 feet high

WINGED EUONYMUS: *Euonymus alatus*
AMUR PRIVET: *Ligustrum amurense*
THREAD RETINISPORA: *Chamaecyparis pisifera filifera* (evergreen)

Tall hedges 5 feet and more

HAWTHORN: *Crataegus* in variety
ALDER BUCKTHORN: *Rhamnus frangula*
COMMON LILAC: *Syringa vulgaris*
CHINESE LILAC: *Syringa chinensis*
DOUGLAS FIR: *Pseudotsuga taxifolia* (evergreen)
AMERICAN ARBORVITAE: *Thuja occidentalis* (evergreen)
CANADA HEMLOCK: *Tsuga canadensis* (evergreen)

Index

Catalog

If you are interested in a list of fine Paperback
books, covering a wide range of subjects
and interests, send your name and address,
requesting your free catalog, to:

McGraw-Hill Paperbacks
330 West 42nd Street
New York, New York 10036